THE

# PUBLICATIONS

OF THE

# Northamptonshire Record Society

FOUNDED IN DECEMBER, 1920

VOLUME XXX

FOR THE TWO YEARS ENDED 31 DECEMBER 1979

Oh read ouer D. John Bridges/ for it is worthy worke:

# Or an epitome of the

fyrste Booke/ of that right worshipfull vo=
lume/ written against the Puritanes/ in the defence of
the noble cleargie/ by as worshipfull a prieste/ John Bridges/
Presbyter/ Priest or elder/ doctor of Diuillitie/ and Deane of
Sarum. Wherein the arguments of the puritans are
wisely preuented/ that when they come to an=
swere M. Doctor/ they must needes
say some thing that hath
bene spoken.

Compiled for the behoofe and ouerthrow of
the vnpreaching Parsons/ Fyckers/ and Currats/
that haue lernt their Catechismes/ and are past grace:
By the reuerend and worthie Martin Marprelat
gentleman/ and dedicated by a second Epistle
to the Terrible Priests.

In this Epitome/ the foresaide Fickers/ &c. are very in=
sufficiently furnished/ with notable inabilitie of most vin=
cible reasons/ to answere the cauill
of the puritanes.

And lest M. Doctor should thinke that no man can write with=
out sence but his selfe/ the senceles titles of the seueral pages/
and the handling of the matter throughout the Epitome/
shewe plainely/ that beetlcheaded ignorraunce/ must not liue
and die with him alone.

Printed on the other hand of some of the Priests.

TITLE PAGE OF THE EPITOME OF MARTIN MARPRELATE, PRINTED AT FAWSLEY IN 1588

# THE PURITANS IN THE DIOCESE OF PETERBOROUGH

## 1558–1610

BY

W. J. SHEILS

Northampton

1979

© Northamptonshire Record Society
ISBN 0 901275 40 9

Published by the Northamptonshire Record Society,
Delapre Abbey, Northampton NN4 9AW

*The publication of this book has been assisted
by a grant from the Twenty-Seven Foundation*

Printed by Butler and Tanner Ltd, Frome, Somerset

IN MEMORY OF MY PARENTS

# CONTENTS

# LIST OF PLATES, MAPS AND TABLES

# ACKNOWLEDGEMENTS

A first book, arising as this one does out of a thesis prepared for a higher degree, necessarily involves the author in several debts. Firstly Sarah has cheerfully allowed the intrusion of the puritans into an already busy household for longer than either she or I care to remember, but my interest in the period goes back even further. H. C. Oram first showed me that there were several competing theories to explain the breakdown of the Tudor state. My interest in the problem was sustained by Professor Gerald Aylmer and Dr Claire Cross, both of whom have continued to show an active interest in my work since my return to York. As a research student I had the good fortune to be supervized by Professor Patrick Collinson, who with Dr Cross has read the entire manuscript and improved it not a little, and by the late Professor James Cargill Thompson. It was at this time that I also benefited from the weekly exercises held at the Institute of Historical Research under the moderatorships of Professors Hurstfield and Bindoff respectively; they not only taught me much about research, but also provided me with an insight into the value of corporate endeavour such as the puritans themselves were engaged in.

More immediately I am grateful to the officers of the Society for the chance to correct the errors of interpretation and of fact which were in the original thesis. Dr Edmund King has proved a patient and perceptive editor and has done much to see the book through the press. Mr Anthony Fletcher made valuable comments on an early draft of the work and Dr David Smith gave practical help at a vital stage. The original research was assisted by grants from the Fenton Trust and the General Research Fund of the University of London, whilst the Twenty-Seven Foundation have made a generous grant towards the cost of publication. No historical research can be carried out without the help of archivists and custodians of records and I am grateful to those in charge of the offices where I worked, most particularly to Mr Patrick King and his staff at Delapré Abbey. Even so that research still needs typing and Mrs Joyce Beach and Mrs Edna Meadows proved equal to the palaeographic challenges I posed. Despite all this it is too much to hope that I have avoided errors, and for those that remain I can at least claim sole responsibility. Finally, I should like to draw the attention of readers to the dedication which recalls a debt of an entirely different order to those acknowledged here.

# ABBREVIATIONS

| | |
|---|---|
| *A.P.C.* | *Acts of the Privy Council of England* (ed.) J. R. Dasent. |
| Baker | G. Baker, *The History and Antiquities of the County of Northampton.* |
| *B.I.H.R.* | *Bulletin of the Institute of Historical Research.* |
| B.L. | British Library. |
| *The Borough Records* | *The Records of the Borough of Northampton* (eds.) C. A. Markham and J. C. Cox. |
| Bridges | J. Bridges, *The History and Antiquities of Northamptonshire.* |
| *Eliz. Puritan Movt.* | P. Collinson, *The Elizabethan Puritan Movement.* |
| *H.I.L.* | *Northamptonshire and Rutland Clergy, 1500–1900* (ed.) H. I. Longden. |
| Lamb. Pal. Lib. | Lambeth Palace Library. |
| N.R.O. | Northamptonshire Record Office. |
| N.R.S. | Northamptonshire Record Society. |
| P.D.R. | Peterborough Diocesan Records (in N.R.O.). |
| P.R.O. | Public Record Office. |
| *V.C.H.* | *Victoria County History.* |
| *Visitations of Northants 1564, 1618–19* | *The Visitations of Northamptonshire made in 1564 and 1618–19, with Northamptonshire Pedigrees from various Harleian MSS* (ed.) F. C. Metcalfe. |

NOTE Dates are given in new style with the year beginning 1 January. The spelling and punctuation of quotations has been modernized where possible.

# INTRODUCTION

ALMOST forty years ago Professor Knappen called for more local studies of puritanism in order to deepen our understanding of the movement. Since then much local work has been done on the history of both the protestant reformation and puritan activity, most particularly for the counties of Sussex and Lancashire, each with two monographs dealing with different phases of the reformation. The diocese of Peterborough has not yet been the subject of extended treatment and this calls for some explanation. From the work of Knappen and that of subsequent writers on Elizabethan politics and religion it is clear that the area covered by the diocese was of paramount importance in the history of provincial puritanism. It was a region of marked religious polarization in which catholic and puritan were in close contact with each other, more so perhaps than in Lancashire where the religious divide was reflected in clear-cut geographical groupings. In Northamptonshire the two opposing groups lived side by side and such proximity was itself a dynamic influence on religious attitudes. It is no surprise that the county which housed the extremist puritan Marprelate Press should also have been the residence of one of the principals in the Gunpowder Plot 16 years later. The chief recusant families of the area have already been the subject of study, and it is the purpose of this book to place our knowledge of the more celebrated confrontations between the puritans and the leaders of church and state more firmly in their local context.

Recent local studies have led to a redefinition of Knappen's original problem, which he phrased as follows: 'further attention to puritan local history is essential if any sound conclusions are to be reached on the vexed question of the strength of the party at any given period'.[1] It is clear now that to view puritan activity as the work of a party, with all the organization which that implies, offering a comprehensive alternative to the episcopal church established by law is mistaken. Puritan activity embraced a wider section of the community than the vanguard of intellectual preachers supported by powerful lay patrons which, in the reign of Elizabeth, sought to bring about a national reform either through parliament or by establishing an *ecclesia in ecclesia* with its own discipline and organization.

Local studies show that the activity which was centred on the capital and parliament, where Northamptonshire men were prominent, drew strength from a variety of local experiences and situations. From them emerged individuals who, while sharing the broad aims of further reform of the established church,

[1]M. M. Knappen, *Tudor Puritanism* (Chicago, 1939), 518; for Sussex see R. B. Manning, *Religion and Society in Elizabethan Sussex* (Leicester, 1969) and A. J. Fletcher, *A County Community in Peace and War, Sussex 1600–1660* (1975); for Lancashire, C. Haigh, *Reformation and Resistance in Tudor Lancashire* (Cambridge, 1975) and R. C. Richardson, *Puritanism in North-West England* (Manchester, 1972).

differed in the level of their commitment to reform, and disagreed about the appropriate means by which it could be brought about, and even, ultimately about the precise form that reform should take. Most would have supported some loose form of presbyterianism, but the puritans, or 'precisians' as they were also called, were not always precise about their long term objectives. So diverse were the strands that, in a recent lecture to the Northamptonshire Record Society, Professor Elton remarked that the word 'puritan' had become such a protean term in historical writing that it served very little useful purpose. In this Professor Elton is part of a long tradition among historians going back even further than Thomas Fuller, who wished the word 'were banished common discourse'.[2] Contemporaries too objected to the term, it being in origin, like many other useful labels, intended as a term of abuse. The word has, however, entered common discourse among historians and, although it is fair to say that it is used as a protean term yet, faced with a protean beast, the historian has no other tool to use. In the context of late 16th-century England the problem seems to be not so much to find a more useful terminology to describe the varieties of puritan, but rather to find any terms at all to describe those protestants who were not puritan. The word 'Anglican' is wholly anachronistic, except perhaps for a few intellectuals on the episcopal bench, and 'Arminianism' only began to infiltrate the hierarchy at the very end of our period. When the Northampton preacher Percival Wiburn described the puritans as 'the hotter sort of protestants', he not only provided a general description, but also offered a key to understanding the success of the puritans in reaching a wide sector of society. I have already suggested that the parliamentary puritan activity drew strength from a more diffuse and localized experience throughout the country; so also that experience developed within the framework of a strong Calvinist theology which was shared by the establishment for most of our period. Whatever the differences between the hierarchy and the puritans on matters of ecclesiology and pastoral activity, they shared a common theological outlook. This shared outlook has to be borne in mind when considering the inconsistencies and illogicalities that become apparent from a study of the relations between the governors of church and state and the puritans.[3]

Sharing a common theology does not necessarily lead to understanding or tolerance of each other and, although it is misleading to define the views of the hierarchy and the puritans simply in terms of opposition, the puritans were a separate entity and some attempt has to be made to provide, if not a comprehensive definition, then some criteria for recognizing a puritan. Otherwise the danger of conflating the terms 'protestant' and 'puritan' remains. Support for a presbyterian form of church has been mentioned as one test for the puritans and, for the years between 1558 and 1610, this would encompass most of them provided the system was not applied too rigidly. For a substantial minority of puritans the full presbyterian system was the desired aim, but their attention to organizational details and the unrealistic nature of their ambitions engendered an exclusiveness and extremism which alienated many of their fellow puritans. Although presbyterianism remained an important rallying call for the puritans

[2]Quoted in C. Hill, *Society and Puritanism in Pre-Revolutionary England* (1964), 13; Professor Elton's remarks were made in a lecture at the Annual General Meeting of the Society in 1976.

[3]Most recently discussed in an important article by N. R. N. Tyacke, 'Puritanism, Arminianism, and Counter-Revolution' in C. S. R. Russell (ed.), *The Origins of the English Civil War* (1973).

in times of crisis, most of them would have settled for a substantial reduction in matters of ceremonial and a reformed system of episcopacy which produced smaller diocesan units served by bishops who were in close touch with the parochial clergy in their charge.

The repeated failure to get concessions such as these from the government led some of the puritans to turn away from matters of ecclesiastical polity by the end of the period, and to return to more fundamental issues. J. S. Coolidge has recently attempted to identify some of the salient features of puritanism, and writes: 'Puritanism as a distinct and militant movement within the Anglican church originates, then, in concern for the communal aspect of Christian experience . . . while the ceaseless nurture and growth of faith within the church is their [the puritans] incessant theme. As they understand that process, it is all but inconceivable *extra ecclesiam*.' In this passage Coolidge, in identifying their concern for the 'communal aspect' of Christian experience, helps one to understand the stress the puritans placed on the role of the local community in church discipline and government, whilst the ceaseless growth of faith was brought about by regular and public preaching to laity and by frequent catechizing and prayer in the godly household.[4] That they sought to do this within the framework of a church many of whose leaders feared the 'democratic' tendencies of local initiative and considered the regulation of spiritual life in a hierarchical mode was bound to lead to tensions. The history of those tensions is the subject of this book.

In individual cases of course the tensions between puritan attitudes and authority could be resolved in widely differing ways, and the careers of two Rutland puritan clerics can here suffice as examples. Both Robert Johnson and Thomas Gibson, rectors of North Luffenham and Ridlington respectively, entered the diocesan ministry in the mid 1570s after the first confrontation between the puritans and the bishop. Johnson was identified early as a nonconformist, and both he and Gibson played leading roles in the puritan exercise based at Oakham in the 1580s. Johnson indeed organized a famous fast at Stamford in 1580 in defiance of the authority of both Lord Burghley and the bishop. Both clergymen appear to have remained aloof from the political activity of their puritan brethren at this time and both chose to educate their sons at the recently founded Emmanuel College, Cambridge where puritan theology was paramount under the master Dr Chaderton. Emmanuel itself had local roots, being founded by a Northamptonshire landowner Sir Walter Mildmay. It was celebrated for its puritan outlook and was to educate many of the leading 17th-century puritan divines.[5] Perhaps through Mildmay's influence, Johnson's career was advanced in 1591 by promotion to the archdeaconry of Leicester, which he held with his rectory until his death in 1625. Johnson's puritan principles remained with him and also survived among his descendants. His son Abraham entered the legal profession and in 1618 was sheriff of Rutland, a position he used to establish a 'lecture by combination' in the town at Oakham where puritan clergy from neighbouring parishes provided regular preaching on Sunday mornings and afternoons. Johnson's grandson, Isaac, who was brought up by his grandfather at Luffenham, found the events of the 1630s too much for him and, with many like-minded men, removed himself from the Laudian church by emigrating to

[4]J. S. Coolidge, *The Pauline Renaissance in England* (Oxford, 1970), 147.
[5]For Emmanuel College see H. C. Porter, *Reformation and Reaction in Tudor Cambridge* (Cambridge, 1958), 238–242; for Johnson and Gibson see below pp. 38–39, 45–46, 48–50, 63.

America.[6] The career of Thomas Gibson was less dramatic; he appeared regularly before the diocesan courts for his nonconforming activities and published one sermon preached at the Oakham exercise. He survived in his benefice until 1605, when the enforcement of the Canons promulgated by archbishop Bancroft proved too much for his conscience and he was deprived for refusal to subscribe. Here too, however, his influence outlasted his career, deprivation may have been little more than the opportunity for retirement, for he was succeeded as rector of Ridlington by his son, also Thomas, whose ministry continued the tradition established by his father.[7] These examples illustrate two important points, the discrepancies in the treatment of individual cases by authority, and the persistence of the puritan tradition once established.

It is in accounting for the persistence of that tradition that the justification for local studies of puritanism lies, for it is only in creating a picture of the wide range of patronage networks, the connections between clergy and laymen of all social groupings, the professional relations between the clergy themselves, and the contacts between the godly laity that the diversity of the puritan experience becomes intelligible. Professor Collinson has written that the historian of puritanism in the 1590s and after 'will be concerned with a persistent tradition, and yet with something more diffuse, lacking in specific and short-term objectives . . .'[8] The evidence from the diocese of Peterborough suggests that the tradition was in many important respects diffuse from its very inception in the early 1570s.

---

[6]H.I.L., viii. 31; E. A. Irons, 'Mr Abraham Johnson', *Rutland Archaeological and Natural History Society, 10th Report* (1913), 59.
[7]See p. 86.
[8]*Eliz. Puritan Movt.*, 466.

# 1  A NEW DIOCESE

*Institutions and personnel*

THE diocese of Peterborough was itself, like puritanism, the creation of the reformation. The circumstances of its creation out of the enormous medieval see of Lincoln and the wealth of the dissolved abbey of Peterborough created a number of institutional and administrative problems which seriously impaired the effectiveness of the diocesan authorities as agents of ecclesiastical control. The problems of enforcing the edicts of the church courts were universal in the post-reformation church in England but in a poorly-endowed see, with the episcopal city placed in fenland at one extremity of the diocese, they were likely to be particularly acute. Writing to his brother Robert in 1595, Sir Thomas Cecil described the bishopric as follows, 'The place is of small revenue, and but for the title of a bishop, I think few will affect it but to step forward to a better'. Only Gloucester, of all the English sees, was considered to be poorer. The problems posed by poor endowment have been discussed at length elsewhere and, though they never reached the depths of dissarray and corruption that characterized administration at Gloucester, they were serious.[1]

As the centre of a wealthy abbey Peterborough had seen some prosperity in the middle ages, but the dissolution of the monastery created an economic vacuum in the community which the new cathedral was never able to fill. As late as the 18th century Defoe could relate the contrast between the riches of the monastery and the poverty of the cathedral and wrote of Peterborough, 'This is a little city, and indeed 'tis the least in England'.[2] More damaging than the low economic fortunes of the town was the isolated geographical position of Peterborough in relation to the rest of the diocese. The diocese was coterminus with the counties of Northampton and Rutland, and the fenland town had little in common with the arable uplands and great sheep pastures of the western regions of the diocese, from which it was separated by a large tract of forest, the royal forest of Rockingham. In the middle ages the ecclesiastical government of the area was based at Northampton, a more central and more readily accessible town where the political administration of the county was also most usually to be found. The economy of the fens had little to do with the midland shires from which emerged a thrusting group of landlords, improving their estates and desirous of playing an increasing part in the local government system and,

[1] A more detailed discussion of the problems resulting from poor endowment is found in my article 'Some Problems of Government in a new Diocese; the bishop and the puritans in the diocese of Peterborough 1570–1630', in R. O'Day and F. M. Heal (eds.) *Continuity and Change; Personnel and Administration of the church in England 1500–1640* (Leicester, 1976), where detailed references are given. For Gloucester see F. D. Price, 'Bishop Bullingham and Chancellor Blackleech' in *Transactions of the Bristol and Gloucestershire Archaeological Society*, xci. 175–198.

[2] D. Defoe, *A Tour through the Whole Island of Great Britain* (Penguin edn., 1971), 417.

indeed, in national affairs. It was with families such as the Spencers, Knightleys and Ishams that the impoverished bishop of Peterborough was placed among the leaders of local society. If the puritans were able to gain support from such quarters, then the bishop and the institutions over which he presided would be seriously hampered in the defence of the established church.

Of these institutions one, the archdeaconry of Northampton, had medieval antecedents, but longevity did not guarantee efficiency. Early in Elizabeth's reign the archdeacon William Binsley was forced to sue the widow of his registrar in Chancery because she had retained her husband's working papers. Not unnaturally, the absence of those papers seriously impeded the work of the archdeaconry officials, but the widow proved defiant before the court and, whatever the outcome of the case, it is true to say that the survival of archdeaconry records before 1570 is very scanty. Binsley himself was to be the subject of a lawsuit involving two other diocesan officials. The charge in question concerned the maladministration of Binsley's will and the defendant was the chancellor of the diocese, James Ellis, whose financial deviousness had also incurred the wrath of the Earl of Leicester, an early champion of the puritans in the county. The plaintiff was John Mottershed, the diocesan registrar, and the case was heard before a local commission for ecclesiastical causes, a body of laymen and clerics intended to bolster the efficiency of the local ecclesiastical courts. Instead the commissioners found themselves, in 1575, sitting in judgement in a suit between two of the principal officials of these local courts.[3] Establishing new institutions was a difficult business, but lack of experience was no excuse and the activities of officials and deputies in later years did little to improve the reputation of the local courts. The very principles on which the church courts were established were under attack from a wide sector of the political nation, so that officials noted for corruption only undermined their authority further. When the hierarchy chose to use the local courts in contentious matters such as the imposition of conformity, then their opponents could exploit the deficiencies of the officials to undermine the system further. This was the case in the diocese by the later years of James I's reign when John Lambe, chancellor of the diocese and arch-enemy of puritanism, chose to remove the court of the archdeaconry from the county town to Rothwell where he lived. The inhabitants of Northampton charged him with a variety of offences including extortion in fees, vexation by excommunicating people who failed to appear before the court because they were not properly advised of its location, and bribery by some of his officials. The case came before parliament in 1621 and again in 1624 when it was heard before the Parliamentary Committee for the Courts of Justice.[4] The truth or otherwise of the allegations need not concern us, but the case highlights the gulf that had arisen between the diocesan officials and the chief inhabitants of the county town, who were able to enlist powerful support for their cause. It was probably the radical nature of Northampton and the local opposition to his Arminian policies which prompted Lambe to remove the court to the less hostile Rothwell in the first place, but in so doing he only aggravated the situation further.

Responsibility for the personnel serving the diocesan administration ultimately rested with the bishop of Peterborough and, during the reigns of Elizabeth and James, three men filled that office; Edmund Scambler (1560–1585), Richard Howland (1585–1600) and Thomas Dove (1601–1630). Despite Cecil's remarks about the see only Scambler managed to 'step forward to a better'; though both

[3]P.R.O., C3/197/26; Sheils, *art. cit.*
[4]*Commons Journals*, i. 630, 634, 697, 709.

of his successors aspired to wealthier sees they were to be disappointed and remained at Peterborough until their deaths. Scambler's early career, though he
did not go into exile during Mary's reign, stamped him with sound protestant
credentials, for he remained in London as a minister to a protestant community
during those dangerous years. After his promotion to the episcopal bench,
possibly through the influence of Robert Dudley, later Earl of Leicester, and
almost certainly with the support of William Cecil, his career seems to have been
characterized by a determination to avoid trouble. He is said to have impoverished the already poorly-endowed see in order to satisfy his patron Cecil, but his
other patron Leicester was probably instrumental in getting the bishop's support
for early puritan activity.[5] It was in 1570 that the only diocesan official to show
any positive support for the puritans, Nicholas Sheppard, archdeacon of Northampton, was appointed, and Scambler himself, like his colleague bishop Curteys
of Chichester, encouraged the establishment of prophesyings in his diocese. The
surprisingly rapid growth of puritanism, and the local crisis of 1574, appear to
have caused Scambler to think again, and the later years of his episcopate saw
him at loggerheads with many of his puritan clergy. Indeed his translation to
Norwich in 1585 brought to an end, by leaving unresolved, a confrontation
between the puritans and their bishop over subscription to the Three Articles
issued by archbishop Whitgift the previous year as a test of conformity.[6]

Into this situation came Richard Howland, a bachelor straight from a senior
university post. Howland was closely identified with the anti-puritan policies
of Whitgift but his patron, Lord Burghley, had no great confidence in his abilities and the bishop was able to achieve little by way of halting the spread of
puritan activity. Held in low esteem by the gentry of the diocese, and required
to make thank offerings to his patron, Howland entertained hopes of a new post,
but they were never satisfied and he died in 1600.[7] The arrival of Thomas Dove
as bishop marked the beginning of an aggressive policy against the puritans in
the locality, which presaged the national policy of archbishop Bancroft. Dove
was one of the representatives of the hierarchy at the Hampton Court Conference in 1604 and his use of patronage, when not influenced by family considerations, shows him to have been a favourer of the emerging 'Arminian' party,
based principally at Oxford University. John Buckeridge, a notable pluralist and
archdeacon of Northampton from 1604 until his elevation to the episcopate in
1610, had been William Laud's tutor whilst at Oxford and was a close friend of
Lancelot Andrewes; the next archdeacon, Richard Butler, had been in the circle
of Richard Neile (later archbishop of York) and, early in James' reign, had been
charged with heresy by his puritan colleagues whilst still a parochial incumbent.
The activities of John Lambe, chancellor of the diocese from 1615 and another
close associate of Richard Neile, have already been alluded to.[8] Under such men
the diocesan authorities were to prove hostile to the puritans, but the outcome
of the confrontation between the Arminian governors of the diocese and the
puritan clergy and their supporters was to be largely determined by the events

[5] See D.N.B. for careers of the bishops; some correspondence between Scambler and
Leicester is preserved at Magdalene College, Cambridge, Pepys. MSS. Papers of State, ii.
389–90, 647–8 and among the Baskerville transcripts, De L'isle and Dudley papers, ii. no. 60
at the National Register of Archives. I am grateful to Dr G. D. Owen for locating the latter
for me.
[6] See pp. 48–50.
[7] D.N.B. sub. Howland, Richard; B.L., Lansd. Ms. 76, ff. 193–194; P.R.O., E 178/1703.
[8] D.N.B. sub. Dove, Thomas, Buckeridge, John; for details of Butler's connections with
Neile I am grateful to Dr Andrew Foster; for Lambe see P.R.O., SP 14/12/96.

of the preceding thirty years, when the diocesan authorities had been less able
and less committed to an assault on puritanism.

The historian tracing the history of puritan activity in a region or locality
draws heavily on the records of the local ecclesiastical courts. Papers of government departments, the central courts of justice, county administration and
private correspondence are all needed to extend the range of such a study, whilst
the puritans themselves provided a sermon literature and private papers which
throw much light on their activities. Unfortunately, in the period under discussion, the literary output of the puritans in Peterborough diocese was not
great in comparison to their colleagues in Essex or their spiritual descendants in
Peterborough itself during the 1620s and 1630s, and it is the appearances of clergy
and laity before the ecclesiastical courts for nonconformist practices which are
often the only evidence for a puritan tradition in a particular locality or parish.
Dependence on these records has three major drawbacks, the first of which is
implicit in the use of the term nonconformist. Appearances before the local
courts laid stress on the negative aspects of puritan activity, the extent to which
they departed from the official line. Whether the declared policy of the leaders
of the established church ever did represent normal practice in a particular
locality at any time is questionable; for instance, when the Canons of 1604 were
imposed on the diocese the mayor and aldermen of Northampton objected that
ceremonial was being forced on the townsmen which had not been practised
for over 40 years. In such a situation it could be the practices of the hierarchy
that appeared as nonconformist in the eyes of the leaders of local society. The
impression given by the court records of puritanism as an essentially nonconformist tradition at odds with generally accepted ecclesiastical usage has therefore to be questioned.[9]

The other drawbacks concern the efficiency of the church courts as a system
of policing and a place of record. Standards were not likely to be high in these
respects, for diocesan administration depended largely on local and parochial
voluntary officials for the presentment and notification of moral and ecclesiastical
offences. The local pressures that could be brought to bear on such officials are
obvious and the sources suggest that they were often effective. In a parish with
a resident puritan squire, a puritan parson and a congregation largely sympathetic to the tradition, the authorities had difficulty extracting information. In a
number of parishes in the west of the diocese where, from other sources, we
know that a puritan tradition was established, the records of the local courts are
silent. Significantly, the local records are much fuller at times when the government was pursuing a vigorous anti-puritan campaign nationally, so that information on activity in the periods from 1588 to 1592 and 1604 to 1606 is comparatively detailed. At such times the local machinery was galvanized into more
rigorous action by a strong central policy, and parochial opponents of the puritans were encouraged to speak out. Concealment of offences was clearly a problem as also was the inertia of parochial officials; the penalty for failure to present
offences, usually excommunication, became less effective as a guarantee of
efficient policing as the period progressed.[10]

[9]Hist. Mss. Com., Salisbury MSS., xvii. 26.

[10]General discussion of these problems is contained in R. A. Marchant, The Church under
the Law (Cambridge, 1969); detailed analysis of the efficiency of the courts in particular
localities can be found in M. Spufford, Contrasting Communities (Cambridge, 1974), 241–271.
Visitation articles survive for the following years, 1594, 1599, 1602, 1605, 1607, 1608, see
bibliography for details.

The final drawback relates to the survival of records. As a record keeping body the diocesan administration from 1570 was efficient and only one important source, the files of cause papers relating largely to instance business, that is to say actions brought before the court by one party against another on matters of probate, matrimonial law, and tithes, has been lost. Whilst not grievous to a study of puritan activity the loss of these records limits discussion of how puritan clergy got on with their parishoners over questions such as tithe, where opposing religious views of clergy and laity might have been at the bottom of an otherwise economic issue. A more grievous loss is the very fragmentary survival of records prior to the 1570s, when the difficulties of establishing institutions in a new diocese caused heavy attrition on the records. In addition those cause papers relating to matters of discipline, among which nonconformity would be included, do not survive at all. The circumstantial evidence which such papers can provide, usually through the testimony of witnesses, often fills in the local context in considerable detail, and their loss means we know little about many lay puritans apart from their names. Attempts to place those individuals within the context of their local community are therefore restricted.

## The Diocese

Although much of our information on puritan activity derives from the records of the church courts and, in such records, the sense of confrontation looms large, the success of puritanism did not depend solely, or even very largely, on the inability of the church courts to enforce uniformity. The puritan tradition was far more than a reaction against the establishment and, in this sense, the concept of *dissent* is misleading. In some places at certain times, such as the coastal towns of East Sussex and some industrialized settlements of south Lancashire in the early 17th century, the puritans comprised the establishment, in the *real* sense of having *local power* rather than in the *formal* sense of holding *ecclesiastical office*.[11] That this was true in parts of the diocese of Peterborough will become apparent, but before relating the events of that story some discussion of the geographical features of the area and of its social and economic structure is necessary.

Professor Everitt has eloquently reminded us of the importance of the diversity of provincial life and stressed the individuality of each locality.[12] Yet among this variety some general outlines do emerge and the diocese can be divided into six main regions. The principal division, between the highland west and the Nene valley of the east and north-east, is immediately apparent from the legend of Christopher Saxton's map of Northamptonshire in 1576. The western uplands was a region of great inclosures during the early Tudor period when much arable land was turned over to the extensive sheep pastures on which the fortunes of the Spencers and the Knightleys were based. At Fawsley the church and Hall stood alone in a park-land grazed by 2,500 sheep but, notwithstanding the inclosures, the area was densely settled with many nucleated villages dominated by strong seigneurial families, albeit of relatively recent origin.[13] The other

[11]Fletcher, *A County Community*, 70–74; Richardson, *Puritanism in North-West England*, 13–17; but see also C. Haigh, 'Puritan Evangelism in the reign of Elizabeth I', *English Historical Review*, xcii. 30–58, which underlines the difficulties of evangelizing the mass of the people.

[12]A. Everitt, *Change in the Provinces, the Seventeenth Century* (Leicester, 1969), 6–8.

[13]For Spencers see M. E. Finch, *Five Northamptonshire Families, 1540–1640* (N.R.S. xix, 1956) 38–65; and also K. J. Allison, M. W. Beresford, and J. G. Hurst, *The Deserted Villages*

highland area, around Northampton, was not so dominated by its great land-lords and had not suffered the transfer to sheep raising, remaining largely an arable and cattle-raising area for the county town which was famous as a marketing centre for livestock. Much arable land remained on these plateaux and it was the upland zone and the excellent farming land of the Nene valley, stretching between Northampton and Oundle, that impressed John Norden on his travels through the area in 1591. He found the county a prosperous one 'adorned both with salutary and profitable seats, many and notable sheep pas-tures, rich feedings for cattle, fertile corn grounds, and large fields greatly en-riching the industrious husbandman. No shire within this land has so little waste grounds, for there is not in a manner any part thereof, but is farmed to some profitable use.' Moreover the county contained 'plenty of Towns, Parishes and Villages, which are so universally dispersed that in every two or three miles at the most, is found a place of ease to the wearisome traveller'.[14]

Norden may well have been less impressed with the large tract of forest area, known as Rockingham Forest, stretching north and west of Oundle into Rut-land, or the similar area in the south-east corner of the county, whilst the sparsely populated fenland area looking across the Soke to Peterborough still needed much drainage work to realize its full agricultural potential. Both fenland and forest were less densely populated than the uplands and the presence of resident gentry of the first rank was less obvious, but whereas the fen villages were small, the forest villages were, for the most part, larger than elsewhere in the county and were growing in size during our period.[15] A greater proportion of the population in forest villages than elsewhere in the county were poor and de-pended on cottage handicraft industries for their livelihood in addition to farm-ing and sylviculture. The forest areas attracted many of those people no longer needed for work in parishes converted to pasture and these pockets of immigrants, in addition to the generally larger population and the more fragmentary occupa-tional pattern of forest villages, made for less cohesive communities. Brigstock was one of the largest parishes in Rockingham Forest, and had a small decayed market. There was no dominant landlord, the village being part of the royal demesne, and of 52 landholders recorded in 1607 only two were farming over 100 acres and another ten had more than 30 acres. In such communities the husbandmen and smaller farmers had the place to themselves and could develop a more independent turn of mind.[16] When he replaced the deprived rector in 1605, the new incumbent of Brigstock, George Sharpe, noticed this.

> I find all the chief of the parish, with many of the inferior sort on both sides depending, to consist of puritans, I hope something conformable, and of papists, I fear refractory and obstinate. Between both there is outwardly scarce a show of humanity, but inwardly mortal and unchristian malice of the rest, many rebukeable for their dissolute courses, others to be pitied for their very beggarly estates. I am grieved that where there is no agreement with con-

---

*of Northamptonshire* (Leicester, 1966) esp. p. 11. For a general topographical discussion see J. M. Steane, *The Northamptonshire Landscape* (1974), 25–30.

[14]J. Norden, *Speculi Britanniae Pars Altera, or a Delineation of Northamptonshire* (1720), 24.

[15]For a discussion of this see P. A. J. Pettit, *The Royal Forests of Northamptonshire, 1558–1714* (N.R.S. xxiii, 1968), 141–145; A. Everitt, *The Pattern of Rural Dissent: the Nineteenth Century* (Leicester, 1972), 41 includes suggestive remarks about the religious climate of woodland areas.

[16]Pettit, *The Royal Forests*, 164–174.

trarities, nor any communion with different religions, he whose part is to reconcile shall find his labours uneffectual or intolerable. My duty shall not be wanting.

He did however go on to ask his patron, Robert Cecil, for permission to remain at Cambridge a further five months in order to take his B.D. degree.[17] In such communities religious attitudes could not be imposed from above, whether by clergy or by gentry. This may explain the less cohesive character of puritanism in this part of the county when compared with the west or with Northampton town, for here the reformation often had to be planted without the support of squire; but once planted its hold was tenacious, as the survival of the 'Old Dissent' in these regions illustrates.[18]

In the fens the influence of the Dean and Chapter, and the presence of the cathedral city provided a bulwark against puritan growth in all but a few communities, but in Rutland, the influence of great landowners like the Harringtons and the Cecils did much to promote puritanism. In this sense the squirearchy and magnates of Rutland played a similar role to that of their friends and peers in the west of the diocese, but it was support for a markedly different stamp of puritan activity, for Rutland did not see the fully politicized puritanism of the *classes*, those clerical meetings of the 1580s which sought to establish a fully presbyterian church in England. The character of puritan activity in the west of the region was to differ from that in Rutland or the forest areas, whilst in the neighbourhood of Northampton it was the county town that was to play an important part in local religious life. As a prophesying centre in the 1570s and the location of a *classis* in the 1580s Northampton provided a regular meeting place for the clergy and the godly of the neighbouring parishes throughout the period and, indeed, it was attendance at the market-day lectures that often brought the first contact with puritan ideas to inhabitants of the rural hinterland. There were fifteen other market towns in the diocese and, of these, eleven were identified with puritan activity at some stage between 1570 and 1610. Some of them were centres of prophesyings and exercises, others had endowed lectureships, and two, Kettering and Daventry, were *classis* centres. Not all of these towns dominated their surrounding villages in the way that Northampton did, but their puritan tradition survived into or was revived in the early 17th century when weekly 'lectures by combination', provided in turn by clergy of the surrounding villages, were established in several places.[19]

The diocese lay on a number of important routes and it was the network of communications which kept these urban centres in touch with each other, and with the rest of the kingdom. It was along these routes that not only commodities, but also news and ideas were transported. The position of Daventry, at the cross-roads of an important west–east route, used by Welsh drovers taking livestock to the Midland markets, and the main road from London to radical Coventry and the north-west made it a natural home of puritan ideas. When the godly townsmen had no services to their own liking in the neighbourhood they could take themselves the ten miles or so along Watling Street to the famous

[17]Hist. Mss. Com., *Salisbury MSS.*, xvii. 67–68.
[18]Everitt, *Pattern of Rural Dissent*, 41–42.
[19]A. Everitt, 'The Marketing of Agricultural Produce' in J. Thirsk (ed.) *The Agrarian History of England and Wales*, iv. 473–475; P. Collinson, 'Lectures by Combination: Structures and Characteristics of Church Life in 17th-Century England', *B.I.H.R.* xlviii. 198–199, discusses Northamptonshire lectures.

puritan exercise at Southam in Warwickshire in 1574.[20] In addition to these market towns a number of decayed towns like Brigstock, Byfield, Weedon Bec and Culworth became notable puritan centres and once again their location on major routes may have been important. Some of these communities enjoyed a temporary economic recovery, and the fairs at Culworth may have revived during this period because of the greatly increased cattle trade between Wales and Northampton.[21] It was perhaps in these small urban communities with their varieties of trades and their network of communications, that independence of mind was best fostered in the absence of wealthy urban oligarchs or powerful landed gentry. Certainly these towns were to provide a home not only for puritan activity, but for dissent in the centuries following the Restoration, and the independence of 'the baser sort of men' who 'wade through the world with good countenance in their calling, least beholden generally to the monied men of any other shire whatsoever that I know' struck Norden forcefully on his travels through the county in 1591.[22]

At the same time Norden could not fail to observe that, 'No shire within this land is so plentifully stored with gentry, in regard whereof this shire may seem worthy to be termed the Herald's Garden.' More recently it has been observed that Northamptonshire provides a *locus classicus* in support of the 'rise of the gentry' argument and certainly at the outbreak of Civil War over 70 per cent of the leading landowners had moved into the county, or emerged as landed gentry, since the reign of Henry VII.[23] The classic example is that provided by the Spencers of Althorp, formerly Warwickshire yeomen-graziers whose concentration of sheep pastures saw them rise through the gentry and enter the peerage in 1603.[24] Lesser families, such as the Drydens, Pickerings and Samwells, first began to play a part in county affairs during the reign of Elizabeth and were to emerge among the leaders of the Parliamentary County Committees during the Civil War. Even greater families, whose names were to become almost synonymous with the county, the Ishams of Lamport, the Montagues of Boughton, and the Mildmays of Apethorpe were relatively recent arrivals in county society, having made their fortunes in commerce, the law, or in government service. The same could be said for the two principal Rutland families, the Cecils of Burleigh and the Harringtons of Exton.[25] The diocese had never been the place for backwoodsmen from the shires uninterested in politics. Whatever the complexion of government, men from this area were always to be found playing a prominent part in national affairs. In the reign of Mary the Privy Council included local men like John Lord Mordaunt, Sir Thomas Tresham, and Sir Edward Griffin of Dingley. The accession of Elizabeth curtailed the careers of these men, but other local gentry took their place, Sir Walter Mildmay and later Sir Christopher Hatton both played prominent parts in government at various times, whilst the contribution of William Cecil to the Elizabethan system of government was unparalleled.[26]

With excellent communications to the capital, and relatively easy access to

[20]P.D.R. X608/13 f. 77v.

[21]Everitt, *Pattern of Rural Dissent*, 32.

[22]Norden, *Speculi Britanniae*, 32.

[23]*Ibid.*, 28; A. Everitt, *The Local Community and the Great Rebellion* (1969), 20–22.

[24]Finch, *Five Northants. Families*, 38–65.

[25]See pedigrees in O. Barron, *VCH Northamptonshire Families* (1906).

[26]For Mary's Privy Council see *A.P.C.* v. *passim*, and for Tresham see Finch, *Five Northants. Families*, 57–62. The careers of Cecil, Hatton, and Mildmay have all been subjects of recent biographies noted in the bibliography.

both universities, the local gentry were well placed to keep in touch with political and intellectual developments. Not only were some in government service, but men from the area also figured prominently in parliamentary activity, particularly in the opposition to anti-puritan legislation by the government. In addition to the county seats there were four boroughs providing a total of eleven parliamentary seats in all, and very few of these were held by outsiders with no close affiliation to the county. On the other hand Northamptonshire men represented boroughs all over the place; in the parliament of 1593 for instance William Lane of Horton was M.P. for Gatton in Surrey, Edward Stafford of Blatherwycke represented Winchester, William Tate of Delapré represented Corfe Castle in Dorset, and George Downhall sat for the Cornish borough of East Looe.[27] That parliament was by no means untypical and, in an area free from the control of ancient baronial families, a vigorous gentry of strong views and relatively recent origin provided a ready audience for puritan preaching, and indeed for catholic missionary activity.

*Antecedents*

The diocese had always enjoyed the advantages of relatively ready access to the capital and the universities. Whether earlier movements for reform had planted a tradition in the region on which the puritans could build is hard to say, for the evidence is unfortunately fragmentary. Most interesting, but furthest removed in time from puritanism, is the evidence for Lollard growth in the decades before and the years just after the Oldcastle rebellion of 1414. The pattern of Lollard activity provides some parallels with the later 'political' puritan activity, both of which grew out of gentry patronage in the west of the diocese and quickly infiltrated the governing classes of the county town. The principal Lollard patron in the 1380s was Sir Thomas Latimer, who held lands in Leicestershire and at Braybrooke and Chipping Warden, which became an important Lollard centre. Inhabitants of the neighbouring villages of Byfield and Eydon were involved in the 1380s and in the rising of 1414 and a continuing tradition of Lollard activity over some 30 years cannot be ruled out in this small area. Latimer also held lands in the suburbs of Northampton and a sizeable proportion of the town governors, as well as many of the commons of the town, became infected with Lollard heresies. In 1393 a dispute among the town governors led to a charge of Lollardy against the mayor John Fox, who was removed from office. The bailiffs and commoners attempted to re-elect him in 1395, but the King intervened to quash the election; Fox, however, was again elected mayor in 1399. Not much is known of events in Northampton during the Oldcastle rising but in the west the town of Daventry, where image-breaking was noted, became implicated in the plot, and two inhabitants of nearby Byfield were executed and their heads displayed on the gates of Coventry and Northampton 'to discourage any rebels remaining there'. The roads connecting Byfield, Northampton, and Coventry must have been the same route along which the illicit and scurrilous Marprelate Press was trundled some 175 years later when Sir Richard Knightley housed it at Fawsley before its removal to Coventry. A Northampton man, the bookbinder Henry Sharpe was a principal figure in the distribution of those puritan broadsides. The distance in time between the two

[27]The boroughs were Peterborough (2), Northampton (2), Brackley (2), and Higham Ferrers (1). Details of 1593 are taken from E. E. Trafford, 'Personnel of Parliament, 1593' (Unpublished London M.A. thesis, 1948), biographical appendices.

events was a long one but, at Byfield adjacent to Fawsley, there still exists a public house, 'The Cross Tree', which is said locally to get its name from a group of people who used to meet for services in the woods to avoid 'the Pope's officials'. If this refers to the Lollard groups and if such an oral tradition can survive to the present (assuming it was not revived in the 19th century) then some of the 16th century inhabitants of the locality must also have been aware of it.[28]

Tantalizing as these parallels are it is difficult to do more than present the facts as they emerge from fragmentary sources. The gentry household at Fawsley does not immediately look like the spiritual descendant of a group of Lollard farmers and peasants, but we do not know what effect puritan preaching had on the farming community of that locality in the later 16th century. The records are silent on that point. We do know however that plenty of puritan preaching went on at Byfield and adjacent parishes and if it aroused much local opposition it was rarely the sort that was recorded. Whatever conclusions can be drawn from such patterns Lollardy as a dissenting force seems to have disappeared from the locality soon after Oldcastle's rebellion. Apart from a short period of activity in Northampton in 1427 and 1428, it did not preoccupy the minds of the diocesan officials or their superiors.[29]

✗ The next recorded stage in puritan pre-history concerns the reception of reformed ideas in the locality from the 1540s onwards. The area did not like Lancashire produce a small group of university-trained men with local family connections to provide an intellectual vanguard of reform and such evidence as exists tells us little of the views of the leaders of local society. Some of the younger generation, William Cecil and Walter Mildmay, were to be identified with the Tudor state and, as it was to turn out, hence with protestantism, but their attitude in the early years of the reformation is not always clear.[30]

The surviving records do not focus on the leaders of local society, but on the laity lower down the social scale. The picture they give is fragmentary and begins with the visitation of 1546. The episcopal visitors uncovered articulate critics of transubstantiation and devotion to images among the inhabitants of Oundle, one of whom, significantly, had first come across these ideas on a visit to the capital. At Oakham, the archdeacon ordered the parish priest to intervene in order to restrain the 'many readers and meddlers with the Bible, which have no authority thereto'. Small conventicles of protestants were also uncovered in the rural parishes of East Carlton and Lowick, and at both places it was the shared experience of Bible reading which brought the groups together. At Carlton they met in the house of Robert Barker, a smith, and at Lowick several parishioners were said to read the Bible 'not only unto themselves, but also unto audience' and one of them, Thomas Ripon, was accused of being 'a common converter of the people from the laws and ordinances of the church'.[31] These scattered incidents hardly make for a tradition and the almost total loss of local court records between 1546 and 1570 makes it difficult to trace the growth, if indeed there was one, of protestantism among the laity. There was one heresy case noted in the reign of Mary, and it may be significant that it concerned an inhabitant of Oundle, but even that indefatigable collector of evidence the

[28]This material is taken from C. Kightly, 'The early Lollards 1382–1428' (Unpublished York D.Phil. thesis, 1975), 86–110, 141–151. I am grateful to Dr Kightly for his enthusiastic discussions of this material.
[29]J. A. F. Thomson, *The Later Lollards 1414–1520* (Oxford, 1965), 97–98.
[30]Haigh, *Reformation and Resistance*, 163–174.
[31]P.D.R., Archd. Ct. Bk. 3, ff. 27v., 35v.–39, 65v., 69v.

martyrologist John Foxe recorded only one instance of martyrdom in the county, concerning a shoemaker of Syresham.[32]

In the absence of records of local courts the principal surviving source for the progress of protestantism is the probate records, for testators about to dispose of their worldly possessions invariably took the opportunity to also make a statement, usually in the form of a preamble to the main body of the will, concerning their soul and the after-life. The evidence from wills is beset with difficulty for, although in most cases it is relatively easy to establish whether a preable reflects conservative, catholic, or protestant attitudes, it is hard to establish how far the preamble reflects the views of the individual. Wills were invariably drawn up when death was imminent and, in such circumstances, the attitude of the scribe responsible for writing the document could be more influential than the views of the testator. To judge from the regularity with which clergy are listed as overseers to wills, or head the names of witnesses, it is clear that they were often called upon to act as scribes but, even in rural communities, literacy was not confined to the clergy and a testator could call on any of a number of possible scribes, be he parson, schoolmaster, squire, or one of the increasing number of literate yeomen and craftsmen in each locality. Indeed, as the century progressed, the evidence from witness lists in the registered copies of wills, suggests that the role of the clergy, although still important, declined. With some small degree of choice it is likely that any testator would choose to entrust the solemn task of writing a will to an individual in whom he had some confidence, so that the wording of the preamble was generally likely to reflect the views of the testator, even if at one remove. The loss of the great majority of original wills makes the task of identifying local scribes impossible, but the survival of the registered copies of these wills permits some discussion of the religious preambles.[33]

Most preambles lack spontaneity or individuality and are expressed in conventional formulae but, clearly, references to the Virgin Mary, the saints, and prayers for the dead can be taken to reflect catholic attitudes whilst emphasis on the sufficiency of the passion of Christ can be identified with protestantism. Between these positive statements are a number of neutral formulae whereby the testator merely bequeathed his soul to God or to 'God, my maker and redeemer', and also a number of transitional statements, like that of William Ley of Marston Trussell, dated 8 January 1549, 'I give and bequeath my soul to almighty god, through the merits of whose passion I do hope and trust to be after this the changes of this my transitory life, one of the elect children of salvation, praying to his blessed mother, Our Lady Saint Mary, and all the holy company of heaven to pray for me.' Such confused and neutral statements can be used to show the breakdown of the hold of conventional catholic piety, but do not provide sufficient material to establish the arrival of a protestant tradition in any locality. A random sample of 282 wills proved in the archdeaconry of Northampton between 1549 and the accession of Mary, provides the basis for the following discussion. Of these wills over half, 148, were broadly catholic or conservative, but among these, were a small number, 18, which made no mention of the Virgin Mary and a further 16 which included references to God as 'maker and redeemer' or, as in the case of William Houghton of Orlingbury, reflected the same kind of theological confusion noted above in William Ley's

[32]V.C.H. Northants., ii. 38; P.D.R. ML 556, f. 198v.
[33]For a discussion of wills as a source for lay religious sentiment see M. Spufford, 'The scribes of villagers' wills in the 16th and 17th centuries and their influence', *Local Population Studies*, vii. 28–43.

will.[34] The distribution of these wills indicates a transitional stage in the reformation at Yelvertoft where the wills of three husbandmen, John Ashby, Maurice Wells, and Henry Barker all reveal a combination of conservative and protestant statements in different forms of words. The same can be said for two wills from Kingsthorpe, just outside Northampton, and of two from Uppingham, where Amice Wilson sought 'all the elect of him [Christ] to pray for me'.[35] Of these conservative wills, it can be said that a few individuals in some communities were already on the road to protestantism at this date, even if they had not yet arrived. The next largest groups of wills were not yet fully protestant either, but neutral. Some 87 preambles merely referred to 'God' or 'God, my maker and redeemer' and, although some, like that of John Young of Daventry went a little further by describing God as 'his only maker and redeemer', it is making the evidence stretch too far to say these statements were proof positive of the acceptance of protestant ideas.[36]

This leaves 47 wills with positive protestant preambles, that is to say wills which refer to the sufficiency of Calvary in the act of salvation, to salvation by faith, or to election. Most of these, like that of Richard Welford, a husbandman of Earls Barton, follow a common formula referring to the passion. 'I bequeath my soul to Almighty God, in whom only I trust, by the merits of Christ's passion to be saved and annexed to the blessed company of heaven,' and few are as individual as that of Thomas Goodman of Weston, whose preamble read, 'I bequeath my soul into the hands of my saviour and redeemer, lord and god of truth, who has redeemed [it], of whose grace and merits in all cases unworthy of myself. So do I, calling the Kingdom of heaven by his mercy, only to him be all praise.' Other wills from Earls Barton and Mears Ashby suggest the reception of protestant opinions among the laity of these localities[37] and at Raunds a different tradition, possibly introduced by the incumbent William Taverner, stressing the role of faith in the means to salvation was established.[38]

The Bible reading noticed in the visitation of 1546 clearly influenced Margery Roberts of Wardley in Rutland, who bequeathed her soul to Almighty God 'in whom I believe, as the holy word of god does teach me'. At Braunston near Daventry, Barrowden and Moulton wills with reference to the Calvinist doctrine of election were recorded, and other protestant statements came from Grendon, Bozeat, King's Cliffe, Barnack, Walgrave, and Oakham.[39] Most of these refer to individual examples about which it is difficult to generalize, but a sufficient percentage of the whole sample, 16.6 per cent, were protestant enough to suggest that in some localities, the reign of Edward VI had witnessed the growth of reformed ideas. Whether this was confined to or directed by the parochial clergy is uncertain, but there is enough individuality among the formulations of belief to suggest that the laity were not passive recipients of religious opinion. Indeed in a minority of protestant wills, 17, clerics are not listed at all among overseers or witnesses in the register copies. As a proportion of the protestant wills this is 35.4 per cent, significantly higher than the conservative wills where clergy were among the witnesses in 78.6 per cent of cases.

The evidence from the reign of Mary suggests that the years from 1553 until

[34]These wills are taken from P.D.R. Will volume K; the wills are numbered consecutively and are referred to by number not folio unless otherwise stated; K 260, 493.
[35]Ibid. K 339, 382, 489, 500, 515, 523, 662.
[36]Ibid. K 434.
[37]Ibid. K 311, 361, 365, 464, 660.
[38]Ibid. K 278, 513, 516.
[39]Ibid. K 289, 432, 449, 459, 462, 472, 479, 517, 647.

1558 put protestant opinions underground in this diocese as elsewhere. Religious preambles in this period tended to reflect the fuller statements of medieval catholic piety and the Virgin was reinstated in almost every example of a catholic will. To take an example of one year, 1558 the last year of the reign and that in which Elizabeth acceded to the throne on 17 November, of 224 wills made in that year only 11 contained positive protestant preambles and the proportion of wills of a neutral nature also declined to 20 per cent of the total. What the wills of 1558 and 1559 do show, however, is that the protestantism noted in Edward's reign had survived in some localities, notably at Earls Barton, Wardley, and Raunds.[40] Survival rather than advance was the first ambition of protestants under Mary, but some parishes had their first protestant wills recorded in this period. In the light of future developments, three wills are worth particular mention. A wealthy glover at Towcester, Thomas Pratt, made a will in 1556 with a firmly protestant preamble[41] and at Northampton Richard Wilkinson, an innholder, bequeathed his soul 'into the merciful hands and custody of god, my maker, redeemer, and preserver', a preamble of a neutral sort. However, among the witnesses was Nicholas Herman, curate of All Saints church and possibly a Cambridge graduate of the 1530s who, having been a fellow of Gonville and Caius College, worked in the diocese of Worcester during the reign of Edward VI. The overseer of the will was Mr Rand, described as a 'very old friend' and it is these connections which suggest the emergence of a protestant group in the county town, for Alice Rand, whose will is dated 17 May 1563, provided one of the very earliest idiosyncratic statements of protestant belief to emerge from the diocese. The preamble suggests that the reality of the reformation came to Alice from relatively undirected study, and its individuality epitomizes the kind of attitudes likely to emerge from a clandestine body of protestants meeting informally together during persecution; the phraseology can owe nothing to anybody but Alice herself and reads:

> I bequeath my soul to the everliving god, in the confession of Jesus Christ to be son of the everliving god, acknowledging also three persons in trinity and one god in essence, with all other articles of the catholic faith contained in god's book, the Old Testament and the New; trusting [that] I enjoy the fruition due by Christ's merits and only sacrifice, utterly without my deserving; acknowledging also, while I have time in this world, if I do not work justly the law of god, hate and abhor sins, that then my faith is but presumption, dead and fantastical. But when life faileth I have no other refuge but the same anchor and rock, Jesus Christ, who died for my sins, who rose for my justification, with my immortal soul. I doubt not that my mortal body, after the general day, shall live with the father immortal and holy ghost forever; desiring the ones that I have offended in this life to forgive me for charity's sake, advertising all them that have offended me that I heartily forgive them as I would be forgiven at Christ's hands, to whom all praise honour and glory, Amen.[42]

Such a statement shortly after Elizabeth I's accession can hardly have emerged from nothing, and a small circle around the Rand family may provide us with a first glimpse of the protestant reformation at Northampton.

In some communities therefore, the transition from catholic to protestant

[40]These wills are in P.D.R. Will volume Q 268, 269, 273, 276, 290.
[41]*Ibid.* Q 146.
[42]*Ibid.* P 27, Q 105; *H.I.L.* vi. 151.

doctrine was still incomplete; in many others there was no evidence to suggest that it had started to have any effect on the laity, but in a few localities a protestant tradition had been planted during Edward VI's reign and had survived the Marian campaigns. Much stress has been laid on the initiative of laymen and women in matters of religion, but the reception of protestant ideals was impossible without clerical evangelizing. The emergence of protestantism among the parish clergy remains, in the absence of court records, obscure, and the only glimpse we have is through the institution act books. These show that in the early years of Mary's reign 34 priests were deprived; most of these would have been deprived for marrying during the reign of Edward VI and for their refusal to separate from their wives under the new regime.[43] The motives for clerical marriage were several and, in many cases, it must have represented a declaration of acceptance of protestant doctrine; it was an action impossible to reconcile with traditional teaching. Although only two of the deprived clergy can be positively identified with parishes with known protestant inhabitants, their numbers, well in excess of 10 per cent of the total parish priests in the diocese, suggest a strong involvement of the clergy with new ideas.[44] They were not grouped in one locality, but dispersed fairly evenly throughout the diocese, and some of them at least must have remained in their own communities to sustain any congregation they might have acquired.

[43]P.D.R., Inst. Bk. I, ff. 49v–58; an incomplete list is printed in *Northants. N & Q* (Old Series), ii. no. 175, followed in *V.C.H. Northants*, ii. 38.
[44]Greatworth and Dallington.

## 2 EARLY GROWTH 1558–1576

*The settlement of religion*

THE accession of Elizabeth I on 17 November 1558 led to a reversal of religious policy and the return of a protestant government. However, by the cautious attempt to offend as few people as possible, the settlement itself emerged as a compromise acceptable to many but desired by few. It returned England to the theology of the Edwardine reformation, but retained a liturgy slightly more conservative than the later experiments of Edward's reign. In matters of church government the hierarchy and the church courts, though financially weakened in the preceding half-century, remained intact. To many contemporaries the settlement of 1559 and the 39 Articles of 1563 represented, in effect, a document for further discussion.[1] This attitude was particularly true of the returning Marian exiles who filled many important posts in government, church, and the universities left vacant by the change of regime. The settlement of religion was carried through peaceably and this was due in some measure to its conservative and reconciling nature. It owed much more, however, to the goodwill of those entrusted to carry it through; for a number of men, like John Jewel bishop of Salisbury and author of *An Apology of the Church of England*, had serious misgivings about accepting positions of authority in the church, and only did so in the belief that the settlement represented a *terminus a quo* in matters of religion. These men, often influenced by personal contact with the continental reformation, desired further reform in both liturgy and church government and, in the interests of protestant evangelism, were generous in their interpretation of their responsibilities when it came to imposing uniformity through the church courts. It was to these men, such as Edmund Grindal, bishop of London and later archbishop of York and Canterbury in succession, that the government of the church was entrusted in the 1560s, and they had their counterparts at the universities who trained a new generation in the need for further reform. Only in the mid 1570s did it become fully apparent that this view of the settlement was not shared by the Queen, who saw the settlement much more as a *terminus ad quem*. By that time some younger ecclesiastics who sympathized with their monarch's view were beginning to climb the hierarchical ladder, to emerge at the top in the 1580s. To this group the settlement and the 39 Articles were the crucial test of uniformity.[2]

The short term success of the Elizabethan settlement in providing for a peaceful change in matters of religion was not due to the virtues of the *via media* and their natural appeal, but to confusion over the precise status of the terms of settlement. Did they provide a document for further discussion or a definite statement of the ecclesiastical polity of the English church? In that confusion

[1]The problems posed by the settlement are discussed at length in *Eliz. Puritan Movt.* 21–50.
[2]R. Robinson (ed.) *The Zurich Letters* (Parker Society, 1842–1845), i. letters nos. ix, xvii, lxiv, lxix, lxxiii for example.

lay the germ of long-term disagreements. In the years immediately following the settlement, however, this sort of discussion was largely confined to the intelligentsia among the ranks of the clergy and the more far-sighted of the laity involved in national politics. The ease with which the settlement was carried through in the localities rested partly in that confusion, but also owed a lot to a truism of provincial life; it was one thing for Crown and government to legislate and quite another business to bring that law into effect. The only professional administrators were ecclesiastics working with poorly-financed institutions; secular administration was in the hands of local gentry at the county level, and voluntary officials in the hundreds and the parishes. At all levels the local administrators were more likely to reflect the prejudices of their environment rather than the policies of the government. In such circumstances it is hardly surprising that the diocese of Peterborough was not transformed into a protestant community overnight.

Soon after his return to England in 1559 Edmund Grindal wrote to his friend Conrad Hubert, preacher at Strasbourg, reporting on the state of religion in England; progress was slow and the chief difficulty was the 'great dearth of godly ministers', and in this the diocese of Peterborough was no exception.[3] The years following Elizabeth's accession did not see deprivations among the parish clergy of the same order as under Mary and between 1559 and 1564 only sixteen clergy were deprived for refusal to conform to the terms of the settlement. In addition to these men, only two of whom were graduates, a further seventeen clergy resigned and some of these, such as Edmund Perton of Plumpton, were Marian appointees who may have resigned because of the religious changes.[4] The rest of the parochial clergy remained with their cures, though in some cases their commitment to the religion of the new regime was likely to be minimal. Under Mary the issue involving deprivation was marriage and, as such, was clear cut; if married a priest had either to separate from his wife or his calling and there was little scope for 'trimming'. In the early days of Elizabeth's reign the issue was not clear cut and some men like Thomas Fox, vicar of Weedon Lois, chose to acquiesce rather than lose their livelihood. Fox remained in his parish until his death in 1570 but his will, with its mention of the Virgin Mary and the saints, shows him to have been entrenched in conservative attitudes, hardly surprising in a man who had first entered the living in 1524. Another recruit to the diocese in the 1520s, Thomas Mowmforth, rector of Aldwincle All Saints was, by the time of his death in 1568, still ambiguous about his theological loyalties, commending his soul

> unto Christ Jesus, my maker and redeemer and saviour in whom and by the merits of his blessed passion is all my whole faith, full trust, and hope of clear remission and forgiveness of all my sins, and by the same to be saved and to have the fruition of his presence in Joy for ever. Beseeching the blessed virgin our Lady St Mary, mother to our saviour Jesus Christ, with all the celestial company of heaven to pray for me.

Such men were unlikely to bring about the reformation Grindal had in mind.[5]

These two examples do, of course, refer to old men unlikely to change their views late in life, but the chief problem of the diocese in the 1560s was the ab-

---

[3] R. Robinson (ed.) *The Zurich Letters*, ii, letter no. viii.

[4] H. Gee, *The Elizabethan Clergy and the settlement of Religion 1558–1564* (Oxford, 1898), 22. To his list add Richard Raynes of Lutton and Robert Kyrley of Southwick; P.D.R., Inst. Bk. I, ff. 75v, 79, 84–103; Vis. Bk. I, f. 63.

[5] *H.I.L.*, v. 103; x. 13; P.D.R., Will Volume, S 135, T 1.

sence of a group of younger, able and committed clerics ready to counter the influence of the conservatives. Of 229 parish clergy known to be serving parishes in the diocese in 1560, only 39 are known to have been at university and almost half of these were pluralists; some such as George Neville, archdeacon of the East Riding, or William Mowse, Dean of Arches and vicar-general to the archbishop of Canterbury, had responsible posts elsewhere and were unlikely to attend to their parochial responsibilities. The percentage of graduates in the diocese was lower at this date than that obtaining in the dioceses of Worcester and Exeter, although they were both much further removed from the universities.[6] It was the responsibility of the new bishop, Scambler, to attempt to improve standards of recruitment to the parish clergy and to lessen the debilitating effect of pluralism and non-residence on pastoral care. In 1560 there were 48 pluralists in parochial livings and 86 parishes were served by incumbents who did not reside or had responsibilities elsewhere. Not all cases of pluralism were incompatible with a proper standard of pastoral care and John Pratt, who held the adjacent livings of Corby and Weldon, could probably serve his congregations adequately. Nevertheless, pluralism was a serious problem not made easier by the shortage of clergy; at the same survey in 1560 twenty-one livings remained vacant. Scambler himself made some attempt to check the worst abuses of pluralism by checking on dispensations for plurality, and also tried to ensure at least some standards of learning among the clergy. Two aspiring clerics are known to have been refused appointment by the bishop because of deficiencies in learning, one to the mastership of St Leonard's Hospital and another to the rectory of Ufford. The problem of finding able ministers remained grave; the official survey in 1560 listed 166 parochial clergy and found that only nine of them were preachers.[7] This was a small force to bring about a reformation in the diocese and, dispersed as they were, their influence was likely to be minimal. Indeed some of them had originally received preaching licences in Mary's reign and only in two parishes, Finedon and Kettering, can one find early examples of protestant laity in parishes served by preachers.[8]

The difficulties of the church in the years following the settlement of 1559 ensured that the religious policies of the government would be slow to influence the laity. The decade following Elizabeth's accession is marked by the almost total absence of evidence for commitment to protestant ideals from the laity, except in a few localities. The impression given from the probate evidence of the archdeaconry court at Northampton is one of a retreat from catholicism and conservatism, but this was not accompanied by an obvious advance of articulate protestantism. Many of the clergy serving in the diocese at this time had served their congregation in Mary's reign also, and the caution of churchwardens in retaining expensive items of furniture, such as rood screens, as long as they were likely to be restored does not suggest a commitment to reform.[9] This lack of commitment, probably born out of the uncertainty and confusion of the religious changes of the previous decades, is amply underlined by the preambles to wills proved at Northampton in the early years of the reign; conservative statements of belief declined rapidly after 1560, but most testators chose fairly

[6]The figures are compiled from *H.I.L.* and Corpus Christi College, Cambridge, MS 122. Figures for Worcester are in C. Hill, *Economic Problems of the Church* (Oxford, 1956), 207 n. 1, and for Devon in A. L. Rowse, *Tudor Cornwall* (1941), 324.

[7]Corpus Christi College, Cambridge Ms. 122; P.D.R., Inst. Bk. II, f. 6; Bridges, i. 417.

[8]E.g. P.D.R., Will Volumes, P 333, 348; R 94.

[9]G. Anstruther, *Vaux of Harrowden* (Newport, 1953), 77–79. He also identifies 41 Marian clergy serving in the diocese in 1570, *ibid.* 75.

c

noncommittal statements, bequeathing their souls simply 'to God' or 'to God, my maker and redeemer' to replace the earlier pious sentiments. The proportion of protestant preambles remained at little over 10 per cent of the total until 1566 when references to 'Christ's passion' or to 'the elect' began to increase, so that by 1569 wills of that nature represented almost 30 per cent of the total. Although

**Table 1**   Religious Preambles of Wills Proved at Northampton 1558–1569

|      | Conservative | | Neutral | | Protestant wills | Uncertain |
|------|------|------|------|------|------|------|
|      | GMS | GS | G | GMR | | |
| 1558 | 153 | 14 | 22 | 22 | 11 | 1 |
| 1559 | 114 | 17 | 45 | 29 | 24 | 4 |
| 1560 | 58 | 37 | 38 | 28 | 27 | 3 |
| 1561 | 5 | 15 | 10 | 9 | 10 | 1 |
| 1562 | 5 | 9 | 15 | 17 | 7 | |
| 1563 | 5 | 2 | 34 | 12 | 9 | |
| 1564 | 3 | 2 | 56 | 10 | 11 | |
| 1565 | 4 | 4 | 41 | 8 | 7 | |
| 1566 | 5 | 6 | 33 | 18 | 14 | 2 |
| 1567 | 6 | 13 | 22 | 30 | 19 | 1 |
| 1568 | 6 | 6 | 29 | 29 | 21 | 4 |
| 1569 | 1 | 5 | 30 | 27 | 27 | |

*Key*   GMS   God, Mary and the Saints
        GS    God and the Saints
        G     God
        GMR   God, my maker and redeemer

*Source* P.D.R. Will Volumes (1st Series), P, Q, R, S.

the statistics are likely to be distorted by the uneven geographical spread of the wills, it seems clear that the protestant reformation really began to take hold among the laity in the diocese only in the later 1560s. It was foundations laid in this early period that aided the sudden growth of puritan activity in the diocese after 1570, and it is worthwhile examining some of the communities and personalities involved in laying these local foundations.

The early appearance of a protestant tradition at Earls Barton on the banks of the Nene about eight miles east of Northampton has already been mentioned, and that tradition was maintained in the 1560s through the influence of the vicar, Henry Neale. Neale may have been a graduate and had ministered at Earls Barton since 1542 to a congregation which appears to have been consistently protestant from the reign of Edward VI. His views are reflected in the wills of the farming community he served, and when making his own testament in 1570 he followed an orthodox protestant preamble with small bequests for the poor in the neighbouring parishes of Great Doddington and Wollaston in addition to a bequest of 26s. 8d. to a preacher to preach four sermons within a year of his death.[10] Among the witnesses to his will were Robert Welford, a member of a family of parish gentry already noted as protestants and later to have separatist connections, and William Anderson, rector of Whiston where the puritans were to establish an important centre in the 1570s.[11] Adjacent parishes

[10]H.I.L., x. 41; P.D.R., Will Volume T 21.
[11]See below pp. 28, 42.

to Earls Barton contained protestant inhabitants and Neale himself probably belonged to a local landholding family at Wollaston. If so then his influence may have been important in introducing advanced protestant ideas to neighbouring gentry; George Carleton of Wollaston was soon to be a prominent political supporter of puritan clergy and Isabel Catesby of Whiston provided support for Percival Wiburn after his removal from the county town.[12]

It is in the Nene valley area that the evidence for the early reception of protestant ideas among the laity is strongest, and another minor landholding family with many family ties among the clergy was to play a prominent part in the area some ten miles north of Earls Barton at Cranford. It was from there that the famous puritan preacher Eusebius Paget hailed, but the leading protestant family was the Fosbrookes, whose influence at Twywell, Islip and Titchmarsh can be seen in the wills from these parishes. A little further south-east the tradition already established at Raunds continued to flourish and influence adjacent parishes on the opposite banks of the Nene.[13] The most important centre of protestant activity at this time was the county town, some 16 miles upstream. The emergence of protestantism at Northampton was noted in Mary's reign, and Calvinist doctrine soon took a firm hold in important sections of the community if the wills of the inhabitants are to be believed. One of the clerics involved seems to have been William Baylie, vicar of St Giles, but the wills of the townsmen indicate an idiosyncrasy and individuality not attributable to one source; many lay great stress on the trinity whilst others express hope in joining 'the elect' or being counted 'among the numbers of those that shall be saved'. The evidence cannot tell us how great was the progress of Calvinism in the town but the will of one prominent citizen, Thomas Collis, a grocer who had served as mayor in 1561, shows that the inhabitants were aware of developments in the pattern of puritan activity elsewhere. His will, drawn up on 1 August 1567, began 'First and above all I commend my soule to almighty god, and to our Lord Jesus Christ through whose most blessed passion and merits I hope undoubtedly to be one of those which at the day of Judgement shall be saved.' Collis then went on to ask for christian burial 'and then and there to have a divine sermon according to the manner now used at funerals. Also that there be given to the preacher 6s. 8d. in money for his pains.'[14] This is the earliest local reference to a funeral sermon, a popular puritan practice in London and elsewhere, and who the preacher may have been is a mystery, but Eusebius Paget of Old was soon to be in demand as a local preacher at funerals. However two clerics in villages just to the south of the town were at that time laying foundations for radical protestant traditions; Thurston Moseley of Hardingstone was a regular witness to the very Calvinist wills of his parishioners, and George Gilderd of Collingtree was continuing the tradition first established by his father John, whose will contained several bequests to the poor of his home county, Yorkshire, and a preamble mentioning 'the elect people of God'. George, the son, had been at Cambridge and was soon to be noted as a nonconformist.[15] The influence of the county town was reflected in other parishes on its boundaries; inhabitants at Great and Little

[12]*Visitations of Northants, 1564, 1618–19*, 118; see pp. 26, 105–106.

[13]E.g. Will Volumes R 160, 205, 586 for Fosbrookes; R 99, 103, 105, 197, T 262 for Raunds.

[14]*H.I.L.*, x. 142–143; several wills could be cited here, mostly from St Giles' parish, they include members of the Wilkinson family (P.D.R. Will Volume S 11, 158). Collis was of All Saints parish (S 94).

[15]P.D.R., Will Volume P 362; *H.I.L.*, v. 243–245, for Hardingstone see Will Volume S 13, 222, 232.

Houghton in the south-east, and at Boughton and Moulton to the north all recorded protestant preambles in the years immediately following the accession of Elizabeth.[16]

Beyond the Nene valley between Northampton and Oundle, protestantism had taken root in Rutland, most particularly in the parishes along the roads between Oakham and Uppingham; Wardley to the west had an early tradition, but preambles from Ayston, Preston, Manton, Ridlington, and Brooke all underline the progress made by the reformation in that region by 1570.[17] Elsewhere, Exton where the Harrington family resided and North Luffenham appear to have been centres, whilst in Northamptonshire a few parishes around Daventry and on Watling Street provide examples of protestant laymen.[18] Throughout the diocese there are examples of individual protestants at this date, but not sufficient evidence to point to a protestant tradition. By 1570 examples of villages where protestant and Calvinist ideas had been received among the laity could be multiplied, but it was only in the Nene valley and the western area of Rutland that those ideas had gained more than a very localized currency. In both areas protestantism had a history stretching back to the beginning of Elizabeth's reign and beyond. Neither locality was to emerge in the forefront of the clerical presbyterian campaigns of the 1580s, and the clergy there were less committed to the *classes*. The slower and more natural growth of protestantism among the people may have militated against the gentry-inspired political puritanism of the south and west, though this is not to say that these regions were less radical. These considerations take the story on rather further than is proper at this stage and, in 1570, the principal problem was to provide the means of evangelizing the county.

## Early growth and first crisis

At the visitation in the spring of 1570 the rector of the Godstow mediety of Pattishall was presented for using the Latin service of Our Lady to the annoyance of his congregation. He was ordered to be present at the next prophesying at Northampton and to accommodate his views to those of the church. Percival Wiburn was to provide a certificate as to his reformation and if none was forthcoming the rector had to appear before the court again on 24 May.[19] This report contains the earliest local reference to the 'prophesying' or 'exercise' held at Northampton and to Percival Wiburn, the founder and moderator of that exercise which was to become a landmark in the history of puritanism both locally and nationally. The exercises were established widely throughout the country in the 1570s and represented the ideals of the moderate reformers who sought not to overhaul or overthrow the system completely, but to remove the more obvious abuses and to improve local standards of clerical learning and pastoral care. Their approach was to provide locally inspired opportunities, based in market towns, for discussion among the clergy and for preaching to the laity. Many bishops, such as Grindal at York and Curteys at Chichester, gave them support and indeed took the initiative in their establishment. At Peterborough Scambler was happy to use the exercises as the local vehicle for sup-

[16]P.D.R., Will Volume R 29; S 30, 39, 132.

[17]*Ibid.* P 349, 393, 414; R 266, 249; S 23, 79, 80; T 31, 48, 49, 81.

[18]*Ibid.* P 391, 408, 415; R 159, 201, 204, 208; S 37 for Exton and North Luffenham. Newnham and Norton by Daventry have good series of protestant wills.

[19]E. A. Irons 'An Episcopal Visitation in 1570', *Northants N & Q* (New Series), ii. 118.

porting and enforcing the verdicts of the conventional courts christian.[20] This was particularly true when the problem being faced was conservatism or catholic sympathies among the clergy. Scambler not only used the Northampton exercise for this, but shortly afterwards was ordering the recantation of a catholic priest to take place in another exercise established at Oundle.[21] The organization, aims, and purposes of these meetings can be best illustrated from the orders drawn up for the conduct of the Northamptonshire meetings in 1571 which were clearly intended to provide an integrated and continuing opportunity for local initiative in matters of clerical discipline and pastoral care, which would work in support of the more distant episcopal authority.

The arrangements for the exercise have been printed on several occasions and need no further repetition here. Having ordered the suppression of 'idolatrous' practices and made provision for the advance of protestantism in the town itself, the authors turned their attention to arranging regular contacts for the clergy of the area. Every cleric, on entering the exercise, was required to subscribe his consent to 'Christ's true religion' and to the discipline of his brethren. His name was then entered on a list and the membership had to take it in turn to act as principal speaker on a text of scripture. A text was treated of at each exercise and the first speaker given 45 minutes to analyse the text and other commentaries; his treatment was then discussed by two other members of the exercise, who were allowed 15 minutes each. The exercise was then concluded by the moderator, an office which circulated among the more learned of the members. This part of the exercise, which was not to last more than two hours, then led on to a more restricted discussion among the learned members about the various expositions they had heard that day. In addition to intellectual criticism, the more learned members also undertook to admonish any moral or spiritual failings of the clergy. Care was taken to ensure that this part of the exercise did not degenerate into abuse and nobody was permitted to move any subject extempore. The consultations ended with 'some short exhortations to move each one to go forward in his office, to apply his study, and to increase his godliness of manners and newness of life'. Arrangements were then finalized for the next meeting, held every Saturday in 1571. A confession of faith followed and failure to observe this or the rules of the exercise were to be punished publicly before the brethren.[22]

It is clear that these rules had episcopal support, but their chief inspiration was Percival Wiburn, a prominent exile in the reign of Mary who had kept in touch with the friends he had made among the continental reformers. He had been involved, with some other London clergy, in an early confrontation with the hierarchy, known as the Vestiarian Controversy, which had taken place in 1566 and had centred on the vexed question of the legality of enforcing the wearing of clerical apparel which many clergy considered 'popish'. Wiburn had suffered deprivation for his stand and sometime later, it is not clear exactly when, he removed himself to Northamptonshire.[23] The reasons behind this move bear some investigation. It has generally been considered that Wiburn's arrival in Northampton resulted from an initiative by some of the gentry of the county

---

[20]*Eliz. Puritan Movt.* 168–176 discusses the exercises at length; for Curteys see R. B. Manning, *Religion and Society in Elizabethan Sussex*, 76–78, 190–191.

[21]B.L., Lansd. Ms. 21, f. 4.

[22]In *V.C.H. Northants.*, ii. 38–39; *The Borough Records*, ii. 386–390; R. M. Serjeantson, *A History of the Church of All Saints, Northampton* (Northampton, 1907), 104–108.

[23]*Eliz. Puritan Movt.* 48, 74, 75, 79–83.

associated with early demands for the reform of the church and linked to each other through connections with the Earl of Leicester. The Earl was clearly behind the establishment of the order and exercise at Northampton where, as we have seen, there were a group of zealous citizens who would welcome the ministrations of Wiburn. Among the gentry involved there was certainly Sir Richard Knightley, who in 1572 was to establish a lectureship at Towcester for Andrew King, another veteran of the Vestiarian Controversy. The expenses of this post were borne by the Earl of Leicester and Bishop Bentham of Coventry and Lichfield as well as by Knightley. Another former London minister, Nicholas Standen was soon to share the leadership of an exercise at Overstone with King, and its patron George Carleton of Wollaston may also have been involved in establishing the Northampton exercise.[24] These men were likely to have had their first contact with puritanism through their visits to the capital on business, administrative, and parliamentary affairs, and it was this contact with the capital that was to prove crucial in forming their views. Less obviously in contact with the capital, but very probably involved in the establishment of puritanism in the county at this date, was Isabel Catesby, the widowed lady of the manor at Whiston. During her time at Whiston the village became a notable centre of puritan activity to which Wiburn retired when removed from Northampton. She may well have been the 'Mistress Catesby' to whom John Field, the London based organizer of puritan activity, addressed himself in one copy of his presbyterian tract, *An Admonition to the Parliament* published in 1572. Her home parish Whiston had already benefited from her piety when, in her more orthodox days, Mrs Catesby and her husband rebuilt their parish church in 1534, placing there an inscription with the conventional request for prayers for their souls.[25]

This group brought Wiburn to Northampton and he met with quick success, due in part to the support he received from important sections of the community, among whom we can mention the aldermanic families of Raynsford, Manley and Coldwell. His success was such that, in addition to the exercise, Wiburn went on to establish the 'order' of Northampton on 5 June 1571. The order was intended to graft the religious life of the community on to its civic institutions after the pattern of the consistory at Geneva so that by 'the bishop's authority and the mayor's joined together . . . ill life is corrected, God's glory set forth and the people brought in good obedience'. This was a radical departure, even by puritan standards, and aroused some vocal opposition from within the town.[26] Scambler acted quickly to suppress the order thereby incurring the wrath of the Earl of Leicester who at the instigation of the mayor and assembly of the town, intervened on Wiburn's behalf. The order was principally concerned with the internal history of the town and, as such, will be dealt with later, but it appears that Scambler also wished to suppress the exercise. This was an entirely different matter and, under pressure from Leicester, the bishop was at pains to promise to reinstate the meeting. It was clear that the main bone of contention between the earl and the bishop was the future of Wiburn. Leicester wanted to have him reinstated as a preacher in the town but the bishop, who accused the puritan of being 'over-studious of innovation', refused to do this unless Wiburn conformed. He did however 'promise your honour that [a] good and godly exercise shall be maintained, at Northampton, either with Mr Wyborne's

[24]P.R.O., SP12/150/42 (1); see p. 28.
[25]*Eliz. Puritan Movt.* 136; Bridges, i. 389–390. Mr V. A. Hatley kindly drew my attention to the Catesby connections.
[26]*Borough Records*, ii. 387; see pp. 120–122.

help or without it'. The bishop went on to point out that there were other exercises or 'conferences of ministers' in the diocese which did not depend on Wiburn's presence, and mentioned two in particular; one at Stamford, which was attended by ministers of Lincoln diocese as well as by clergy from Peterborough, and another in Rutland. Of this latter the bishop went on to say 'there was conference in some parts of the diocese among the ministers even in Rutland, before they heard Mr Wiburn named'.[27] If this was to suggest that an exercise was in existence in Rutland before the establishment of the Northampton meeting, then some reassessment of the process by which puritan ideas spread throughout the area must be made. Rutland puritanism might have drawn strength from the early settlement of puritan activity in Leicestershire under the patronage of the Earl of Huntingdon, as much as from events in Northampton. The Leicestershire puritans, led by Anthony Gilby of Ashby-de-la-Zouche, later developed a tradition of a more pastoral than political nature in their ministry and this was also true of Rutland clerics. Whether the exercise predated that at Northampton or not is unclear, but the early appearance of one in Rutland fits in well with what we know of the emergence of a protestant laity in that area in the 1560s.[28]

The identity of the leaders of the meetings in Rutland and at Stamford remains obscure, for none of the clergy who were later to figure prominently in puritan activity in the area had acquired any livings in the diocese by this date. At Stretton Herbert Fludd, possibly related to the more famous William Fludd and like him an *alumnus* of Peterhouse, Cambridge was already active and may have been rector. His name appears among a list of clergy from the north part of the diocese and from the Soke which is dated 1572 and may be a roll of members of the exercises in that region. Fludd's name is almost at the top of the list which includes the names of others, like William Rowe of Exton, who were later to appear before the courts for nonconformity on matters of ceremonial, but who did not take an active part in more radical departures. The list names 39 clergy, who comprised a large proportion of the ministers working in the area, and the impression gained from it is that the exercises in this region were of a non-partisan nature chiefly concerned to improve clerical standards. Although inspired by the same aims as the puritans they were not dominated by them. The Stamford exercise may well have been led from among the Lincoln diocesan clergy, but Richard Liveley of Maxey was likely to have been one of the organizers. At any rate the importance he attached to his preaching activity had already created a conflict between that and his pastoral responsibilities to his congregation, who presented him in 1570 for being 'somewhat slack in doing of his service by reason of doing his business and preaching abroad'. His influence in the area continued after his transfer to the nearby living of Deeping Gate in Lincoln diocese.[29]

This list is followed by another which is more readily identified with the exercise based at Northampton. There are twenty names headed by that of Percival Wiburn, which is clearly set apart from the rest. Many of those named were later to play a prominent part in puritan confrontations with authority and included two men already noted as inculcating protestant beliefs among their

[27]National Register of Archives, Baskerville Transcripts, De L'isle and Dudley Ms., ii, no. 60.
[28]M. C. Cross, *The Puritan Earl* (1966), 124–139.
[29]P.D.R., ML 560 f. 47; H.I.L. v. 67; ix. 9; Irons, 'An Episcopal Visitation in 1570', 178. He was succeeded at Maxey by his son-in-law.

congregations, George Gilderd of Collingtree and Thurston Moseley of Harding-stone, as well as others like Nicholas Edwards and Nicholas Williamson, who were deeply involved in puritan affairs in the mid 1580s. Robert Cawdry, who was later to introduce his own idiosyncratic and uncompromising brand of puritanism to the Rutland living of South Luffenham, was also included in the list. Despite the presence of these men the Northampton exercise seemed also to have had a wide following in the area from clergy not known for puritan sympathies, although it is true to say that most of those named were among the younger generation of the parish clergy and there was little support from their older colleagues. The other striking feature of the list is the total absence of the beneficed clergy of the county town among the names.[30] However, most of them, like John Roote vicar of St Giles and a former monk of St Andrew's, were of a generation unlikely to be impressed by innovation.[31] The Northampton exercise had a more obviously puritan membership than the others, and the puritans certainly came to dominate its activities in the following years, but they would not have had the platform provided for them unless the exercises com-manded powerful support in the community and regular attendance by a reasonable proportion of the parish clergy.

With or without Wiburn the exercise at Northampton survived his removal from the town to Whiston and became one of a whole network of prophesyings throughout the Midlands. It was however the Northampton meeting that pro-voked the first confrontation between puritans in the provinces and authority which assumed national significance. Information first came to light in the visita-tion of 1573 when details of the exercise at Overstone were uncovered. At the same time it became clear that several inhabitants of Northampton had aban-doned their parish churches following Wiburn's removal, and had attended services at Whiston where he was then resident.[32] On 13 April 1573 Scambler wrote to William Cecil, Secretary of State, asking for advice on how to deal with the growing number of 'diverse young ministers to whom it is plausible to have absolute authority in their parishes'. The bishop may have been refer-ring to the specific case of Roger Trinling, curate of Overstone, who was being intimidated by the puritan faction in his parish, supported by the preachers Standen and King, or to the growing support that there was for the ideas of Thomas Cartwright, the chief intellectual advocate of a presbyterian form of church government with an emphasis on discipline being securely based in the local church community rather than in the episcopal courts.[33] Certainly the Privy Council had had its attention drawn to the printing of illegal books in the county at this time, and the most likely work to attract attention would have been *The Replye* of the presbyterian Cartwright to John Whitgift.[34]

At Overstone the *Book of Common Prayer* had been abandoned completely and replaced by communal psalm-singing followed by a sermon, devotional practices characteristic of later puritanism. Coming so soon after the parliamen-tary confrontation between the government and the puritans, who had tried to get a bill through parliament permitting preaching ministers with charge of a congregation to depart from the prescribed order of prayer if they had episcopal

[30]P.D.R., ML 560 f. 47v. This absence is surprising in view of the character of lay pro-testantism in the town.

[31]*H.I.L.*, xi. 257.

[32]P.D.R., Vis. Bk. 3, unfoliated; B. L. Lansd. Ms. 17, f. 55.

[33]*Ibid.*; P.D.R., X607/8, f. 2.

[34]*A.P.C.*, viii. 93, A. F. Scott-Pearson, *Thomas Cartwright and Elizabethan Puritanism* (1925), 85–106, discusses *The Replye* and suggests that it may have been printed in the county.

permission, Scambler was forced to take the matter very seriously.[35] The events uncovered by his visitation of 1573 led to the first provincial confrontation between puritans and the hierarchy to be of more than local significance. That this was the case was mainly due to the powerful support for the puritans who were threatened by the bishop. Scambler decided to ask his clergy to subscribe to two articles, both of them likely to be repugnant to the more radical puritans. The first demanded not only toleration of the *Book of Common Prayer*, but also an affirmation that all its contents were agreeable to the word of God; the second concerned the ordinal and the ordination of non-preaching ministers, the legality of which was challenged by some puritans. The latter was to be a recurring source of local controversy, and five clergy were threatened with deprivation for refusal to subscribe. The ministers, probably through John Field, were kept in touch with events in parliament and offered to use the Prayer Book and not to preach against it 'until this present parliament'. This was not good enough for the bishop and the five were suspended and three weeks later, on 29 January 1574, they were deprived of their livings.[36]

Scambler's action again brought him into conflict with the Earl of Leicester who had already interfered in the running of the diocesan courts on behalf of one of the deprived, Thurston Moseley, vicar of Hardingstone. Moseley had previously been in trouble with authority and, on 23 December 1572, the bishop had held a special session of his court in order to restore Moseley to his parish because 'The earl of Leicester, by his letters, required the same.'[37] When Moseley was deprived just over a year later Leicester's attitude was hardly likely to alter. Though the bishop, when considering deprivation, expressed concern because the puritan clergy 'be very bold and stout, like men that seem not to be without great friends', he may not have anticipated the extent of the support that these ministers also had among the humbler sort of people. Their congregations had also attempted to intervene on behalf of the deprived clergy, who had a considerable local following for 'the number of those that have been won by preachers are no small number, as it hath appeared when in Billing iij days before the deputation, there did ride to the Bishop above xij, coming with them the hands of xx more. Likewise did the godly of Collingtree deal with the chancellor.'[38] This sort of local support ensured that, although the bishop could deprive the puritan clergy of their livings and their incomes, Scambler could not destroy their local influence. Of those deprived four remained in or reappeared in the locality; William Dawson, rector of Weston Favell, remained as a schoolmaster at Northampton where he attended clandestine services; Thurston Mosely withdrew from Hardingstone to Sywell, a parish adjacent to Overstone where he continued to attend services; Arthur Wake, rector of Great Billing, retained his office as Master of the Hospital of St John at Northampton, through the influence of the town governors, and Eusebius Paget was later identified by John Aylmer, a staunch opponent of the puritans, as one of 'a rank of rangers and posting apostles that go from shire to shire, from Exercise to Exercise' throughout the Midlands.[39] Named as a fellow apostle of Paget was Nicholas Standen, one of the leaders of the Overstone meetings. Only George Gilderd, rector of Collingtree, cannot be traced after

---

[35]B.L. Lansd. Ms. 17, f. 55; J. E. Neale, *Elizabeth I and her Parliaments*, i (1953), 297–304.
[36]A. Peel (ed.), *The Seconde Parte of a Register* (Cambridge, 1915), i. 121–122.
[37]P.D.R., X607/8, f. 73.
[38]Peel, *The Seconde Parte*, i. 122.
[39]Sheils, 'Some problems of government', *Change and Continuity*, 177–178.

his deprivation but, hailing from the same parish, he may well have retired to the position of a private layman in a community where he was known and respected.[40]

It is clear from the distribution of these clergy that it was the exercise at Northampton which Scambler was most concerned with, and indeed three of the deprived had acted as moderators of that exercise at one time or another.[41] The attack on these men, so soon after the removal of Wiburn, must have been a blow to the exercise whether they ceased to attend its meetings or not, but a survey of 1576 shows that the exercise continued to foster nonconformity among the parish clergy. The survey covers the whole diocese but is very optimistic in its assessment of the level of conformity, for only seven of the parish clergy had their attitudes called into question. Four of them were involved in the North-ampton exercise. Arthur Wake, who has already been mentioned; Robert Morris of Brafield on the Green and Nicholas Edwards of Courteenhall were both said to be 'barely conformable'; and John Tymms of Whiston was described as a nonconformist who preached against the law and received many people from neighbouring parishes to the Eucharist and services in the parish.[42] Scambler's attack on the puritan clergy may have been a setback, but they soon recovered their position in the locality.

A principal reason for recovery was the sense of professional competence and mutual support which regular meeting and discussion in the exercise provided. This sort of local collegiality encouraged a self-confidence which was clearly illustrated by the dispute involving a sermon of John Sibthorpe, rector of Ashton. His sermon was delivered at All Saints Northampton, in June 1574, presumably at the exercise. Sibthorpe was charged with preaching 'openly that the word of God and the laws made by the prince do not agree touching the wearing of the surplice', a dress considered popish by puritan clergy but still legal in the established church. Sibthorpe complied with the court order to appear and produce a text of his sermon on 15 July. In making his defence, he placed the authority of the exercise against that of the normal courts when he maintained that he would

> bring in learned men to confirm and justify the same betwixt this and Michael-
> mas next or else offer to recant openly in Allhallows where he preached it,
> saying that Mr Collinson, Mr Sharrocke, and Mr Edwardes have seen his
> sermon and not disallowed it. Wherefore my Lord thought good that they
> should be called to show the cause of that allowance or not disallowance of
> the same.

The mutual examination of doctrine outlined in the original plans for the exer-cises was clearly taking place and Sibthorpe was happy to appeal to the verdict of his neighbouring colleagues. Although the bishop intended to call on the members of the exercise to justify their actions, no record of such a meeting survives and both they and Sibthorpe remained undisturbed in their livings.[43] The case illustrates the degree of influence which the exercise had come to have over a substantial number of local clergy, and suggests that the puritans who dominated that exercise had a wide measure of support among the clergy

---

[40]*H.I.L.*, v. 243.
[41]Peel, *The Seconde Parte*, i. 121.
[42]Lambeth Palace Library, Carte Miscellanee, xiii. 56.
[43]*H.I.L.*, xii. 169; P.D.R., Archd. Ct. Bk. 4, f. 2v.; X608/14, f. 48. Sibthorpe went on to become a *classis* member, as did Nicholas Edwards, see p. 54.

working within a ten mile radius of Northampton. The events of 1574 did little
to retard the spread of puritanism in the area around Northampton, but did
create local antagonism against authority and also provide the puritans with a
cause for complaint about high-handed episcopal action.

The effect of the crisis on the area was small, but in the particular parishes
involved, the deprivations could cause considerable disruption to religious life.
At Old, where Paget had been incumbent, the churchwardens complained that
they still wanted a parson as late as November 1575, and that 'diverse things
hath been out of order for the space of one year and a half and therefore they
want their quarter sermons, the distribution to the poor, and many other things
thereunto, in defalt of Mr Isham the patron'. John Isham, the patron, was an
uncle of Eusebius Paget whose deprivation had, not surprisingly, led to friction
between patron and bishop. Isham accused Scambler of failure to inform him
of the vacancy, though he can hardly have been ignorant of the situation, and
denied neglecting to fill the post. This was probably an attempt at prevarication
in the hope of restoring Paget to the living. In the 22 months since Paget's
deprivation the living had been served by John Smeton, incumbent of the
adjacent parish of Scaldwell. Smeton was a pluralist whose other living at Overstone had been the location for the preaching activities of Standen and King
which had first drawn Scambler's attention to the extent of puritan activity in
the area.[44]

Continuity of services and worship (they were not always identical) in livings
deprived of puritan clergy for one reason or another was usually maintained by
beneficed curates sympathetic to their ideals. The importance of these ministers
to the movement cannot be overestimated, though they make only fleeting
appearances in the records. Paget and Standen represent the leadership among
the 'rank of roving rangers and apostles', but their work and that of leading
puritans who had cure of souls but whose involvement in the movement
necessitated periods of absence from their cures depended on the goodwill and
support of lesser apostles. The adjacent living to Old, Lamport where the Isham
family resided, depended on the ministrations of these men at this time. In 1574
the curate Robert Hipwell was presented for not wearing the surplice and in 1577
was found serving the chapelries of Faxton and Hanging Houghton. His place
at Lamport at that date was taken by William Prettie, later a close associate and
*amanuensis* to Edmund Snape whose activities as secretary to the Northampton
*classis* were not always compatible with serving his cure at St Peter's church in
the town.[45] When a similar crisis occurred in 1584 over subscription to Whitgift's Three Articles the incumbent of Easton on the Hill was deprived and the
cure served by Christopher Cumbrell, another unbeneficed puritan who was
presented in 1587 for unlicensed preaching at Easton on the Hill, at Tinwell and
other unspecified places. There was also some doubt as to whether he was in
orders, but this had been sorted out by 1592 when he was presented for not
wearing the surplice and refusing to church women after childbirth.[46] Men like
Hipwell, Prettie, and Cumbrell made a significant if shadowy contribution to
sustaining local puritans in times of stress, and assisted the leading puritan incumbents in their pastoral functions. Such a second rank of ministers had emerged

[44]P.D.R., Archd. Ct. Bk. 4, ff. 72v., 77v.; Finch, *Five Northants. Families*, 5, n. 4; H.I.L.
x. 141, xii. 205.

[45]P.D.R., Archd. Ct. Bk. 4, f. 5v; Will Volume V, f. 6; X608/13, f. 145; R. Bancroft,
*Daungerous Positions and Proceedings* (1593), 82; H.I.L. vii. 33; xvi. 109.

[46]Peel, *The Seconde Parte*, ii. 91–93; P.D.R., X609/21, f. 86; X610/23a, f. 126.

in the diocese by the mid 70s and their value in keeping contact with the congregations can be shown by comparing the effect of puritan evangelism in this diocese with the situation in parts of Lancashire where puritan incumbents working in a hostile environment were not always able to reconcile their administrative responsibilities towards their puritan colleagues with their pastoral responsibilities to their flocks. As a result their ministry was far less effective than that of their midland colleagues.[47]

## The situation in 1576

If anything, the deprivations of 1574 illustrated the strength of puritanism among the clergy in one part of the diocese; a strength based on gentry and congregational support and helped by regular contacts at the exercises. Within the diocese the events of 1574 marked a change in the relationship between the puritans and the bishop, but nationally the turning point did not come until 1576 when the Queen initiated government action against the exercises in general. Some exercises had, like that at Northampton, become dominated by puritans increasingly active in organizing demands for further reform of the terms of the religious settlement. The organizing talents of John Field in London and the publication of work by the group associated with Thomas Cartwright had provided the more radical puritans with a coherent plan for reform along presbyterian lines and with a network of contacts ensuring that their policy received powerful support among the parliamentary gentry. Attempts to press for reform had already been made in the parliament of 1572, where the strength of support among the gentry may have made some members of the government apprehensive. By 1576 the old idea of reforming episcopacy in order to remove its worst abuses and to provide a more localized and less hierarchical form of ecclesiastical discipline had given way to demands for a fully fledged presbyterian system among more radical puritans.[48]

It was not surprising that the government focused its attention on the midland exercises, and it was fitting that the one which first attracted the attention of the Council was led by one of the deprived Northamptonshire clergy, Eusebius Paget. Paget, with John Oxenbridge, was a moderator of the exercise at Southam in Warwickshire, just outside the diocese, which was claimed to be the best in England 'undoubtedly without exception' by the midland puritans. The bishop of Coventry and Lichfield was apparently unaware of the exercise which was usually attended by some of the neighbouring justices.[49] Although situated outside the diocese, the exercise obviously involved clergy from parishes on its western borders, for Archbishop Grindal addressed himself not only to the bishop of Coventry and Lichfield but also to Scambler.[50] The Southam exercise was clearly a radical meeting but its suppression proved too much for the archbishop and, when he objected to the Queen's demands, he was suspended from office. The stand made by Grindal on behalf of the exercises illustrated that, though some were vehicles for puritan agitation, many churchmen still considered that the majority of such meetings had a valuable role to play in the

[47]Haigh, 'Puritan Evangelism' 30–58.
[48]Eliz. Puritan Movt. 191–208; P. Collinson, 'John Field and Elizabethan Puritanism', in S. T. Bindoff, J. Hurstfield, C. H. Williams (eds.) Elizabethan Government and Society (1961), 127–162.
[49]Eliz. Puritan Movt. 193–195.
[50]B.L. Lansd. Ms. 23, f. 7.

church.[51] Scambler himself had noted earlier that some exercises were of a less partisan nature and represented genuine attempts to overcome the pastoral problems of a church unable to recruit enough ministers with preaching ability or provide many with a parish which combined cure of souls with a decent income for a professional man. The first of these problems was of a temporary nature, partially caused by the religious and demographic upheavals of the middle years of the century and the changing functions of the ministry, but the second and related problem was more intractable. Poor livings and wide discrepancies in clerical incomes encouraged pluralism and non-residence and created poor standards of pastoral care, but the problem could not be overcome without a comprehensive reallocation of ecclesiastical property. Many clergy and laity on both sides deplored the inequalities within the church and many inventive proposals for reform were mooted. These rarely got beyond theoretical discussion for any readjustment of ecclesiastical property would have had widespread repercussions on the propertied classes as a whole, many of whom enjoyed the ownership of advowsons and rectory estates.[52] It was a problem not radically faced until the 19th century and, as a means of papering over some of the more obvious abuses, the exercises were invaluable. They attempted to ensure minimum standards of learning, and very few contemporaries saw in them an attempt to impose presbyterianism surreptitiously on episcopacy. Rather they represented the ideal of the first generation of Elizabethan reformers, bishops, puritan clergy, and gentlemen alike, many of whom had shared the experience of exile in Mary's reign. After 1576 leadership of the established church and of the puritan clergy passed to a new generation with no such shared experience of exile or of the continental reformation. They continued to share a Calvinist theology, but this did not prevent great differences in attitudes to ecclesiastical polity.

The Southam exercise must have involved some Northamptonshire clergy or justices for Grindal to have written to Scambler, but their names remain obscure, although Sir Richard Knightley can most certainly be counted as present. Attention to the court records reveals little evidence of nonconformity among the parish clergy at this date; only three cases of refusal to wear the surplice are noted between 1574 and 1578 and only at Barby did the incumbent, John Ford, display a more thoroughgoing attitude. He was presented in 1576 for refusing to wear the surplice, for not following the prescribed order of baptism, and for administering the communion to members of his congregation while they remained standing. This practice, later a characteristic feature of puritan worship, followed the precedent of the order of Northampton and its adoption by Ford hardly justified his description as a conformist in the diocesan survey in 1576.[53] Information on the clergy at that date is therefore scanty and we learn rather more from the activities of a group of laity, 16 in all, from the market-town of Daventry. The parishioners were presented on 6 October 1576 for travelling to services at Southam, Fawsley, and other unspecified places. Southam was ten miles west of Daventry and the journey, even if combined

[51]See S. E. Lehmberg (ed.), 'Archbishop Grindal and the Prophesyings', *Historical Magazine of the Protestant Episcopalian Church*, xxxiv, 87–145 for the attitudes of several bishops.

[52]For a discussion of this aspect see C. Hill, *Economic Problems of the Church*, 50–76, 132–167. Anstruther, *Vaux of Harrowden*, 75 discusses high mortality among diocesan clergy in the years between 1556 and 1561.

[53]Knightley was a trustee for Warwickshire preachers, P. Collinson, *Letters of Thomas Wood, Puritan 1566–77* (*B.I.H.R.* Supplement, 1960), p. xxviii; at Clay Coton and Moreton Pinkney, P.D.R., Archd. Ct. Bk. 4, ff. 49, 71; X608/13, f. iv.

with a visit to market, would have involved a full day's outing. Daventry's position on a network of routes communicating with prophesying centres such as Southam, Coventry, Banbury, and Leicester meant that market contacts with those towns could have introduced puritan ideas to those laymen presented. They may also have come down from the gentry, for Fawsley was rather nearer to Daventry, some four miles to the south, and Sir Richard Knightley, the resident squire, must have provided a local centre of worship similar to that provided by Isabel Catesby at Whiston.[54] We do not know which clergy operated from the house at this date, but Fawsley was to become a celebrated centre in the 1620s when the aged John Dod retired there.[55] The information from Daventry illustrates the likely range of influence of a celebrated exercise like that at Southam, which could attract laity from ten miles around to its sermons. It was precisely such 'gadding to sermons' which so alarmed John Aylmer, soon to share the leadership of the established church with John Whitgift during the years of Grindal's suspension.

Elsewhere in the diocese our information is equally scanty. In Rutland the most prominent puritan at this date was Robert Cawdry, who had had experience of the Northampton exercise; but the court records reveal little information beyond a few references to clerics refusing to wear the surplice. In one instance the issue of principle over this matter became so heated between Thomas Day, rector of Clipsham, and his churchwardens, that the incumbent removed the offending garment from the church in 1575.[56] The great advance of puritanism among the Rutland clergy was yet to take place, and can be attributed to a number of young men introduced into livings in the area by the Harrington and Cecil families. One of these was Robert Johnson of North Luffenham, who had already attracted the attention of the diocesan authorities by 1576 when he was described as a nonconformist.[57] For the most part however this group had yet to make an impact on the diocese. In the eastern part of the diocese such information as we have is very fragmentary; two clerics, John Deacon of Finedon, a parish adjacent to the important recusant centre at Harrowden, and William Gulson of Thrapston, a small market-town on the east of the Nene valley were both described as nonconformists in the 1576 survey, though only Deacon ever appeared before the church courts.[58] Both of them may have participated in the Oundle exercise and Thrapston was later to become a puritan centre, but such isolated examples can hardly be evidence for a settled puritan tradition in the area. Some local families of minor gentry status; the Fosbrookes, the Neales, the Pagets, and the Pickerings had already shown evidence of committed protestantism and were soon to produce puritan clerics from younger sons, but as yet only Eusebius Paget had attracted the attention of the authorities for his nonconformity.

By 1576 the exercise in the county town had encouraged substantial support for puritanism in its rural hinterland, a support able to withstand a determined attack by the local courts in 1573 and 1574. Elsewhere in the diocese matters had moved more slowly. In the western regions where there was gentry support the Southam exercise was on the way to establishing a local following similar to

    [54]P.D.R., X608/13, f. 77v.
    [55]W. Haller, The Rise of Puritanism, (New York, 1957), 58, 218.
    [56]P.D.R., Archd. Ct. Bk. 4, f. 65v.
    [57]Lambeth Palace Library, Carte Miscellanee, xiii. 56.
    [58]Ibid.; P.D.R., Archd. Ct. Bk. 5, f. 43v.; Gulson was later a puritan in Leicestershire, D. C. Chalmers, 'Puritanism in Leicestershire 1558–1633' (Unpub. M.A. thesis, Leeds 1962), 93.

that at Northampton, but information about the area is more sketchy and there is no evidence for the same cohesion among the puritan clergy and laity that was found at Northampton. In Rutland and the northerly reaches of the Nene valley isolated examples of puritan nonconformity came to the attention of the authorities, but that is all that can safely be said. Nationally the events leading up to Grindal's suspension placed a much wider range of nonconformist activity in a different context; where prior to 1576, some of the less important matters of ceremonial may have been fudged in order to advance the cause of reformation, after that date the authorities were much more concerned to search out and prosecute clergy who departed from the *Book of Common Prayer*, who refused to wear the surplice, or who indulged in additional forms of worship not specially authorized by the hierarchy. Their policies were by no means successful and nonconformity still flourished, but the sense of common purpose which had led to compromise between the early puritans and the first generation of Elizabethan bishops was disrupted.

# 3   1577-1583: A PAUSE FOR BREATH?

ARCHBISHOP Grindal's sequestration created a vacuum at the head of the established church until his death in 1583. The direction of policy was assumed by John Whitgift and John Aylmer, bishops of Worcester and of London respectively, both of whom were prepared to adopt a more aggressive policy against puritan nonconformity. They were however fairly new recruits to the episcopal bench whose position depended largely on the fact that they shared the Queen's opinions in matters of religion.[1] Inexperienced, and enjoying a position based on a fairly informal arrangement, the two bishops faced obstruction from some of their older episcopal colleagues and also from members of the Privy Council, notably Lord Burghley, anxious to avoid a further continuation of the upheavals of 1576 and 1577. As long as the archbishop remained alive some doubt remained as to where precisely authority lay within the church and, in such a period of uncertainty, Whitgift and Aylmer concentrated on consolidating their position within the established church, largely through influencing senior ecclesiatical appointments.[2] As a result, the six years prior to Whitgift's appointment as archbishop did not see any major confrontation between the hierarchy and the puritans, and even the parliament of 1581 was moderately quiescent, directing more of its attention to legislation against the Catholics.[3]

Historians have consequently tended to pass over these years fairly rapidly, but the events in the parliament of 1584 and the puritan outcry against the Three Articles imposed by Whitgift soon after his translation to the archbishopric of Canterbury, indicate that these years were formative ones in the development of puritanism. Whitgift and Aylmer may have set about consolidating their position within the established church, but the puritans, faced with the destruction of 'the promise of Grindal's church' looked to their own organization also. In 1584 the outcry against Whitgift's attempts to impose subscription to his Three Articles was far more widespread and vocal than the opposition to royal policy in 1576. During the intervening years the puritans had increased in numbers by the introduction of new recruits from the universities, had forced close links with prominent members of local society, and had re-formed the regular meetings of clergy temporarily suppressed in 1576. Not much of this activity was reflected in national affairs until 1584 but in the diocese of Peterborough, as in many others, local events can be traced in some detail.

## New recruits and patronage

The importance of placing a few prominent puritan clergy in key positions,

[1] See V. J. K. Brook, *Whitgift and the English Church* (1964 edn.), 78–79; *Eliz. Puritan Movt.* 205–207.
[2] *Eliz. Puritan Movt.* 201; R. A. Houlbrooke, 'The Protestant Episcopate 1547–1603', in R. O'Day and F. Heal (eds.), *Church and Society in England; Henry VIII to James I* (1977), 83–84.
[3] Neale, *Elizabeth I and her Parliament*, i. 378–404.

usually in market-towns, has already been remarked upon. That a few of the more prominent local gentry were responsible for these initiatives is undeniable, but the surviving records suggest that, in the years prior to 1576, it was personal contacts between clergymen which were of most importance to the spread of puritanism. Apart from the activities of a few notables like Sir Richard Knightley, lay patronage was not yet significant in creating a puritan group among the rank and file of the parochial clergy. Given the conservatism among the gentry at the beginning of Elizabeth's reign this should cause no surprise, but in the late 1570s and 1580s lay patronage helped to transform the character of the parochial clergy. Whether the gentry acquired their taste for puritan preaching and pastors through attendance at the earlier exercises, or through contacts with the universities, the Inns of Court and the capital is unclear. Among families like the Knightleys, the Montagues, the Harringtons, and the Fitzwilliams, contact with the capital appears to have been crucial,[4] but among the lesser known families, those of Dallyson, Sheffield and Fosbrooke for instance, local contacts seem to have been most important, whether through a member of the family attending the universities or through personal contact with puritan clergy or the more substantial puritan gentry.

This transformation did not come about through the agency of two or three individuals who controlled large amounts of ecclesiastical patronage; the pattern of patronage in the diocese was fragmentary and no family possessed more than seven advowsons.[5] This contrasts with the situations in Essex and in Leicestershire, where the Rich and Hastings families could foster puritanism in large areas of their counties through the extensive patronage they owned.[6] In Northamptonshire, where over half of the livings were in the hands of the local gentry, there was no cabal organizing ecclesiastical preferment on a county-wide basis, but a series of more local contacts operating in particular regions and, ultimately, involving a comparatively large section of the landowning class.

In the west of the county these contacts were organized around the Knightley family which was patron in four livings. Three of them, Plumpton, Fawsley, and Byfield were served by a succession of puritan clergy from 1580 whilst the fourth, Bugbrooke, was held by the absentee rector of Exeter College, Oxford for most of the period. Knightley's appointees were to be most closely involved in the presbyterian *classes* of the later 1580s and had been for the most part educated at Oxford.[7] Christ Church, Oxford produced a number of puritan clergy under the leadership of its first Elizabethan dean, Thomas Sampson, and the college was patron of the living at Badby, where the Knightleys were lords of the manor.[8] In this parish a vigorous puritan tradition took root despite confrontation between the family and the godly among their tenants over inclosures.[9] A junior branch of the Knightley family lived at Preston Capes where their close relatives, the Lanes were patrons. The earliest attempt to place a puritan in that living met with fierce opposition from the parish, some of whom objected to their incumbent John Elliston, who countered by claiming that the attack was inspired by catholics. Elliston was consequently replaced by Robert Smart, no less a puritan but less controversial, in June 1585, but presumably he

[4] For discussion see below pp. 116–117.
[5] The Cecils and Harringtons each had seven in Rutland.
[6] M. C. Cross, *The Puritan Earl*, 122–142; C. Hill, *Economic Problems of the Church*, 56.
[7] For a general survey giving details of patronage see Lamb. Pal. Lib., Carte Miscellanee, xiii. 56; *H.I.L.* x. 73.
[8] M. H. Curtis, *Oxford and Cambridge in Transition* (Oxford, 1959), 191–192; Baker, i. 255.
[9] See below pp. 134–136.

D

remained in the area until April 1586 when the Knightley living at nearby Plumpton fell vacant and he was preferred. His answer to articles concerning simony, which all new incumbents were required to answer, indicated the close contact between puritan cleric and patron for 'he hath been acquainted with his patron about four years past, the first cause of their acquaintance was, as he thinketh, by this examinates preaching'. Elliston's successor at Preston Capes also enjoyed the favour of the Knightleys, some of whom were godparents to his children.[10] The Knightley family and their Lane neighbours were supported by less influential families such as the Andrews family of Charwelton and the Foxes of Chacombe so that, between 1576 and 1584, sufficient clerics were placed in that part of the diocese to ensure the continuity of the radical tradition established by the Southam exercise. This generation of clerics, John Barebone, Robert Smart, Simon Rogers, Edward Sharpe, John Elliston, William Proudlove and others proved to be the mainstays of the *classis* of Daventry in the late 1580s and also continued to lobby for a presbyterian form of church government in the early years of the reign of James I. Their local influence was such that even after the *classes* had been dissolved and their leaders imprisoned, William Proudlove was reinstated to the Crown living at Weedon Bec in 1596 after his release from prison.[11]

In Rutland two families, the Cecils and the Harringtons, controlled over one-third of all livings and the strength of puritanism in that area can be attributed directly to their support. The first prominent puritan to gain a living in the diocese was Robert Johnson of North Luffenham in 1574, and his patron to what was a Crown living is most likely to have been Sir Walter Mildmay, with whom he remained on close terms.[12] Thereafter, it was parishes in the gift of the local families which became centres of puritan activity. By 1576 Cecil had placed the radical puritan Robert Cawdry at South Luffenham where a consistently troublesome pastorate was ultimately ended by the High Commission in 1588. Despite his uncompromising attitudes he retained the support of his patron for longer than he had reason to expect. After deprivation Cawdry remained in the locality, publishing works of an edifying and catechetical nature in the early 17th century one of which, *A Treasorie or Storehouse of Similies* was dedicated to Sir John and Sir James Harrington for the 'manifold courtesies and benefits which I found and received, now more than thirty years ago (when I taught the grammar school at Oakham in Rutland, and sundry times since) of the religious and virtuous lady, Lucy Harrington, your Worship's mother and my especial friend'.[13] Humphrey Wildblood, another puritan, was ordained at the request of Thomas Cecil and presented to the living of Great Casteron by Burghley in 1574. As a result of Whitgift's articles of 1584 Wildblood and a colleague, Edward Wilkinson of Tinwell, were suspended and threatened with deprivation. Their livings were sequestered temporarily until 'making their journey to London for their remedy, and their taking advice of Sir Thomas Cecil who is their patron, who went himself to the Archbishop, and of him received a letter to the Bishop to restore them until he heard further from him'. They remained in their parishes.[14]

[10]Peel, *The Seconde Parte*, i. 295–296; B.L., Sloane Ms. 271, f. 72v; P.D.R., Inst. Bk. III, f. 7.

[11]See below pp. 59–60; B.L., Lansd. Ms. 445, f. 81.

[12]B.L., Lansd. Ms. 443, f. 207; Irons 'Mr. Abraham Johnson', *Rutland Archaeol. and Nat. Hist. Soc. 10th Report 1913*, 57.

[13]For Cawdry see Peel, *The Seconde Parte*, ii. 202–208 and below pp. 61–64; R. Cawdry, *A Treasorie or Storehouse of Similies* (1600), dedicatory epistle.

[14]H.I.L. xv. 75; P.D.R., Inst. Bk. II, f. 5v; Peel, *The Seconde Parte*, ii. 92.

This sort of local support was reflected in governmental circles where Burghley did much to moderate the anti-puritan policies of Whitgift. His attitude may have owed as much to political commonsense as to religious convictions, for the policies of the Archbishop were likely to provoke a major confrontation with parliament in 1584. When the crisis of the *classes* was about to break, Burghley could still make a speech in the Lords attacking pluralism and non-residence in terms unflattering to the bishops but, in central government, his actions were mostly aimed at moderating anti-puritan policy rather than advancing the puritan cause.[15]

Together with Cawdry, Johnson, and Wilkinson, the most celebrated of the Rutland puritans was Thomas Gibson, from 1576 Vicar of Ridlington, a living in the gift of the Harrington family. Like some of his colleagues Gibson was saved from deprivation in 1584 by the intervention of his patron and remained at Ridlington until he refused to subscribe to the Canons of 1604 and was deprived the following year. Two other Harrington appointees were also deprived at that time, one of them being Robert Cuthbert who served Exton where the chief Harrington residence was located.[16] Members of the Harrington family also gave support to local initiatives like the puritan fast held at Stamford in 1580 in defiance of Burghley's instructions, but the character of their contribution needs to be distinguished from that of the Knightleys.[17] The clergy of Rutland were as outspoken in attacking abuses within the church as their Northamptonshire colleagues and continued to meet and discuss after the suppression of the exercises, but they never exhibited the same organized lobby for presbyterianism that was so characteristic of the *classes* of Northamptonshire and Warwickshire. In this the influence of the patrons, who were more closely identified with government than with parliamentary opposition, either in the initial selection of clergy, or in moderating their actions, was important. As the events of 1584 indicated, the relationship between many of the Rutland puritans and their patrons was as close as that of the group around the Knightley family. Some of the Rutland clergy did, in fact, belong to local families: the Brownes of Tolthorpe, who were related to the Cecils, not only produced the celebrated separatist Robert Browne, but his elder brother Philip, who enjoyed the family living of Little Casterton from 1590 until his deprivation in 1605. Another local puritan was Sampson Sheffield, who held his family's living at Seaton.[18]

Elsewhere in the diocese the situation was more complex, and puritans seeking preferment had to look to a number of patrons, each with very small amounts of patronage. The extensive estates of the Griffin and Tresham families, both catholic, were counterbalanced by the property accumulated by Sir Walter Mildmay to the north of Oundle. However, he was not able to acquire much in the way of advowsons and only one of his livings, Warmington, had a succession of puritan clerics.[19] The first of them, William Bollinge, was presented in 1573 having already served the living of Southwick where a puritan tradition was to emerge under the influence of the patron, George Lynne. Bollinge was

[15]Neale, *Elizabeth I and Her Parliaments*, i. 398–400; Conyers Reed, *Lord Burghley and Queen Elizabeth* (1965 edn.), 293–300.

[16]Peel, *The Seconde Parte*, ii. 92; P.D.R., Inst. Bks. II, f. 17; IV, f. 13 and v.

[17]J. Field, *A Caveat for Parson's Howlet and the rest of his darke broode* (1581), sigs. Gvii^v–Hij; *V.C.H. Rutland*, ii. 129.

[18]See below pp. 100–101 and Peel, *The Seconde Parte*, ii. 204; F. I. Cater, 'Robert Browne's Ancestors and Decendants', *Transactions of the Congregational History Society*, ii. 154; B.L., Sloane Ms. 271, f. 25v.; *V.C.H. Rutland*, ii. 215.

[19]For the strength of catholicism in the area see G. Anstruther, *Vaux of Harrowden, passim*.

later made a chaplain to the puritan Margaret, Lady Zouche, prior to his deprivation in 1576.[20] He was succeeded at Warmington by the nonconformist Michael Cuthbert, who in turn later moved to the parish of Etton where Sir William Fitzwilliam was patron. Cuthbert's relationship with his patron was a close one and acknowledged by a bequest in his will, dated 10 September 1587.[21] When seeking to replace Cuthbert at Etton Fitzwilliam sought out his Essex connections and presented Giles Whiting, a deprived minister of London diocese, to the living on the recommendation of two leading London puritans, Richard Greenham and Thomas Crooke. Crooke had been a lecturer at Gray's Inn and it may have been there that Fitzwilliam had his first contact with puritanism.[22] William Fosbrooke of Cranford was another local man who attended Gray's Inn and his half-brother John later married a daughter of George Lynne of Southwick. John was himself Rector of Cranford St Andrew and later to be a *classis* member.[23] The Browne family of Tolthorpe in Rutland have already been mentioned and it may have been through marriage with a daughter of the house, Dorothy, that Gilbert Pickering, squire and patron of Titchmarsh, came into close touch with puritanism. From 1583 Titchmarsh remained a puritan centre.[24] It was through these sort of links that such families in the east of the diocese accumulated a network of livings for puritan clerics.

Another source to be tapped was the extensive range of Crown livings in the diocese and the example of the corporation of Northampton is discussed in Chapter 8. In the eastern region there was a fairly substantial crown living at Little Oakley which became the object of dispute in 1584 between the puritans and their opponents. Richard Baldock, a puritan, was supported by two junior members of the Montague family, William and Thomas, whilst his opponent Robert Norbury had crypto-catholic affiliations. Norbury claimed to have been inducted by John Holmes, vicar of Wellingborough and a licensed preacher, in Easter week 1584 but was harried from his living soon afterwards by the Montagues and a group described by him as a band of rowdies from Brigstock, Boughton, and Weekley. They claimed that Baldock had been inducted by Christopher Green, a schoolmaster employed by the Montague family, and had read the required articles in Little Oakley church where Norbury's supporters snatched them from him. Baldock's case rested on the fact that Norbury had been presented to the living some seven years earlier but had not resided, and a neighbouring cleric, John Backhouse of Thorpe Achurch, was called in to testify as to Norbury's insufficiency for his calling. As a result Norbury was called before the Bishop and departed from the diocese, leaving Baldock in possession until deprivation in 1605. He subsequently resided at Little Oakley where he died in 1632, 'a godly old minister'.

There were some other attempts to force unacceptable clerics to leave in favour of puritan ministers,[25] but more often puritan clergy were introduced to fill genuine pastoral needs. The local puritan godly were instrumental in inviting William Fleshware to fill the hitherto vacant curacy at Abington, on the out-

[20]P.D.R., Inst. Bks. I, f.7; II, f. 21v 12.

[21]*Ibid.*, II, ff. 20, 50; H.I.L., iii. 329.

[22]P.D.R., Misc. Bk. VIII, f. 80v; for Crook and Greenham see R. G. Usher, *The Presbyterian Movement 1582-9* (Camden Soc. 3rd Series vii), pp. xxxviii, xlii; see below p. 116.

[23]*Visitations of Northants. 1564, 1618-19*, 89-90; *Gray's Inn Admissions Registers*, ed. J. Foster (priv. pd. 1889), col. 73; see below p. 117.

[24]Cater, 'Robert Browne's Ancestors and Descendants', 154.

[25]P.R.O., E134/27 Eliz. E8, T6; for other examples see STAC 8/42/6, Sheils, 'Thesis' 138-139, 146, and 'Some Problems', 182.

skirts of Northampton. At Cransley the local squire, Edward Dallyson, had offered as early as 1570 to supplement the income of the poor living 'if an honest man may be there appointed, to be made worth xij *li*. or thirteen pounds'. The curate at that time was said to be a drunkard who neglected the services, and in 1585 the living was still void, but was soon filled by the puritan Leonard Pattinson, whose income was subsequently secured by Dallyson in his will.[26] In this case the motive was not so much to further a party cause, but rather to secure a decent and regular ministry.

In the years between 1576 and 1584 an alliance was formed between puritan clerics and local gentry through the patronage system. It was not an alliance dependent on the attitude of one or two powerful figures, but one which affected many sectors of the landowning community. In some cases it represented something of a party interest determined on a presbyterian form of church government, but it also drew strength from the need to secure a preaching ministry. Scambler's attack on the puritans in 1574 incurred the wrath of a few powerful individuals with governmental influence, but local events during Grindal's suspension were to ensure that subsequently vigorous episcopal action against the puritan clergy would be followed by widespread protests from the local gentry. The links between the puritan clergy and local society were sustained and developed right up to the outbreak of the civil war, but it was in the years between 1576 and 1584 that they were first formed. Puritan activism may have been less apparent during those years, but by 1584 it had become a more widespread and well-connected phenomenon.

*Passive resistance*

The first confrontation between the puritans and the diocesan authorities had taken place against the background of a local commission for ecclesiastical causes, a court of local laymen and ecclesiastics which could lend weight to the normal diocesan courts through its powers to fine or imprison offendors. The crown turned to such local prerogative courts in order to bolster the declining status of the courts christian whose power of excommunication, although still important in dealing with minor moral offences, proved to be ineffective when dealing with persistent moral offenders or when trying to enforce uniformity. The use of a *significavit*, whereby the church could turn offenders over to the secular arm for punishment was cumbersome and, as puritan sympathies grew among the leaders of local society, unlikely to be helpful in the matter of uniformity.[27] If the local commission was designed to deal with the early phase of puritan activity, and its foundation just after the suppression of the order of Northampton is suggestive, then it soon got distracted from its task. It did indeed deal with some of the more vocal opponents of the hierarchy in the county town, among them Henry Sharpe the bookbinder later to be involved in the Marprelate tracts scandal, but much of its time was in fact occupied by charges of corruption against the diocesan chancellor, James Ellis, charges which, if not puritan inspired, had reached the ears of the Earl of Leicester. Thus the commission, in dealing with local maladministration, only served to further the decline in respect for the local courts christian and from 1579 the enforcement of uniformity

[26]For Abington see Sheils, 'Thesis', 177; for Cransley see Irons, 'An Episcopal Visitation in 1570', 204; *V.C.H. Northants.*, iv. 167; P.D.R., X611/29, f. 47v.; P.R.O., P.C.C. wills, Drury 49.

[27]R. A. Houlbrooke, 'The Decline of Ecclesiastical Jurisdiction under the Tudors', in O'Day and Heal, *Continuity and Change*, 239–257, esp. 245.

was left once more to the Bishop and his officials.[28] Occasionally more important offenders, such as the Northampton preacher Francis Merbury in 1578, Robert Cawdry in 1588, and the *classes* leaders in 1589 were sent for trial before the provincial court of High Commission in London, but the effectiveness of this court depended on it remaining aloof from the more mundane problems of enforcing uniformity.[29] Its existence as a prerogative court was coming under increasing attack from the common lawyers in parliament, many of whom had puritan sympathies, and its use by Aylmer often led to vocal political opposition. In this context the main responsibilities for the policing of the diocese fell to the Bishop through his local courts and regular visitation.[30]

Whether a general decline in their status, local corruption, or disenchantment after the events of 1574 and 1576 was the principal cause, the years between 1577 and 1583 are marked not by confrontation but by an indifference to the local courts and visitation system. This indifference, expressed in an unwillingness to attend visitation when called, can be attributed to the puritan clergy and laity who, having lost an archbishop in whom they had some confidence, were less willing to acquiesce in the normal ecclesiastical procedures after Grindal's suspension. Such a policy of non-recognition of the local courts and of visitation procedures had already become apparent at the visitation of 1577 when seven of the parochial clergy were presented for non-attendance. Of these seven, five had puritan connections or were in parishes with nonconforming traditions: William Wood, incumbent at the Knightley living of Plumpton, had already attracted the attention of the local authorities for nonconformity; Ralph Fosbrooke of Cranford St Andrew came from a local family of firm protestant persuasion and was soon to be a *classis* member; John Tymms of Whiston had been named as a nonconformist in the survey made in 1576; and, although nothing is known of two others, they both served in parishes affected by the earlier crisis. Hardingstone had been deprived of its incumbent in 1574 and Wollaston included the residence of George Carleton, founder of the exercise at Overstone. Whiston was obviously at this date still one of the leading puritan centres and its incumbent Tymms not only failed to appear but was also charged with refusing to subscribe to the articles of religion.[31]

By midsummer of 1582 the lack of cooperation had become more pronounced, and was extended to include the puritan laity in addition to some clergy. The churchwardens of Whiston, Castle Ashby, Ashton near Roade, Barby, and the Northampton town churches, all parishes served by puritan clerics at this date, were charged with failing to appear. In addition Richard Person, one of the churchwardens at Wootton where Francis Wigginton, a less famous brother of Giles, was curate, was presented for the same offence.[32] In addition the incumbents of Whiston, Castle Ashby, and the county town also failed to appear as did their puritan colleagues at Plumpton, Lamport, and Abington. Further to these known puritans a number of other clergy, many from parishes subsequently identified with puritanism, were also negligent in appearing before

[28]Sheils, 'Some Problems', *ibid.*, 177–179.

[29]Hist. Mss. Com., *Various Collections*, iii. 3–5; Peel, *The Seconde Parte*, ii. 202–208; and see below pp. 52–59. The loss of the court records makes it difficult to assess precisely how much business was transferred from the diocesan courts, but the local references are few in number.

[30]For opposition from the common lawyers see Neale, *Elizabeth I and her Parliaments*, (1957), ii. 267–278. No visitation articles survive prior to 1594.

[31]See Sheils, 'Thesis', 90–91; for references see P.D.R., X608/13, ff. 7v., 139; 14, ff. 23–24v.

[32]P.D.R., X608/16, ff. 7–8, 9v., 27v–28.

the Bishop's officials. The extent of the practice suggested that the situation was a serious one for the diocesan authorities and, although none of the clergy were deprived, some of the offending churchwardens were excommunicated.[33] By 1583 most interested parties would have been aware of the direction in which Whitgift was taking the church, and there must have been widespread dissatisfaction among the numbers of new recruits to the diocese, as well as from some of the older clergy.

The extent of the problem was not made clear by the evidence for nonconformity which the diocesan authorities had managed to collect between 1577 and 1582. Few cases of any note came before the local courts. Events in Northampton came to the attention of the Privy Council and one of the preachers, Francis Merbury, was sent for trial to the High Commission in London, but the evidence from the rest of the county is fragmentary.[34] In Rutland Henry Colset the incumbent at Easton on the Hill was charged with not wearing the surplice during divine service, with preaching without licence, and with permitting his parish clerk, a layman, to perform what puritans considered the 'idolatrous' ceremony of churching women. Churching after childbirth was to trouble the scruples of a number of godly women in the diocese and fell into that category of services which some puritans were prepared to entrust to the laity. Colset was treated lightly by the courts and dismissed with a warning as to his future conduct, but it proved to be a warning of substance as he was the only one of the parish clergy to be deprived as a result of the enforcement of Whitgift's articles in 1584.[35] A few other cases of nonconformity were reported from the west of the diocese; in one parish in Brackley deanery, probably Gayton where John Chawner was parson, the minister was presented for saying divine service whilst under excommunication; at Preston Capes, where John Elliston fell out with his parishioners over tithes, the vicar was presented for departing from the *Book of Common Prayer*; two other new recruits to the parochial clergy, Andrew King of Culworth and Henry Bradshaw of Norton, were presented for a whole range of puritan practices in 1583. Their offences included discarding the surplice, not following the order of the *Book of Common Prayer*, not baptizing or burying in accordance with the Injunctions of 1559, and refusing to observe holy days.[36] Of the puritans in neighbourhood of the county town only Giles Brooke of Kislingbury was presented for nonconformity.[37]

The paucity of information from that region can partly be explained by the lack of cooperation from clergy and churchwardens at visitation. It was parishes in the neighbourhood of Northampton and in the west of the diocese that were most affected by this and for the rest of the period diocesan officials had trouble eliciting information about puritanism in those areas. With greater numbers of people refusing to answer interrogatories and articles, little positive information got through to local court officials, and the extent of the evidence for nonconformity in the period of Grindal's suspension gave little warning of the strength of the local opposition to Whitgift's articles in 1584. However, consideration of that evidence in the light of the non-appearance of some clergy

[33]*Ibid.*, ff. 8 and v., 27v–28v. Other places involved included Stoke Bruerne, Culworth, Barby, Brixworth, Lamport, Yelvertoft, Warmington, and Titchmarsh, all soon to be known puritan centres.
[34]Hist. Mss. Com., *Various Collections*, iii. 3–5.
[35]P.D.R., X608/16, f. 65v.; Peel, *The Seconde Parte*, ii. 92.
[36]P.D.R., X648/1, ff. 114v., 140a, 148, 150; Peel, *The Seconde Parte*, i. 291–296.
[37]P.D.R., X648/1, f. 118a.

and officials in the visitations of 1577 and 1582 makes the picture rather clearer. With the advantage of hindsight the historian can see that events, including the influx of new recruits brought in by patrons predisposed to puritanism, were building up to some sort of crisis. Contemporary opponents of puritanism of the stature of Bishops Whitgift and Aylmer also realized that the suppression of the prophesyings had been only the first battle in a long campaign.

### Fasts and exercises

Considerable stress was laid on the importance of the clerical contacts made at the exercises in the early 1570s in the spread of puritanism among the parish clergy. Earlier in this chapter it has been suggested that the patronage system as operated by the local gentry began to take an increasing part in that growth. Nevertheless, having experienced the benefits of the exercises, many clergy were reluctant to abandon them entirely after their suppression and wished for alternative means of keeping in contact with each other. In addition some of the new recruits to the diocese had been near contemporaries at both Magdalen College and Christ Church, Oxford, and links formed at university were unlikely to be dropped by close neighbours sharing the new responsibilities of pastoral care.[38] From 1577 the legality of formal meetings of the clergy was in doubt within the province of Canterbury, but in many places regular, if less formalized, contacts were kept by ministers in several localities. The evidence is of its nature fragmentary as such meetings could have remained within the law only by claiming an informal and transitory existence, but to many contemporary observers it was common knowledge that such meetings took place.[39] Within the diocese the exercise at Oakham continued and details survive to show that the puritan clergy were the dominant element. In 1583 Robert Cawdry was inhibited from preaching outside his own parish as a result of a sermon preached at Oakham in which 'he uttered many indiscreet and opprobrious words against the ministry comparing them that had two benefices to such as had two wives'. It is interesting that the charges were brought against Cawdry by four of his parochial colleagues in the area, one of whom, William Rowe of Teigh, was himself later presented for nonconformist practices. Rowe's nonconformity only extended to scruples over wearing the surplice, but what is important is that the exercise at Oakham was becoming a divisive influence among the parochial clergy of the area.[40] This was in marked contrast to the situation in Rutland mentioned by Bishop Scambler ten years earlier when the conference in that part was compared favourably with that at Northampton by the bishop. Much of the antipathy between the puritans and their orthodox colleagues was based on the uncompromising attitude of the former to a non-preaching ministry. Cawdry had touched upon that point in his own sermon, claiming that a non-preaching minister could have no proper calling in the church. Another puritan delivered a sermon at Oakham along the same lines. The preacher Thomas Gibson, incumbent at Ridlington, had published his sermon, *A Fruitfull Sermon, Preached at Occam . . . 2 Nov 1583*, because of the opposition it had aroused 'in the county where I dwell'.[41]

---

[38]See below pp. 96–98.        [39]*Eliz. Puritan Movt.* 210–215.

[40]P.D.R., X608/15, ff. 124, 125v, Rowe's accomplices were Robert Green of Market Overton, William Dalby of Burley on the Hill and Richard King of Cottesmore. Cawdry subsequently preached in a similar vein at the exercise at Uppingham, Peel, *The Seconde Parte*, ii. 207–208. For Rowe's nonconformity see P.D.R., X609/23, f. 156v.

[41]T. Gibson, *A Fruitfull Sermon, Preached at Occam . . . 2 Nov. 1583* (1584), 5v–6.

The issue of the ministry was central to the dispute between puritans and their orthodox fellows and will be dealt with at greater length later. The attack on non-preaching clergy obviously undermined the standing of such men among their congregations and by 1583 some of the Rutland clergy were prepared to make a counter attack on the puritans through the local courts. The issue of preaching was also important in the western borders of the diocese where the practice of 'gadding to sermons' had not died out after the suppression of the exercises. In this region the counter attack was possibly inspired by the diocesan authorities themselves. Simon Gibbes, Rector of Boddington, had been a fellow of Corpus Christi College, Cambridge and a university preacher. He was, therefore, one of the more prominent of the orthodox parochial clergy and, serving a cure with a puritan squire in John Wake, was well acquainted with the strengths of the puritans. On 28 June 1583 he preached a sermon at Eydon, in the heart of Knightley country, in which he inveighed against the practice of deserting parochial services in order to attend sermons. He likened 'Those who [were] accustomed to repair to sermons abroad and might hear the word read at home' to 'The children of Israel who, being fed with *manna* by the Lord, murmured and would have stronger meat; and [the] Lord sent them quail and choked them'. These were strong words against the puritans spoken in their own territory, and the details of the sermon survive on a loose leaf in a diocesan court book.[42] The notes were presumably taken by a member of the congregation who may well have had puritan sympathies for he made a memorandum to send the details to Mr Rogers, probably Simon Rogers the puritan minister of Byfield.[43] If so the sermon was surely not left unanswered and the issue of preaching was likely to have been as contentious in the west as in Rutland. Indeed, it also involved the laity of the region in due course, for in 1590 Joan Green of Welton was refused the sacrament by her puritan minister for complaining that 'Mr Sharpe and Mr Barebone had preached so long at Badby that they had brought all to nought, and that Welton was almost as bad. And that it was a merry world before there was so much preaching.'[44]

Another opportunity to allow puritan clergy and their followers to meet together was the public fast. Whereas within the catholic church fasting was essentially a private or a household devotion, among protestants it was seen as a public and congregational exercise. In the early 1580s the practice became widespread and the combination of bad harvests, fear of papists and, in 1580, a mild earthquake, provided plenty of excuses for public fasts which the puritans seized with alacrity. Percival Wiburn made particular mention of fasts held in the diocese of Lincoln, and it was at Stamford, a town situated in that diocese but with a suburb in Peterborough diocese, that the most celebrated fast took place in 1580. The Stamford fast became the subject of a pamphlet by Robert Parsons, the Jesuit, who used the occasion to challenge the loyalty of the puritans. His tract, *A brief discours contayning certayne reasons why catholiques refuse to goe to church* brought replies from the London organizer of the puritans John Field, and from Percival Wiburn, the old Northampton campaigner.[45] The principal

[42]H.I.L. v. 209; P.D.R. X648/1, loose leaf between ff. 167 and 168.
[43]For Rogers see below p. 58.
[44]P.D.R., X610/24, f. 23v.; Archd. Vis. 7, loose leaf between ff. 19 and 20.
[45]The main outlines and context of the fast are discussed in *Eliz. Puritan Movt.* 216–217. The pamphlets on which our knowledge is based are J. Howlet (pseudonym for R. Parsons), *A brief discours contayning certayne reasons why catholiques refuse to goe to church* (Douai, 1580); J. Field, *A Caveat for Parsons Howlet and the rest of his darke broode* (1581); and P. Wiburn, *A Checke or Reproofe of Mr Howlet's Untimely Schreeching in her Majestie's Eares* (1581).

mover behind the fast appears to have been Robert Johnson, Rector of North Luffenham and an organizer of the Oakham exercise. He encouraged the burgesses of the town to proclaim a fast in June 1580, but their plans were reported to Burghley, the Lord of the Manor, who commended their motives but condemned any action they might take without episcopal permission. Bishop Cooper of Lincoln gave cautious approval, appointing the town preacher and one other Lincoln cleric as preachers. The burgesses prevailed upon Lord Zouche of Harringworth to approach Burghley on their behalf and 'considering that the exercise was now already appointed and warranted' went ahead with the fast, which was conducted by 'the godly learned preachers about them'.[46]

Equivocal as their support was the burgesses took little heed of Cooper's instructions, and when the fast did take place the preachers were Robert Johnson, who turned up with 'six or seven other preachers' of the diocese of Peterborough, and the puritan Rector of Market Deeping, Richard Lively who, as Rector of Maxey, had probably been a leader of the Stamford exercise in the 1570s. If Parsons is to be believed then the preachers voiced their defiance in inflammatory tones, but when Field produced his book in defence of the fast he provided a number of testimonials as to the good behaviour and sound doctrine of the participants. Sound doctrine and inflammatory phrases were not incompatible and there may have been some radicalism at Stamford (which had a congregation of Dutch refugees) which the tenseness of the circumstances encouraged.[47] Whatever the details of the proceedings, the testimonials throw a great deal of light on the local context of such events. Testimonials were provided, not surprisingly, by five of the burgesses, by Robert Crosdale, a Lincolnshire incumbent and, more importantly, by the excluded town preacher John Hanson and by Nicholas Sheppard, the Archdeacon of Northampton and formerly president of Burghley's old Cambridge college, St John's. Sheppard's testimonial suggests that the sermons cannot have been too inflammatory, and Parsons was accused of deliberately exaggerating the language and tenor of the sermons and

> that he hath very much abused the preachers in this his report, by setting down that which they never uttered; and that in truth, there was nothing then & there taught, which was not spoken with all loyal and dutiful obedience, and in good terms, and which might, without just occasion of offence given, have been preached before any estate in this land, both for the manner and matter thereof.[48]

In addition testimonials were supplied by Lord Zouche, who rode over from Harringworth for the occasion, by Francis Harrington, the Recorder of Stamford, and by Toby Houghton, a minor gentleman living at King's Cliffe. Houghton's testimony illustrates the way in which the godly gentleman approached such events, for he had made extensive notes on the sermons, neither of which was 'twelve or ten hours long, nor yet much above five hours, which time was thought to be little enough for them'. He was able to refer to his notes in some detail and to affirm that nothing was said 'against the good and godly government of the estate of this our Realm of England'.[49]

[46]Field, op. cit. sigs. G. ii–iiij; B.L., Lansd. Ms. 102, f. 185.
[47]Field, op. cit. sigs. G. iiij[v]–vii give a resumé of Liveley's sermon; A. Rogers (ed.), The Making of Stamford (Leicester, 1965), 65.
[48]Field, op. cit. sigs. G. vii[v]–H.
[49]Ibid.

The Stamford fast provided the puritan clergy of Rutland and Lincoln with the opportunity to make a show of strength, which illustrated that the contacts established in the early 1570s had not been completely destroyed. The puritan clergy had developed a confidence which was even prepared to incur the displeasure of Burghley. The events at Stamford were perhaps exceptional in their ramifications, but more typical in their context. Puritan clergy in the early 1580s displayed a confidence based partly on their academic superiority over their colleagues and partly on the knowledge of the extent to which they could depend on local lay support. That support had been built up slowly before 1576 and more quickly thereafter; it provided some shelter against harassment from the ecclesiastical courts and an adequate compensation for the rift that was emerging between the puritan ministers and their conforming colleagues.

*Whitgift's Three Articles and their aftermath*

GRINDAL's death in July 1583 and the translation of John Whitgift to the Archbishopric of Canterbury in September has recently been called 'a decisive climacteric in the history of the Reformed Church of England'. The new Archbishop quickly justified the fears of the puritans and their supporters and on 29 October he issued his famous Three Articles as part of a series of articles introducing a number of reforms to the Church. Attention focused on the Three Articles which had to be subscribed to by anyone wishing to exercise any ecclesiastical function. Scambler of Peterborough was involved in the compilation of the articles, which touched on the Royal Supremacy, the Book of Common Prayer, and the 39 Articles. Those dealing with the Supremacy and the 39 Articles were generally acceptable to all churchmen, provided subscription to the latter was limited to merely doctrinal matters in accordance with the statute of 1571. It was the second article, 'That the Book of Common Prayer and of ordering bishops, priests, and deacons containeth nothing in it contrary to the word of God. And that the same may be lawfully used; and that he himself will use the form of the said book prescribed in public prayer and administration of the sacraments and none other,' which proved the stumbling block, not only to the most radical of the presbyterians but to a wide spectrum of clergy seeking further reform in the ceremonial as well as the government of the church.[1] Whitgift must have known this would be the case, and thenceforward any ambiguity there may have been in the attitude of the hierarchy towards the puritans was removed. The issue of the Three Articles throughout all dioceses in the realm was an uncompromising demand that all clergy wishing to practise their ministry should conform.

Similar articles had been imposed before in particular dioceses, and were responsible for the crisis at Peterborough in 1574, but they had never been generally applied. The attempt to impose such a standard of uniformity, never previously attained in the Elizabethan church, was not only unrealistic, but also brought with it the danger of uniting all the strands of puritanism in common cause at the very time when differences within the movement were beginning to emerge. These differences, not so much over aims but over the methods to be employed in achieving reform, were cast aside in the face of Whitgift's policy, which he had been able to force through the Privy Council partly through the indisposition of two senior councillors, Francis Walsingham and Lord Burghley. Opposition to the articles was widespread throughout the Home Counties, East Anglia, and the Midlands, involving not only the clergy but a

---

[1]*Eliz. Puritan Movt.*, 243–272, discusses the details of the confrontation. Already by this date the ministers of Kent received substantial support from the gentry, but no evidence for concerted action was noted in the diocese though there were a number of cases of individual clergy being protected.

large section of their lay supporters. In the diocese of Peterborough about 45 of the parochial clergy, almost one-sixth of the total, refused to subscribe to the articles at first and, according to the puritans, some were 'suspended, other some admonished, and the rest reserved to await further suspension and deprivation when the Bishop shall see good'.[2] Surviving local sources do not give the names of those so threatened but John Field, the puritan organizer in London, gathered some details in preparation for a collection of case histories detailing the sufferings of the puritans at the hands of authority. The names we have come from Rutland, from where some of the puritans travelled to London to seek support from their patrons the Cecils, father and son. Edward Wilkinson of Tinwell and Humphrey Wildblood of Great Casterton used Cecil to obtain letters from the archbishop himself ordering the diocesan authorities to delay sentence of deprivation; a sentence which Thomas Gibson of Ridlington claimed would be invalid when he found himself before the High Commission. All of these men must have come close to deprivation but there were many others, as Robert Cawdry pointed out in a letter to Burghley, who had submitted to the Book of Common Prayer despite believing that 'some points are unlawful and others inconvenient'.[3]

The confrontation dragged on for some months but, in the summer of 1584 Burghley and Walsingham were able to bring pressure on Whitgift to moderate the terms of the subscription. Faced with a crisis likely to lead to mass deprivations throughout the country, the two elder statesmen offered Whitgift their support in later dealings with the radical ringleaders if he was prepared to allow a form of subscription acceptable to many nonconformists. This was achieved and puritans were allowed to subscribe to the articles and insert a proviso referring the *Book of Common Prayer* to the judgement of divine law. By assisting puritan consciences in this way, and by promoting Scambler out of the diocese to the wealthier see of Norwich, the crisis was averted at Peterborough as elsewhere. Of the diocesan clergy only Henry Colset of Easton on the Hill was deprived for his refusal to subscribe.[4]

The events of the year following Michaelmas 1583 progressed in an unsatisfactory way. There were few deprivations and a major confrontation was averted, but only with considerable loss of face by ecclesiastical authority. Nor did the compromise do much to win support for Whitgift; the parliament called in November 1584 provided further opportunity to plead the cause of the preaching ministers. Organization and leadership was lacking however and the Queen was able to control tactics whilst, at the same time, allowing the commons to lay the failings of the church at the door of the bishops.[5] The outcome of Whitgift's policy in this first year was resentment and widespread dissatisfaction with the state of affairs among a sizeable minority of articulate clergy and laity. By aiming at the unattainable the Archbishop, far from arresting the growth of puritanism, merely provided it with a unity based on opposition to his actions. By drawing together all strands of nonconformity in this way Whitgift provided the more thoroughgoing presbyterians with the opportunity to influence their less committed colleagues in an anti-establishment direction. Subsequently forced to moderate his policy by the pressure of the

---

[2]Peel, *The Seconde Parte*, i. 241; P.R.O., SP. 12/172/1; B.L., Add. Ms. 22473, ff. 14–15.
[3]Peel, *The Seconde Parte*, i. 241, ii. 92.
[4]Burghley's contacts with the puritans and his influence with Whitgift are detailed in *Eliz. Puritan Movt.*, 265–271; for Colset see Peel, *The Seconde Part*, ii. 262.
[5]Neale, *Elizabeth I and her Parliaments*, ii. 81–83.

opposition, the Archbishop had further undermined the authority of the church. The years following 1584 were marked by a policy of containment which involved attacking the more radical puritan leaders in the hope of discouraging their colleagues. Such a policy avoided major confrontation without dealing with the situation out of which such confrontation might arise. The Archbishop had to be satisfied with a situation which modern politicians might well describe as an acceptable level of dissent. Although it may not have been immediately apparent, what made the events of 1584 a climacteric in the history of the reformed church in England was the fact that what had previously been regarded as disagreement within the church came to be characterized as dissent by much of the hierarchy. One important consequence of this was that the puritans began to give even greater attention to their internal organization rather than to relations with the establishment.

For some years John Field had been acting in the capacity of organizing secretary in London to the puritan clergy throughout the South-East, East Anglia, and the Midlands. His industry ensured that petitions were organized on behalf of suspended clergy; that contacts were kept with leading laymen, particularly the parliamentary gentry; and that puritan clergy in different parts of the country maintained some contact with each other's activities. Whether Field's work was considered of central importance by many of the country puritan clergy was debateable but his value to the more politically determined presbyterians was unquestioned.[6] The events of 1584 not only increased the contact between provincial puritans and the capital, but also revived contacts in their own localities. These new contacts differed from the earlier exercises in that they were restricted to the clergy, and to the puritan clergy at that. Arrangements were not formalized immediately, but once the puritans of the diocese decided to produce a survey of the parochial clergy, similar to those produced by their colleagues in Warwickshire and Oxfordshire in 1586, some sort of local secretariat must have been established. The need for a preaching ministry was one of the mainstays of the puritan platform together with the removal of idolatrous ceremonial and the demand for a presbyterian form of church discipline. The surviving returns from Oxfordshire and Warwickshire show that the puritans were now expressing opinions about their orthodox colleagues in language that could only further the antagonism between the two parties locally. The issue over church government may well have been paramount in the dispute between the establishment and the puritans nationally, but in the local context it was the conflict over the legitimacy of non-preaching ministries which drove a wedge between the puritans and the rest.[7] Unfortunately the Northamptonshire survey does not survive in any form, but the summary of the Rutland survey, if not its details, has been left on record. The Rutland puritans deputed the task of compiling the survey to Edward Wilkinson of Tinwell whose findings were as follows:

| | |
|---|---|
| Churches and Chapels with charge of souls | 48 |
| And of them there be prebends and Appropriate | 18 |
| There be to serve these churches preachers according to their gifts | 14 |
| And of them dwelling upon their charge in Rutland there be double beneficed | 6 |

[6]P. Collinson, 'John Field and Elizbethan Puritanism', in S. T. Bindoff, et al. (eds.) Elizabethan Government and Society, 127–162.

[7]P.R.O., STAC 5/A 49/34, Johnson's evidence; for examples of surveys elsewhere see, Peel, The Seconde Parte, ii. 88–177.

And that be non-resident 5
The rest be simple although some of them be sufficiently learned, and
  are in number 29
Whereof five of them at the least serve two charges.[8]

The findings of the survey are very similar to the situation uncovered by
Bishop Howland's primary visitation of 1585. Such agreement from two anta-
gonistic sources suggests a reasonable measure of objectivity on the part of
Wilkinson.[9] One interesting feature of the survey, granted that it was presented
in summary and not in detail, is the temperate language of the document. There
are no references here to the 'idle shepherds' or 'dumb dogs' that figure in the
other surviving surveys. Despite the controversies that had surrounded the
preaching of Cawdry and Gibson in 1583, Wilkinson was prepared to admit
that some of his less able colleagues were sufficiently learned. The Bishop's
visitation of 1585 had uncovered no scandalous abuses, and pastoral standards
seem to have been high in Rutland at this time. Indeed, between 1576 and 1585
the only complaint about negligence from Rutland was made to the Archdeacon
in 1581 by the churchwarden of Bisbrooke, where they occasionally had 'a
drunken evening prayer'.[10] The report of Wilkinson may have reflected a healthy
pastoral situation, or it may tell us something of the character of Rutland
puritanism. The puritan clergy of that county did not, or more accurately are
not known to have followed their fellows in Oxfordshire, Warwickshire, and
Northamptonshire in organizing themselves into *classes*.

### The classes

The *classes* of the late 1580s have been said to have formed a church within
a church, presbyterianism within episcopacy. The impetus to organize along
these lines was increased after the return of Thomas Cartwright to England in
1585 and work began on a *Book of Discipline*. Drafts were made in 1585 and
1586 and in the latter year a revolutionary bill was introduced in parliament,
sponsored by M.P.s from the Midlands and East Anglia, asking that the *Book of
Common Prayer* be replaced and the Genevan liturgy be authorized in the English
church. The organization which had gone into raising petitions and securing
the election of particular M.P.s, and the sweeping nature of the changes proposed suggest that the presbyterian element had prepared this campaign
thoroughly. Parliamentary activity ended with a royal assertion of prerogative
in matters ecclesiastical and the imprisonment in the tower of five members,
including Peter Wentworth, M.P. for Northampton.[11] Meanwhile work on the
*Book of Discipline* continued, and the puritan ministers meeting in London during
the Parliamentary session probably carried copies back to the provinces at the
end of 1586. With the book went a form of approbation maintaining that it
agreed with the word of God, and that regular meetings should take place in
'classical conferences', which would send delegates to a provincial assembly held
every six months. In addition to these superior assemblies parochial institutions
were to be altered to enable the establishment of an eldership along presbyterian

---

[8]Peele, *The Seconde Parte*, ii. 92; there is some confusion in the versions of the document
and the information given might also cover the deanery of Peterborough as well as Rutland.
[9]P.D.R., Vis. Bk. IV, unfoliated.
[10]*Ibid*., X608/14, f. 39.
[11]Neale, *Elizabeth I and her Parliaments*, ii. 145-165.

lines, and it was through these institutions that ecclesiastical discipline was to be exercised.[12]

The *Book of Discipline* received a very mixed reception among puritans in different parts of the country and Professor Collinson has recently provided the definitive story of its progress. Many puritans sympathized with its programme, but were uncertain about setting up such an obvious *ecclesia in ecclesia*. Another assembly was called and met at Cambridge in September 1587 to discuss organizational problems and the issue troubling many puritan conferences, what to do when faced with the choice of subscription to the *Book of Discipline* or deprivation. It says much for the determination of the members, who included John Barebone and William Fludd as representatives from Northamptonshire, that most of the time was spent on organizational problems rather than on troubled consciences. Nevertheless the assembly was aware that the responses to the *Book of Discipline* were equivocal in many areas, but the participants took little account of the diversity of the tradition they claimed to represent. Its activities have recently been described as 'the deliberations of a body which held itself to be the provincial assembly of a nascent English presbyterian church', and the mood of the representatives was to press on with its policies, notwithstanding the doubts of some of the membership. Whether that policy was a wise one or not remains to be seen. Northamptonshire, however, was one county in which it had considerable success.[13]

The activities of the Northamptonshire *classes* in the crucial years between 1587 and the Star Chamber trial of the leaders in 1591 are the best documented of all such meetings. Many of the leaders of the movement were based in the county, and evidence given before the courts by William Proudlove of Weedon Bec, Thomas Stone of Warkton, Edmund Snape of Northampton, Edmund Littleton sometime of Brixworth, Andrew King of Culworth, and John Johnson of Northampton provides a mass of detail, some of it contradictory.[14] Johnson was vicar of All Saints, Northampton and by 1590 had fallen out with the *classes* and turned queen's evidence. His testimony is by far the most detailed but needs to be balanced by the more noncommittal answers of the defendants and in particular those of Thomas Stone. Stone also provided the government with information, but his willingness to testify appears to have been prompted by the desire to record some defensive account of events in the light of Johnson's defection. Johnson claimed that he had withdrawn from the *classis* at Northampton before the matter of the *Book of Discipline* was raised, and could give no evidence about the nature of any subscription made to its terms. It would appear that the Discipline was subscribed in Warwickshire late in 1587 or early the following year and was carried from there to Northamptonshire where the ministers had already divided themselves into three *classes*, at Northampton, Daventry, and Kettering, in eager anticipation. The Daventry meeting was smallest in number, but represented a cohesive group of Knightley protegés; its membership comprised Simon Rogers of Byfield, Edward Sharpe of Fawsley, John Barebone of Charwelton, John Elliston of Plumpton, Andrew King of Culworth, Robert Smart of Preston Capes, and one representative of an older generation of nonconformists, William Proudlove of Weedon Bec. The personnel of the Northampton *classis* included three of the town clergy, John Johnson

---

[12]*Eliz. Puritan Movt.*, 317–318.

[13]*Ibid.*, 318–329, esp. p. 320 based largely on the evidence of the Dedham minute book and the testimony of John Johnson of Northampton before the Star Chamber.

[14]Principally in P.R.O., STAC 5/A 49/34 and 56/1.

**MAP 1**  The Distribution of the Puritan Clergy

*Key*

OAKHAM    Prophesying centres
Byfield    Parishes served by *classis* members
X          Parishes served by puritan clergy

*Note*

Where the only evidence for nonconformity comes from appearances before the local church courts, two appearances for offences other than merely neglecting the surplice have been necessary for inclusion.

of All Saints, Edmund Skinner of St Sepulchre's, and Edmund Snape, a 'chief-man', curate at St Peter's. In addition the rural clergy comprised three members of the older generation, John Sibthorpe of Ashton, John Spicer of Cogenhoe, and Nicholas Edwards of Courteenhall and five others; Edmund Littleton of Brixworth, Henry Bradshaw and Nicholas Lack, curates of Horton and Wellingborough respectively, Ralph Harrison of Grendon, and William Fleshware of Abington. The separatist John Penry, who had married into a Northampton family, was also a visitor to the *classis*, which drew its support almost entirely from clergy serving parishes to the south and east of Northampton itself. Two other visitors to the Northampton *classis* were Thomas Stone of Warkton and Robert Williamson of Titchmarsh, the moderators of the *classis* based at Kettering. This *classis* had a more fitful existence than the others and included long-serving clerics like Ralph Fosbrooke of Cranford St Andrew, Edward Massey of Thrapston, and Leonard Pattinson of Cransley. Other members included Hugh Okes of Weekley and John Davies of Pilton, whilst Brian Atkinson, formerly curate of Grendon, and Thomas Baxter of Draughton also maintained contacts with the *classis* and its members.[15]

The division of the county into three meetings was carried out at the suggestion of William Fludd, an unbeneficed clergyman working in the county who attended the different *classes* 'like an apostle or patriarch' who 'did ride much abroad to hear and see what was done in most places, so as whatsoever he directed was commonly concluded and followed'. Fludd may earlier have held a living in the county at Ashby St Ledgers, but between 1587 and 1589 he resided at Northampton. He attended the Cambridge meeting of 1587 as a representative of the county, and did so again in 1589, when he also attended the puritan synod held at London. He remained in the diocese for twenty years, his ministry based on the approval of other 'godly and learned men', with the support of George Carleton and others of the local gentry, some of whom regarded him as a 'patriarch', in much the same light as did the clergy of the *classes*.[16]

In addition to the three *classes*, the puritans established a meeting not provided for in the *Book of Discipline* but one reminiscent of the order establishing the exercises in 1571, that is an assembly of the whole shire attended by two delegates from each *classis*. The assembly was regularly attended by Snape, Barebone, Stone and Williamson, none of whom held livings in the diocese before 1581. The assembly met, usually every six to eight weeks, to discuss matters beyond the scope of the individual *classes*, and to keep in touch with events elsewhere. They elected their own moderator, who was said to have authority over all the other *classes* until the next meeting of the assembly, and conducted correspondence with puritan leaders like Lawrence Chaderton in Cambridge, Walter Travers in London, and John Gellibrand in Oxford. Snape usually acted as corresponding secretary for the county and the assembly issued advice to the *classes* so that they might 'the better direct themselves and their churches accordingly'.

[15]P.R.O., STAC 5/A 49/34, Johnson's evidence; Stone's evidence sets out deliberately to contradict and modify Johnson's at some points, and also lays stress on the date at which Johnson removed himself from membership, putting it after the reception of the *Book*. Much of the detail given by Johnson does indeed suggest that this was the case. The material was written up from the point of view of the establishment in R. Bancoft, *Daungerous Positions and Proceedings* (1593). See also T. Fuller, *Church History of Britain* (1845 edn.), v. 163–169.

[16]P.R.O., STAC 5/A 49/34 Johnson. For Fludd see *Eliz. Puritan Movt.*, 324–325, 397–398; for his standing with the gentry see N.R.O., Isham Correspondence, 3480, letter from Thomas Isham.

Johnson's testimony is the principal source for the conduct of the meetings. They were held in private houses in the towns where they were located, once at Mr Davies' in Kettering, and began with the election of a moderator by secret ballot after a prayer for guidance. Thus elected, the moderator took charge of the meeting and a roll was called, latecomers sitting in order as they came. The work of the moderator was to set out the questions to be discussed and, following the discussion, to make a summary of the debate. Matters requiring censure were also taken up by the moderator, whose authority lasted until the next meeting, which was usually to be held within three weeks; the date of that meeting was always fixed before the *classis* disbanded. The moderator was empowered to call the *classis* together sooner if urgent business required dispatch. Although the membership of the meetings, and indeed the spirit also, had changed, the forms of the earlier exercises had not been forgotten.

The ministers, early in 1588, drew up their own rules and kept a register book, unfortunately no longer extant, by which they were bound to submit all matters of doctrine and discipline to the censure of their brethren in the *classes*. A common fund was established, contributed to by all the membership, in order to defray the costs of any minister employed on the business of 'the church'. This was the framework established by the *classes*. It remains to discuss how far the system represented a fully fledged 'church within a church' with an independent discipline. In that discussion three key issues came out at the trial of the leaders in 1591. First, the nature and extent of subscription to the *Book of Discipline*; second, the establishment of an eldership in the parishes; and finally, the use of discipline and censure among the membership.[17]

The authorities were able to prove that the ministers of Warwickshire had formally subscribed to the *Book of Discipline*, but evidence from Northamptonshire was more fragmentary, the chief source being Thomas Stone of Warkton. Johnson had claimed that he had left the *classis* before the *Book of Discipline* had been introduced to the county and, although other defendants in the Star Chamber denied this, he provided no evidence on this issue. The tone of his deposition does however stress the autocratic and institutionalized aspects of the *classes* and he maintained that early in 1588 each member had to 'promise under his hand to submit himself to be obedient to all such orders and decrees as should be set down by the same *classes* to be observed'. Most of the defendants in the trial denied that the subscription was to any particular order of discipline, which was viewed merely as a set of recommendations to be carried out as far as the law allowed. These sort of reservations were stressed by Stone in his account of the reception of the *Book of Discipline*, he claimed 'that there were many persons of the said assemblies which did not at any time subscribe to the said discipline and yet nevertheless did give their voices in the same assemblies' and he further pointed out that Snape had received letters from himself and others in the county expressing 'certain doubts or scruples whereof the said ministers wished to be resolved'. The voluntarism of the *classes* proved to be a valuable defence in 1591 and Stone's evidence suggests that the membership was careful to keep within the letter of the law, even though the stress on discipline must have taken them beyond its spirit as seen by the Queen and Whitgift. Stone maintained that to his knowledge none of the defendants before the Star Chamber had either 'by writing, printing, or teaching, taught, approved or set forth anything in the said *Book of Discipline* or in any part thereof'. Edmund Littleton, by the time of

[17] *Ibid.*, Johnson and Stone.

the trial an incumbent in Bedfordshire, suggested that things had gone a little further and that

> Mr Snape, Mr Proudlove & such others as were with him in the said two several meetings before specified . . . did agree to put the said articles & discipline in execution & practise so far as the present state of the Church of England now established would suffer & not enforce [it] to the contrary, that is to say till the magistrate did enjoin or enforce them to leave the practising of the said discipline. And they did agree also to guide themselves by the said Book of Discipline and according to it with the same limitations . . .

The distinction between legality and illegality was evidently a fine one in the minds of many of the presbyterians.[18]

Discipline at the parochial level involved establishing the eldership, comprising laymen called elders and deacons, which surpervised the moral life of the congregation and also some of its social needs. The godly laity were thus involved in local church government alongside their ministers. This form of parochial institution was quite illegal and Bancroft in his government-inspired attack on the presbyterians, *Daungerous Positions and Proceedings* published in 1593, claimed that the eldership had been formally established at Kilsby in the west of the the county. This was said to have involved the nomination of six parishioners who were thought fit 'to determine and end all matters of controversy in the town'. If so, it did not correspond very closely to the formal eldership of the reformed churches, even if it shared that spirit. It would appear that at Kilsby the minister chose to rely on and give special confidence to a small band of godly in his congregation. If that entailed an eldership then the practice must have been current in several places and certainly existed at St Peter's in Northampton. The curate, Edmund Snape, was in the habit of confiding in a few of his favoured parishioners and in 1589 called four of them 'into the great seat of the parish church' where he reported some *classis* business to them, indicated his intention to cast off episcopal ordination in order to seek validation of his ministry by the election of the congregation, and spoke inflammatory words about the removal of the whole order of episcopacy. The men entrusted with this news were to give evidence against Snape in the Star Chamber in 1591 when Richard Holmes testified about the disciplining of the daughter of a Mr Nelson, whom he described as an elder or deacon. The implication was that some form of eldership was in existence in 1588, but in answer to another article Holmes stated that Snape 'and those of his faction in his congregation had purposed and determined to have made choice of some elders or deacons or both amongst themselves, but that matter was prevented by the said Mr Snape's imprisonment'. Clearly there was some confusion in his mind as to how far things had been taken, but it was not difficult to graft a form of eldership on to the existing parochial office of churchwarden in order to evade the law without incurring its penalties. How effectively such an eldership could exercise discipline over parishioners unwilling to cooperate is hard to say.[19]

Among the godly themselves Johnson, in his evidence, suggests that discipline was so exercised. He described it as a 'secret kind of excommunication' and said that persistent offenders were denied the sacrament by their ministers. Here

[18]P.R.O., STAC 5/A 49/34, Johnson and Stone.

[19]R. Bancoft, *Daungerous Positions*, 116–117; P.R.O., STAC 5/A 49/34, Johnson's evidence, and A 27/33. In both cases 'the discipline' ran into difficulties when coping with the transgressions of kinsfolk of elders.

Johnson referred to the case of Mr Nelson the elder (again the term was used), whose servant was compelled to make 'public confession of his offence' before getting absolution from Snape. Whether this sort of parochial discipline was exercised elsewhere we do not know, but two *classis* members, Ralph Fosbrooke and Euseby Walker were presented at the visitation in 1590 for withholding spiritual comfort from members of their congregations. Walker had refused the communion to a woman who had railed against the preaching of John Barebone and Andrew King, his *classis* colleagues.[20] Discipline of the laity brought with it exclusiveness and withdrawal from the wider community, an exclusiveness which Johnson made much of in his testimony. Talking of the close cooperation between the puritan ministry and laity, Johnson provided Bancroft and the authorities with a valuable semantic point. The issue centred on the application of the term 'brethren' or 'brother' by members of the *classes* and their followers. He claimed that

> when the word brethren is used to those of the laity, thereby is meant those that generally join with the brethren ministers for the said discipline and do submit themselves to the ministry of some of the classes ... these brethren, viz. both minister and people, are called the godly brotherhood denying in very deed the name of a brother to be proper unto any but unto such as are of their own faction and opinion ...

This was more than a mere form of words in the minds of many puritans, and Snape's congregation had heard him preach along the same lines when he spoke of the church as 'a chosen generation' which comprised 'here one and there one picked out of the prophane and common multitude and put apart to serve the Lord', these it was who made 'The Church of God, and not the general multitude.'[21] These words, with their emphasis on a gathered church set apart from the rest had separatist and congregational overtones somewhat at odds with the presbyterian platform of the *classes*. How far the puritans at this time stood apart from their fellows is difficult to say; the term brother may well have been used by puritans to underline their shared beliefs rather than in the exclusive sense suggested by Johnson. It so happens that the only reference to the term 'brethren', used in this context, in the wills proved at Northampton comes from the very period in which the *classis* was active. On 10 May 1587 Richard Hobbes, a husbandman from Cotton on the outskirts of Northampton, made his will appointing as overseers Edmund York, John West, and Henry Godlie, whom he described as 'my loving friends and brethren in Christ'. Henry Godly was a brother-in-law of the *classis* member John Penry and was himself involved in radical activity in the town. Edmund York, who was styled Mr, figured prominently among the disaffected puritans in his own parish of Hardingstone during the 1580s, being presented regularly, with other members of his family, for not attending his parish church but going to All Saints, Northampton instead. Hobbes' wife was the first inhabitant of Hardingstone to be presented for absenting herself from the communion after the deprivations of 1574. Hobbes was clearly one of the godly in the parish and, in his will, associated himself with his fellow puritans. Whether he used the term 'brethren' in the same sense as suggested by Johnson's evidence is uncertain, but its appearance at that date

[20]P.R.O., STAC 5/A 49/34, Johnson; P.D.R., X610/23a. f. 54v; 24, ff. 23v-24.
[21]P.R.O., STAC 5/A 49/34, Johnson; see Bancroft, *Daungerous Positions*, 120-121; for Snape see P.R.O., STAC/A 27/33.

and in that company is suggestive, even though no further examples can be found.[22]

The idea of a 'gathered church' on congregational lines may have been important at the parochial level, but the *classes* were clearly designed to impose a regular and structural form of discipline upon the clergy. Discussion of doctrine and censorship of faults had been introduced before the arrival of the *Book of Discipline*, and three cases involving clergy are recorded. One of them may well have occasioned Johnson's estrangement from the Northampton *classis* for, according to Stone, he was censured by the moderator for a misdemeanour 'to the great scandal of the ministry'. Stone maintained that the censure 'mentioned in the said *Book of Discipline* was practised upon the said Mr Johnson before named in one assembly held at Northampton as aforesaid, but the same censure was not so practised by virtue of [the] authority or by the prescript of the said book, but was a thing voluntarily done and proceeded unto'. The implication is that this took place after the arrival of the *Book of Discipline* and that Johnson continued to be a member of the *classis* for rather longer than he admitted. The fact that another *classis* member, Edward Lord of Wolston in Warwickshire, chose to get married at Johnson's church of All Saints in 1589 also suggests that relations remained cordial at that date.[23] Another Northampton member, Nicholas Edwards of Courteenhall, was also censured by the *classis* for using the cross in baptism, but the case to which the authorities gave most weight did not concern censure of a member, but rejection of an application for membership. John Hocknell had been presented to the living of Wootton by Bartholomew Tate in 1588 and sought the approval of the Northampton *classis*. His living was encircled by parishes served by *classis* members and it may have been local pressure which influenced Hocknell's decision. He was asked to preach before the *classis* whose members, after some discussion, decided to withold acceptance from him until he pursued a course of further study. Hocknell refused to accept the decision of the members, was instituted to his living in the normal fashion, and remained there until 1616 unmolested by the diocesan authorities and not troubling them with nonconformity.[24]

Hocknell's case illustrates both the local prestige which the *classes* could have, and also their limitations. They could never impose their edicts on unwilling laymen or uncooperative clergy without making their opposition to the established church more explicit than they cared to. Their treatment of Hocknell also brings us away from the organizational preoccupations of the *classes* to their concern for the ministry. In 1588 the old tactic of compiling a survey of the ministry was tried again in preparation for the parliament to be called. The survey was compiled on a deanery basis and Edmund Littleton was responsible for making the return for Haddon deanery. According to Johnson he brought in 'a most railing discourse against every minister which was not of that fraternity'. The *classes* then sent up representatives to London at parliament time, Simon Rogers being accompanied by Thomas Settle of Northampton. Others attended meetings at Cambridge in 1589 and Stone and Barebone were present at a gathering in London shortly before the arrest of Thomas Cartwright, the intel-

[22]P.D.R., Will Reg. V 523; Archd. Ct. Bk. 5, f. 36a; X648/1, ff. 78v., 118a.

[23]P.R.O., STAC 5/A 49/34, Stone; W. P. W Phillimore and H. I. Longden (eds.), *Northamptonshire Marriage Registers* (Parish Register Society, 1909), ii. 2. It may have been Johnson's indebtedness that caused the estrangement with his colleagues, N.R.O., Minutes of the Town Assembly, 1549–1627, f. 232.

[24]P.R.O., STAC 5/A 49/34, Stone; Bancroft, *Daungerous Positions*, 83, 113–114; B.L. Harl. Ms. 64, f. 54; P.D.R., Inst. Bk. III, f. 24; *H.I.L.* vii, 41.

lectual leader of the movement, at that time serving in Warwickshire. Attendance at such meetings was financed by the *classes*, which were sufficiently politicized to appoint deputies to fill any vacancy caused by the arrest of any member and also, presumably, arranged for the discharge of the pastoral responsibilities of delegates.[25]

The uncovering of the movement and the subsequent trials of the leaders before the High Commission and Star Chamber have recently been dealt with in detail.[26] Attention was drawn to the activities of the Midland *classes* by the publication of the Marprelate tracts, a series of scurrilous pamphlets attacking episcopacy. The press on which the tracts were printed was given a temporary home at Fawsley by Sir Richard Knightley in the autumn of 1589 before being removed along Watling Street to Coventry. The tracts, which boasted of the strength of puritanism in Northamptonshire and challenged the mayor and constables of Northampton to apprehend those involved in their publication, helped to tighten a net already closing on the puritans. Snape was so apprehensive that he hid his books in the house of one of his congregation but some of his personal papers were seized, as was much incriminating evidence about the Warwickshire *classes* when the house of Edmund Littleton was searched. Against the background of the Marprelate tracts, publication of which lost a lot of political support for the puritans, the *classes* were uncovered and suppressed. Many preachers were interrogated before the High Commission in the winter of 1589–1590 and most of the details were pieced together in the spring and summer of 1590. On 11 July 1590 the High Commission removed Edmund Snape from his ecclesiastical offices, and degraded him from orders for life, the latter sentence being mitigated to a suspension of ten years. By the following spring the government decided to transfer the trial of nine of the leaders to the more powerful Star Chamber—five of these nine being Northamptonshire clerics, Edmund Littleton, Andrew King, Thomas Stone, William Proudlove, and Edmund Snape. Their position was not made any easier by the actions of some of their erstwhile followers, and others on the fringe of the movement. The curious so-called Hackett conspiracy, which involved two known puritan laymen declaring a semi-literate peasant from Oundle as king of Europe, provided the government with plenty of ammunition with which to attack the ministers with subversion. The extent of their involvement with Hackett, which focused mainly on the elusive figure of Giles Wigginton, was made much of by the government, but it is unlikely that Hackett got any positive support from them. Nor were they in any position to influence the actions of the three so-called conspirators. Hacket, about whom more will be said later, was executed for treason and the affair could hardly have come at a worse time for the puritans.[27]

Snape and Proudlove attempted with some success to organize petitions on their behalf from their former congregations. King, Stone, and Proudlove had been deprived by the spring of 1591, but the trial in Star Chamber dragged on into 1592. The defendants all suffered periods of imprisonment but retained some powerful support in government circles. Once satisfied that the movement had been broken, the government ensured that no vindictive sententences were promulgated. Indeed, one of the defendants, William Proudlove, was restored

[25]P.R.O., STAC 5/A 49/34, Johnson, Stone.
[26]*Eliz. Puritan Movt.* 403–431;
[27]W. Pierce, *An Historical Introduction to the Marprelate Tracts* (1908), 67–73; M. Marprelate, *An Epistle to the Terrible Priests of the Confocation House* (1967 facsimile edn.), p. 28; *Eliz. Puritan Movt.* 413, 417; for Hackett see below pp. 136–139.

to his former living in 1596 and Snape never lost contact with his Northampton-shire colleagues. Those *classis* members not arraigned before the Star Chamber were able to remain in their livings once the movement had been dismantled.[28]

The *classes* of the diocese involved 28 of the parochial clergy as members, and a few others as sympathizers, for a period of little over 18 months. The movement had the political aim of establishing a presbyterian form of church government within episcopacy, but the legal implications of this resulted, as Thomas Stone suggested in evidence, in varying degrees of support among the membership. William Proudlove and Nicholas Lack, curate at Daventry, went as far as renouncing their episcopal orders entirely and seeking a calling from their congregations, others did not go so far.[29] Some parishes witnessed the establishment of an eldership in spirit if not formally. Concentration on the political and organizational concerns of the *classes* reveals that, in the diocese, the control of policy was in relatively few hands, six or seven men usually nomi-nated as the assembly and accustomed to act as moderators in their own *classis*. Such concentration on organization probably reflects the priorities of the *classes* themselves but, although Northamptonshire is the best documented of the counties where *classes* are known to have existed, membership involved less than half of the known nonconforming clergy of the diocese. The meetings were considerably smaller than the less politically active *classis* at Dedham in Essex, a more amorphous meeting mostly comprising graduates of Cambridge rather than the Oxford men who were dominant in Northamptonshire.

Despite their involvement in politics, the original impetus to the *classes* was the desire for further reformation of the established church along lines prevalent on the continent. This reform did not come about simply through changing the ecclesiastical polity, but also required a revolution of doctrine and worship. This the members undertook and, in evidence, Andrew King provided the authorities with an intimate insight into the devotional life as practised in his own parish of Culworth. Having called his congregation to hear a sermon, 'he chose his text out of Canonical scripture, & usually appointed a psalm to be sung before & after his sermon. And this defendant made before his sermons a con-fession of sins & a prayer for the fruitful receiving & delivery of the word, and prayer after his sermons for a blessing of the word and for all estates.'[30] This expressed a humility not often noted among the presbyterians. Politics appeared to have displaced preaching for a while as the chief priority of the presbyterian faction, but it was their concern for evangelization which identified them with their fellow puritans in the diocese. This common concern provided much sympathy for the presbyterians locally, and before assessing the contribution of the *classes* to the history of puritanism in the diocese, some discussion is required of the activities of those puritans who remained aloof from their meetings.

*Other puritans*

Although the evidence taken by the Star Chamber was rather inconclusive on many important points, it is fairly certain that Johnson and Stone provided full details regarding the personnel of the *classis*. Bancroft, in *Daungerous Posi-*

---

[28]See P.D.R., Inst. Bk. III, f. 34; B.L., Lansd. Ms. 445, f. 4v; Sloane Ms. 271, f. 24; *A.P.C.*, xx. 313–314; N.R.O., Minutes of the Town Assembly 1549–1627, f. 313.

[29]P.R.O., STAC 5/A 56/1 Proudlove, Snape.

[30]For Dedham see R. G. Usher, *The Presbyterian Movement 1582–9* (Camden Society, Third Series, vii), *passim*. P.R.O., STAC 5/A 56/1, King.

*tions and Proceedings*, was eager to implicate as many known puritans as possible in what he regarded as the presbyterian conspiracy. It is therefore reasonable to assume that some important puritan clergy chose either to remain aloof from the *classes* or to keep up only the most tenuous links. Those puritans not involved in the movement have often been characterized as moderate nonconformists who occasionally objected to minor ceremonial like the wearing of the surplice but who were not so fully committed to the more central concerns of puritanism; that is to say, a determination to root out the non-preaching ministry, to remove 'idolatrous' practices from the services, to attack institutional abuses such as pluralism and non-residence, and to seek a more equitable structure of the ministry and reform of episcopacy.

Some men arraigned before the church courts were 'mere nonconformists' like Giles Sharrocke, rector of Crick and a former member of the exercise at Northampton, who was presented for not wearing the surplice in 1585 but troubled the authorities no more. One of an older generation of clerics, Sharrocke may not have been in sympathy with the young radicals of the 1580s. Other incumbents were forced by circumstance to discard the surplice. Edward Fulshurst of Great Oxendon walked 12 miles to say service in his parish in 1587 but found that the churchwardens could provide neither gown nor surplice. Puritanism would need to be a very broad term to include such a man. Other individuals, like Nicholas Latham of Barnwell St Andrew, Oliver Houghton of Easton Mauduit, and John Gibson of Warmington, only attracted the attention of the authorities over the question of the surplice at this time.[31] The problem in such cases is that puritanism is largely seen by the historian through the eyes of the established church, and its eyes were directed for the most part to ceremonial nonconformity. The incompleteness of the evidence is best illustrated by the case of John Elliston of Preston Capes. Without the deposition of his fellow *classis* members before the Star Chamber, and further evidence collected by John Field for his register of puritan sufferings, we would have to rely on the local diocesan courts for details of Elliston's activities. In that case the only information we would get on Elliston would be that he was presented in 1590 for not wearing the surplice, and thus a whole aspect of his career would remain obscure.[32] Other *classis* members do not appear to have ever been troubled by the local courts. Sometimes a presentment for not wearing the surplice can be identified with strong objections on religious grounds; William Cherington, curate of Farthingstone, was charged with not wearing the surplice in 1590 and replied that 'he cannot say service, having on the surplice, with a good conscience'. A fortnight later, on 19 November, his attitude was more apparent when he was suspended for a variety of offences which included neglecting to use the *Book of Common Prayer* and refusing to read the Royal Injunctions.[33]

The clearest evidence that other puritans could be as radical in their attitude to the ministry and abuses within the church as were the *classis* members comes from Rutland. We know that Robert Rushbrooke, schoolmaster at Oakham, had attended one meeting of the *classis* held at Kettering, but in all the charges made against the puritans serving Rutland parishes the authorities made no reference to the *classes*. Even in the lengthy proceedings against the radical Robert

[31]P.D.R., Archd. Vis. Bk. 9, f. 125v.; X609/21, f. 104; X609/23, ff. 126v., 140; 23a, f. 80v.

[32]*Ibid.*, X610/24, f. 73v.; see Peel, *The Seconde Parte*, i. 291-6; P.R.O., STAC 5/A 49/34, Johnson.

[33]P.D.R., X610/24, f. 75v.; 25, f. 6.

Cawdry before the High Commission, he was never charged with membership of a *classis*.[34]

In the later 1580s the chief centres of puritan activity in Rutland were those parishes already mentioned in the first part of this chapter: North and South Luffenham, Tinwell, Ridlington, Great Casterton, and Oakham, where the exercise was based. In 1590 Robert Johnson, Edward Wilkinson, and Henry Hargreaves, who was rector of both Pilton and Whitwell, were presented for permitting an unauthorized minister to preach at Oakham. Some version of the exercise was apparently flourishing in the town at this late date, and was being supervised by the puritans of the county.[35] Johnson's commitment to preaching, already noted at the Stamford fast, continued to trouble the authorities. On 20 November 1587 he was presented by his churchwardens for preaching after being prohibited by the bishop. At that time Johnson was employing a curate, William Laicocke, who also preached unlicensed because, in his own words, he had no need of one since 'when he was made minister by his ordinary, in giving of the Bible unto him, he bade him go and preach.'[36] In 1589 Johnson had allowed the semi-separatist radical Giles Wigginton, at that time exercising an unauthorized and roving ministry based at his home town of Oundle, to preach in his parish. Wigginton had been deprived of his living at Sedbergh in Yorkshire, was one of the prime suspects as author of the Marprelate tracts and, although not a member of a local *classis*, was in close contact with the leadership during their imprisonment in London.[37] Johnson's style of puritanism, which included the practice of distributing the communion after the fashion of a meal, was thoroughgoing and had strong radical connections. This radicalism was, however, a pastoral rather than a political one and did not prevent his promotion to the archdeaconry of Leicester in 1591. His pastoral concern led him to establish two schools, now famous, at Oakham and at Uppingham during the 1580s and to place them under puritan trustees. His new post, which he held with North Luffenham, did not result in any modification of his views. His son Abraham married a daughter of Laurence Chaderton, the first master of Emmanuel College, Cambridge. Chaderton had been a correspondent of the *classis* members, but he later came to symbolize that form of puritanism which concentrated on gradual pastoral reform rather than political action.[38] It was this concern for the pastoral side of evangelization which no doubt prompted Johnson's son Abraham to organize 'a learned godly sermon' at Oakham in 1618. The sermon, delivered on Sundays by neighbouring clergy in turn, was indeed the direct descendant of the exercise of the 1750s. Although puritan in inspiration, these 'lectures by combination' taking place in market-towns were a typical feature of early 17th-century church life.[39] In addition to the exercise at Oakham, the puritans in Rutland continued the practice of fasts, involving attendance by the laity and a show of strength by the clergy. One such fast took

[34]P.R.O., STAC 5/A 49/34, Stone; Peel, *The Seconde Parte*, ii. 202–208. He was later charged with holding private meetings at which the Marprelate tracts were read, B.L., Lansd. Ms. 57, f. 172.

[35]P.D.R., X610/15, f. 6.

[36]*Ibid.*, X608/19, f. 74v.; 21, f. 125.

[37]*Ibid.*, X610/23a, f. 5; B.L. Lansd. Ms. 84, f. 238; Peel, *The Seconde Parte*, ii. 238; see below pp. 136–139.

[38]For Chaderton see H. C. Porter, *Reformation and Reaction in Tudor Cambridge*, esp. 239–241, 398–400.

[39]Irons, 'Mr. Abraham Johnson', 59. For a discussion of these lectures, including several examples from the diocese, see P. Collinson, 'Lectures by Combination', 182–213.

place at Ridlington in 1589 and was supported by the local squire James Harrington and the sheriff of the county. The diocesan authorities were provided with
a full description of the event where

> Mr Holmes did preach upon a private fast in the parish church of Ridlington,
> did continue from ix to iij in the presence of Mr Sheriff, Mr James Harring-
> ton, with others both of town and country, in which sermon the said Holmes
> spoke these words as the like in effect: that the Book of Common Prayer was
> a great idol and full of abominations, as the churching of women and burial
> of the dead, and that they did not belong to (the minister's) office but were
> apish tricks. Then Mr Wilkinson, parson of Tinwell, the said day preached
> and said 'Good brethren, lift up your hearts and pray mightily unto God, and
> believeth this that our brother hath said, for he hath spoken the truth, and
> that we might have reformation of these things.' Then Mr Gibson preached
> and told them that his brethren had spoken the truth, and prayed them to
> believe him and to lift up their hearts mightily to God, and prayed for
> reformation.[40]

Thomas Gibson of Ridlington was prepared to hand his pulpit over to his
colleagues for such events and it is clear that the puritan Rutland clergy kept in
close contact with each other throughout the 1580s. Edward Wilkinson of
Tinwell was accused of preaching in private places and ordered to conform in
1586, along with Thomas Gibson. They were presumably preaching at private
conventicles of the godly, but we have no further details of such meetings, which
drew the puritans together in informal services held apart from their non-puritan
neighbours.[41] Another defendant with Gibson and Wilkinson in 1586 was
Humphrey Wildblood of Great Casterton, and his case provides us with the
only suggestion that the Rutland puritans might have institutionalized their
contact with each other. He had been confronted by a group of female parishioners demanding that they be churched after childbirth, but Wildblood
refused to perform the ceremony, claiming that he had taken an oath against
so doing. This reference pre-dates the establishment of the *classes*, but Wildblood's mention of an oath suggests that, in the aftermath of Whitgift's Three
Articles, the clergy of Rutland were meeting to discuss matters of ceremonial
and that their decisions were regarded as binding in some degree. It is hard to
see any other circumstances in which Wildblood would take such an oath, a
serious business for any puritan, unless he was referring to a personal undertak-
ing made in private.[42] The diocesan authorities did not pursue the matter with
Wildblood at the time but the following year he faced seven charges representing the most comprehensive range of nonconformist practices. The charges were
as follows:

1 that he doth not read common prayer as it ought to be said or sung according as is appointed.
2 that he doth not allow the Book of Common Prayer and the service to be
read as is appointed.
3 that he termeth the gospel chaff, and all other sentences of scripture nothing,
that is appointed by the Book of Common Prayer; but that what he maketh
of his own mind, that is for his purpose, that is godly.

[40]P.D.R., X609/23. f. 216.
[41]*Ibid.*, f. 202; X610/23a, f. 7v.
[42]*Ibid.*, X608/19, f. 69v.

4 that he will not read the Queen's Injunctions and the articles.
5 for not reading the catholic faith [*sic* the creed] which is to be read in the churches at certain times in the year, as the book doth appoint him.
6 that he doth make service against the churchwardens because they present according to their order, calling them rascals, plough-jacks, asses and calves, and not worthy to receive the Holy Communion.
7 that he will not church women according to the Book of Common Prayer.

Despite these offences Wildblood got away with a warning.[43] The charges make it clear that his ministry had divided the parish, but Wildblood's case and those of his colleagues show that, even in the face of local opposition, the Rutland puritans were determined opponents of the *Book of Common Prayer* and persistent in their demands for a preaching ministry. Both concerns brought them into conflict with the diocesan authorities, yet most remained in their parishes for many years to come. Only one Rutland cleric, Robert Cawdry, rector of South Luffenham, was deprived during this period, and his prosecution by the High Commission in 1588 became a *cause célèbre*, espoused by the common lawyers in parliament, who led an attack on the procedures of the court and in particular on the use of the *ex officio* oath.[44] Cawdry's belligerent and uncompromising attitudes had first attracted the attention of the diocesan authorities at the beginning of the 1580s, and continued to trouble them until his deprivation and beyond. Despite repeated appeals to his patron Burghley, Cawdry was finally deprived of his living, but remained in his parish until 1589 when he was again presented for gathering a conventicle which met in private houses to read and study, among other books, the writings of Martin Marprelate.[45] Cawdry not only remained in the parish, but refused to leave the parsonage, and it is interesting that his patron Burghley did not present a new man to the vacancy. That was finally done by Bishop Howland, exercising his right *per lapsum temporis*, who presented William Baylie, one of his chaplains and formerly a fellow of the bishop's old Cambridge college. The rival parties were involved in a fracas over the rye then growing on the rectorial estate, and Cawdry brought an action against Baylie in Star Chamber. Cawdry must have had legal advice and claimed that his deprivation by the High Commission was illegal under the terms of the Act of Uniformity of 1559. This defence depended on a literal interpretation of the Act, which stipulated that the penalty for a first offence in speaking against the *Book of Common Prayer* should be a fine of 100 marks, but the Star Chamber judges were not impressed; they presumably had plenty of examples of Cawdry's opposition to the Book. The case went against Cawdry who remained in the area for some time under the patronage of the Harrington family, until he removed himself to Coventry where he was school teaching in 1604.[46]

The example of these men encouraged other Rutland clergy to dispense with the *Book of Common Prayer* and other ceremonial, and at least three others were presented for such offences in 1589.[47] The influence which the puritan leaders

[43]P.D.R., X609/20, ff. 74v.–75, 202; X610/23a, f. 66v.
[44]Peel, *The Seconde Parte*, ii. 202–208; see C. Hill, *Society and Puritanism*, 344–354 esp. 349–350.
[45]B.L., Lansd. Ms. 57, f. 172.
[46]P.R.O., STAC 5/C 78/3; C 28/36; C 80/40; P.D.R., Inst. Bk III, f. 25. E. A. Irons, 'A Paper on Sir Robert Cawdrie; rector of South Luffenham 1571–87', *Rutland Archaeol. and Natural History Society, 14th report*, (1917) 32.
[47]Robert Rudd, William Rowe, and Richard Swan; P.D.R. X609/23, ff. 155, 156v, 193; X610/23a, ff. 3, 6v.

elsewhere could have on the parochial clergy is nicely illustrated by the case of John Beatniffe, presented in 1587 to the wealthy royal living of Brackley in the south-west corner of the diocese. Beatniffe's appointment was secured by Richard Bancroft and he appears to have been intended as a spearhead in the counter attack by the authorities against the puritans. He was probably a graduate of Trinity College, Cambridge and was marked out to be one of the leaders of the defence of episcopacy and the established church in a strongly puritan area. In 1588 he was chosen to preach the visitation sermon at Towcester, in which he attacked those who left their own parish to hear services and stoutly defended the government of the established church. The sermon was intended for a wider audience and was published in 1588 as part of the growing corpus of anti-presbyterian literature sponsored by Whitgift and Bancroft. With a dedication to Whitgift, Sir Christopher Hatton, Lord Burghley, and Sir Christopher Wray, Beatniffe's star appeared to be in the ascendant.[48] However, the following year he was suspended from office for refusing to wear the surplice and in 1590 resigned his lucrative living. Nor did he find another, but disappeared from the records until the beginning of the 17th century when he resurfaced as a school-master in Kingsthorpe, a suburb of Northampton.[49] Either Bancroft did not know his man in choosing Beatniffe for that particular task or, more likely, once he began to work in a profoundly puritan part of the country, the young clergyman was influenced by those around him and came to share at least some of their views.

Among the Northamptonshire puritans there were a few notable figures not involved in the *classes*. Whiston a celebrated centre in the 1570s continued to be served by its puritan incumbent John Tymms throughout this period. He failed to appear at the visitation of 1590 but may have been in ill health at that time for he was soon replaced at Whiston by Francis Foster, a thorough-going non-conformist who in 1592 provided a haven for 'diverse persons of other parishes ... such as disobey their own minister'.[50] At Oundle the curate Hugh Clarke was not named as a member of any *classis*, but in 1590 was asked by Roger Wig-ston to replace the deprived *classis* member Edward Lord in the Warwickshire living of Wolston. Clarke's appointment was strongly opposed by the bishop of Coventry and Lichfield, but was not withdrawn. He suffered excommunication as a result of his views, but was eventually reinstated through the intervention of Archbishop Whitgift. Whilst at Oundle Clarke's problems were compounded by the local influence of the catholic Tresham family and by the emergence of a separatist group around the mercurial figure of Giles Wigginton.[51] The local influence of this group, some of whose members were in contact with the congregation at Whiston, will be dealt with later; for the moment it is sufficient to say that there were a few puritan centres in the county with radical traditions, which remained outside the *classes*. Giles' brother Francis was curate and schoolmaster at Blisworth and in 1590 was presented for departing from the *Book of Common Prayer*, along with Thomas London, rector of Bradden, and Francis Battie, rector of Aston le Walls.[52] The metropolitical visitation of

---

[48]Ibid., Misc. Bk. viii, f. 80; Inst. Bk. III, f. 16; J. & J. A. Venn, *Alumni Cantabridgienses* (pt. i), i. 118; J. Beatniffe, *A Sermon Preached at Towcester, 1588* (1590).
[49]P.D.R., X609/23, f. 80; Inst. Bk. III, f. 30; H.I.L. xvi. 14.
[50]P.D.R., X610/24, f. 34a; 25, ff. 18v., 19v., 37.
[51]S. Clarke, *A General Martyrology ... Lives of Sundry Modern English Divines* (1651), 389-390.
[52]P.D.R., X609/21, f. 219v.; 23, ff. 81, 98v.

1589–1590 was particularly efficient at uncovering hitherto unknown pockets of nonconformity. It may well have been that churchwardens in puritan parishes were intimidated by the action taken against the *classis* members and proved more willing than usual to present their clergy. The position of the clergy in their parishes may also have been complicated by the encouragement given to any opponents of the puritans by the action of the government. The wardens of Orlingbury certainly had news of the case before the High Commission when they presented Matthew Mapperley for refusing to wear the surplice or use the sign of the cross at baptism. Mapperley was suspended, but the curate put in to serve the parish was also accused of not communicating with the rest of the parish in November of that year. He withdrew to a nearby puritan church.[53]

Such examples could be added to, but the point has been made that puritan activity in the years between 1587 and 1590 was not confined to the *classes*. Indeed their preoccupation with organization and politics may have caused some friction between themselves and other puritans. The puritan clergy of Rutland, most of whom had been recruited to the diocese in the later 1570s rather than the early 1580s, were just as concerned with pastoral reform and renewal of the forms of worship, but refrained from the organization implied by the *classes*. Others like Hugh Clark and John Tymms were in contact with radical clerics but did not join their meetings. This is not to say that the *classes* were unimportant in the more general history of puritanism in the diocese. The influence and prestige of the members could, as in the case of John Beatniffe, be felt beyond their parishes among the laity and parochial clergy of their locality. The *classes* were therefore of central importance, for their members shared the same concern of all puritans for the reform of parish life. For a period of at most three years their attention was almost wholly diverted by a political cause, but that was a relatively short period in the ministry of 17 years which was the average length of time spent by a *classis* member in the diocese. Their political ambition may have been fed by their close contact with some of the gentry and by the very strength of nonconformity in the region. But it was an ambition hopelessly optimistic in the face of determined government opposition. However, for the great majority defeat in the political arena did not bring deprivation and they returned to their pastoral role, where they were ultimately to have a far greater measure of success. This was not achieved without opposition both local and national, and the accession of James I briefly encouraged some to place their hopes in political action again. Puritanism was not suppressed by the defeat of the *classes*, and further advances were made during the 1590s. What was achieved however was a change of direction or, as some would have had it, a return to the fundamental priorities of a tradition. Parochial reform and congregational worship once again assumed central importance in the minds of the puritans. The activities of the presbyterian party in the 1580s were not the climax to the history of Elizabethan puritanism in the diocese of Peterborough, but rather a turning point.

[53]P.D.R., X609/21, f. 190; 23, f. 119; X610/24, f. 31v., 77.

# 5 REVIEW AND REORGANIZATION 1591–1610

*The later years of Elizabeth's reign*

THE events in Star Chamber called for serious rethinking about strategy and priorities among the puritan clergy. For as long as the Queen and Whitgift, with his zealous assistant Bancroft, remained in control of ecclesiastical policy the tactics of confrontation adopted in the later 1580s were likely to prove fruitless. Whatever the strength of their support in parliament, the puritans were not going to achieve the reforms they desired by constitutional means.[1] Equally, attempts to create an organized infrastructure within the church had been discovered and suppressed. Yet, as we have seen, most of the individuals involved in those activities were permitted to remain in the diocese, for the most part undisturbed in their offices and livings. The effect which the failures of the 1580s had on the attitudes of the former *classis* members, and on the relationship of the 'presbyterian faction' with other puritan ministers emerged slowly during the last decade of the century. Some of the activity can be explained by the view that the presbyterians made a tactful withdrawal from the centre of the stage in order to await a more opportune moment but, more importantly, the years of crisis meant that presbyterianism, however much it might be a rallying call from time to time, no longer retained the hold it had previously had on the imagination of many puritan clerics. It was no longer politically possible, and even the former Northampton minister Francis Merbury could claim in 1596 that he knew of no minister in favour of the erection of a presbytery. During the 1590s the ideals of those 'other puritans' mentioned in the previous chapter came into their own once more, and priority was given to the more generalized aims of bringing about the true reformation whereby, in the words of the order of Northampton of 1571, 'ill life is corrected, God's glory set forth, and the people brought in good obedience'. For most puritans this reformation was to start among their own congregations, and puritan literary activity during the period showed a marked swing away from discussions of ecclesiastical polity and towards works concerned with the spiritual and moral reform of the individual, the household, and the congregation. This process, described recently as a 'quiet and often unobserved revolution which would in time effect changes in English society quite as profound as those ever dreamed of by the presbyterians', was already under way in the diocese, but it was 'often unobserved' by diocesan authorities.[2] Consequently even in the 1590s, when the more overtly political

---

[1]Neale, *Elizabeth I and her Parliaments*, ii. 216–222 describes the background to the parliament of 1589 which marked the end of widespread parliamentary support for puritan policies.

[2]*Eliz. Puritan Movt.*, 443; P.R.O., SP 12/38/138 and see below p. 86 n. 73; for a local example of a cleric whose attitude altered in this way see R. Cawdry, *A Short and Fruitful Treatise*.

activity of the *classes* no longer overshadowed other puritan activity, all that the records provide us with are glimpses of the process.

The events of the 1580s probably had most impact on former *classis* members, and it is among them that responses to those events can be best illustrated. Three *classis* members never came to the attention of the authorities for nonconformity again; one of them, Robert Williamson of Titchmarsh, may have altered his views as he proceeded to take his D.D. degree in 1598 and was collated to a prebendal stall in the cathedral in 1605. He acted as a surrogate in the episcopal courts and, in that capacity, was delegated to treat with those puritans whose scruples over the Canons of 1604 threatened the peace of the diocese. His career suggests a change of attitude in favour of orthodoxy even though, as the career of Robert Johnson illustrates, promotion within the church in the early 17th century was not always incompatible with puritan views. The other two clerics, William Fleshware of Abington and William Proudlove of Weedon Bec, did not achieve promotion, but remained undisturbed in their livings. Their ideals may not have altered beyond the fact that they withdrew from political activity. Their commitment to puritan ideals may have been focused on the parish, where they were content to minister as long as they remained untroubled by officialdom. The close relationship between Proudlove and his congregation, which resulted in an appeal being lodged on his behalf while he was in prison and his restoration to his former living on his release, suggests that in his case this was so. It was the response of men like him, content to administer to the godly within their congregations, which ultimately paved the way for that form of puritan expression, called non-separating congregationalism, which later found its intellectual definition in the works of William Ames and John Geree.[3] This quiet revolution could take place in a sympathetic environment without ever attracting the attention of diocesan officials not known for their efficiency.

Where the climate was less sympathetic and a parish contained vociferous opponents of the puritans unafraid to inform the authorities of nonconformity, the situation was less comfortable. Such was the case at Preston Capes, already noted for the opposition aroused by the arrival of its first puritan incumbent John Elliston. His successor Robert Smart had powerful support from the Knightley family, patrons of the living, and he remained immune from harassment by the diocesan courts during the 1580s. However, the success of Bancroft in national policy against the puritans was followed by a local campaign against Smart, who was continually before the diocesan authorities during the 1590s. Whether the opponents of the puritans in the parish drew encouragement from the failure of the *classes* or not is uncertain, what is certain is that Smart spent a great deal of time defending himself in court. On 14 July 1591 he was ordered to observe the *Book of Common Prayer* in all points, but 17 months later was still refusing to wear the surplice. Again in 1595 and 1597 his disregard for the prescribed services was brought to the attention of the authorities. The following January he was presented again for not wearing the surplice, and for not using the sign of the cross in baptism or the ring at weddings. On this occasion he was threatened with deprivation if he failed to conform but no further action was taken, and similar offences were brought to light again in 1600 when Smart

[3] *H.I.L.* v. 57; xv. 111; P.D.R., X609/21, f. 239b; X614/40, f. 82; Vis. Bk. 7, ff. 57v–60; for Weedon see X613/37, f. 71 and Sheils 'Thesis', 187–188; for general discussion of this tradition see P. Collinson, 'Towards a Broader Understanding of the Early Dissenting Tradition', Cole and Moody (eds.) *The Dissenting Tradition: Essays for Leland H. Carlson* (Ohio, 1975) esp. 19–25.

aggressively claimed that the diocesan courts had no authority to proceed against him. At the very beginning of James' reign Smart was suspended, having admitted that he 'doth not use the cross in baptism, nor the ring in marriage, nor any of the ceremonies appointed by the Church of England set down in The Book of Common Prayer, nor the order of The Book of Common Prayer in such manner as is set down by authority'.[4]

The accession of James I had encouraged the puritans to organize petitions from several counties for further reform of the Church of England. Smart was deeply involved in the Northamptonshire activity and kept the letter book of their proceedings. Within his parish his disruptive career continued and at the end of 1604 he was again presented, this time for refusing to administer communion to two of his parishioners who wanted to receive while kneeling and for withholding the sacrament from other parishioners. Not surprisingly, in 1605 the imposition of the Ecclesiastical Canons proved too much for Smart and, with a number of other puritans in the diocese, he was deprived. This did not terminate his ministry and he remained at Preston Capes with a small group of disciples, by that time effectively separated from the national church, and proved troublesome to his successor as vicar, George Webb.[5]

The careers of Williamson, Proudlove, and Smart during the 1590s took different courses; Williamson progressed to promotion within the church, Proudlove returned to his congregation where his ministry was undisturbed, and Smart contrived to serve the godly in a parish which contained some vociferous opponents of the puritans. There was irony in the fact that when Smart's conscience was troubled over the need to subscribe to the Canons of 1604 it was his former *classis* colleague Robert Williamson who tried to bring him and his fellow puritans over to the side of the hierarchy. It is not only the variety of clerical responses that their careers illuminate, but also the capacity and determination of puritan groups to remain within the established church. The deficiencies of the sources are also highlighted. The godly at Weedon remain an unknown quantity because their activities never attracted the attention of diocesan officials, but in the divided parish of Preston Capes our information is much fuller. In the former the godly were able to remain within the church, in the latter they were eventually forced into separation, even if of a temporary nature. Their different fortunes no doubt reflected the theological attitudes of their respective ministers to a large degree, but it is important here to point out how the local context could influence the decision of the godly either to remain within the established church or to 'gather a church' and separate from the rest of a parish largely out of sympathy with the puritans in their midst.

Our picture of events in the 1590s is consequently incomplete and, as the example of Preston Capes shows, our information from court records is more likely to come from parishes in which the puritans did not have things their own way than from parishes like Fawsley, Byfield, Ashton, and Culworth where *classis* members remained undisturbed until the major crisis of 1605. The attitudes of such men were not greatly altered and they were as uncompromisingly opposed to the established order as ever. Recent events were a major set-back for their ambitions but they were not long in recovering their confidence.

[4]P.D.R., Vis. Bk. 5, unfoliated; X610/24, f. 102v., 113; 26, f. 232; X611/27, f. 40; 31, ff. 9v., 46; X612/34, f. 49v.; X613/35, ff. 77a, 81.

[5]B.L., Sloane Ms. 271; P.D.R., X613/37, f. 124v.; X614/40, f. 136v.; Inst. Bk. IV, f. 14; R. G. Usher, *The Reconstruction of the English Church* (London and New York, 1904), i. 264.

Deprived of the chance of creating presbyterianism within episcopacy, they were determined that their case should continue to be represented. One incident is particularly instructive as it shows the presbyterians attempting to control the normal institutions of the church. Throughout Elizabeth's reign the puritans had been accustomed to sending up clerical representatives to lobby support in parliament, and when a new house was called in 1593 they set about finding nominees. On this occasion, before the bishop, they had the audacity to propose, through Thomas Stone of Warkton, that John Barebone of Charwelton and his close neighbour John King of Canons Ashby, a noted puritan centre which as a peculiar jurisdiction was beyond the scope of the diocesan courts, be elected as proctors in Convocation. The nomination was supported by former *classis* members Nicholas Edwards, William Fleshware, and Hugh Okes as well as by William Kitchen, newly instituted to the living of Cranford St Andrew. Coming so soon after the Star Chamber trial this was a provocative gesture which called for reply from the establishment. It soon came and the diocesan chancellor and the Archdeacon of Northampton were elected as proctors, whilst Richard Butler made his first appearance as one of the principal local opponents of the puritans.[6]

In such circumstances the authorities can hardly have been ignorant of the continuing strength of puritanism in its traditional centres, but the court records merely underline the fact that little action was taken by them. Some centres, such as Whiston, where the incumbent Francis Foster was presented in 1592 for a comprehensive list of omissions and departures from the *Book of Common Prayer* and for receiving 'diverse persons of other parishes to the communion, such as disobey their own minister' came to the notice of the courts[7], but for the most part their attention was focused on a new area of puritan growth in the parishes of the north-eastern part of Northamptonshire. Most of these were in the area round Rockingham Forest and in the Soke. At Stanion near Brigstock the curate Anthony Stackhouse was presented for preaching without licence, for not reading the prayers on Wednesdays and Fridays, and for not wearing the surplice. Two months later his colleague at Brigstock was presented for a similar list of offences and for both men these marked the first of a number of appearances before the court. Others to come before the courts for nonconformity included Robert Newman, rector of the nearby living of Luddington, and the curates of Stoke Bruerne and Easton on the Hill. At Harringworth, where Lord Zouche resided, John Turner was presented for not observing the *Book of Common Prayer*. In the soke of Peterborough the incumbents of Northborough and of Peakirk, Robert Chapman and Nicholas Titley, were presented for not wearing the surplice.[8] A more radical stance was recorded further south at Thrapston where a Mr Cranford, possibly James Cranford headmaster of the school at radical Coventry, was alleged to have preached a sermon in which he 'inveighed against the state now established'. Cranford was then serving the

[6]E. A. Irons, 'A Calendar of a Court Book', *Northants. Notes and Queries* (New Series), ii. 171.

[7]P.D.R., X610/25, ff. 18v., 37. Irons, *op. cit.*, 238. This is consistent with the idea that the information comes from parishes where puritans had strong opposition for, in the early years of a puritan ministry, the godly were likely to be in a minority. It is also the case that the godly in this region did not enjoy quite the same gentry protection as did those in the west of the diocese.

[8]P.D.R., X610/23a, ff. 95, 109 and v., 112v., 126, 151, 155; 24, ff. 115v., 121v; Irons, *op. cit.*, 245-246.

cure at Hemington where he was reported for departing from the *Book of Common Prayer*.[9]

The visitation of 1592 was the first to uncover clerical nonconformity on a wide scale in this part of the diocese where the influence of the Montague and Zouche families offered support to the puritans. Five years later the findings of 1592 were confirmed and the incumbents of Fotheringhay and Ufford joined the ranks of those puritans already mentioned. The rector of Little Bowden, Robert Dent, was presented later for administering the communion to some of his parishioners in his own home on Easter Day 1598. Bowden was a living in the gift of the Griffin family and it is not clear whether this group represented the godly withdrawing from the parish or a group of catholic sympathizers.[10] The influence of the Griffins, Treshams, and Vauxs remained strong in the area and, where puritanism emerged, it did so in close contact with catholicism, as the description of Brigstock by George Sharpe in 1605 suggests. Whether the antipathy between puritans and recusants noted by him was characteristic of the area as a whole remains unknown, but events at Oundle, where both catholics and puritans were strongly represented, showed that proximity to the other encouraged extreme attitudes in both parties.[11]

In the more traditional centres of puritanism the diocesan authorities met with mixed success. At Rutland a few cases of refusal to wear the surplice were uncovered, but it was two new recruits to the parochial clergy who caused most concern. Philip Browne, brother of the separatist leader Robert, had been presented to the family living at Little Casterton in 1591. His arrival in the parish caused some dissension not only in the parish, but even within the family one of whom, Francis Browne of Tolethorpe, refused to attend church because of the 'diverse and railing sermons' preached by his kinsman.[12] The kinship ties of the Brownes included Catholic families, a pattern repeated in their relations the Pickerings of Titchmarsh; in such families were found a microcosm of the wider conflict between opposing religious views.[13] The other newcomer was Robert Cuthbert. A member of a Warmington family which produced another puritan cleric, Robert was instituted to the living at Exton in 1597 and was soon in trouble with authority, being presented in 1598 'for not wearing the surplice, nor reading service at any time according to law, but one chapter [of the Bible] and a sermon'. Such a ministry would certainly have found favour with his Harrington patrons and he was able to remain in his parish.[14]

On the western borders of the diocese the attention of the authorities was likewise drawn to newcomers and, with the notable exception of Robert Smart, the senior campaigners of the 1580s were left like their Rutland colleagues unmolested. In this region it was curates, such as Benjamin Langhorne of Bugbrooke and John Wilson of Green's Norton, or newcomers like John Gwynne, vicar of Watford, who were presented by their churchwardens for noncon-

---

[9]Irons, *op. cit.*, 220.

[10]P.D.R., X3588/10, f. 27v.; X610/24, f. 140a; X611/29, ff. 6v., 8, 9; 31, 60.

[11]Hist. Mss. Com., *Salisbury Mss.*, xvii. 67 and see below pp. 136–139.

[12]P.D.R., X612/32, f. 145.

[13]One of the Pickering family was on the fringes of the Gunpowder Plot. Francis Browne may have been a crypto-catholic, his wife was Lucy Mackworth of the recusant family from Normanton, see F. I. Cater, 'Robert Browne's Ancestors and Descendants', 154.

[14]P.D.R., Inst. Bk. III, f. 70; X3588/10, f. 18v.; X613/36, f. 117; *H.I.L.* iii. 329, 331 the Cuthbert family may have received their puritan ideas from the clergy placed in Warmington by Sir Walter Mildmay. More work needs to be done on the transmission of puritanism between generations, it did not always depend on the universities.

formity.[15] In the vicinity of Northampton the county town remained a radical and unrepentant puritan centre. Its influence was further radicalized by the presence of Giles Wigginton in the area towards the end of the century. Wigginton had been an articulate and mischievous critic of the establishment for many years while at the Yorkshire living of Sedbergh. After deprivation in 1585 Giles returned to his native Oundle where he was one of the leaders of a radical group on the threshhold of separatism. The activities of this group will be discussed later, but one of their members was the ill-fated William Hacket, whose religious enthusiasm was to lead to the scaffold. Wigginton had remained in close touch with Hacket to the end, and had also acted as messenger to the *classis* leaders while they were awaiting trial.[16] His reputation had led to his being named as one of the chief suspects for authorship of the Marprelate Tracts, the contents of which reflected his scurrilous and impetuous nature.[17] After the crisis years of 1588 and 1591 Wigginton sought to be restored to his old Yorkshire living and his movements become obscure. He was, however, active in the region in 1597 when on 17 February the churchwardens of Collingtree were presented for allowing Wigginton to preach in their parish on the last Sunday of January 'through their ignorance, and further because he showed their curate Mr Wigginton, his brother, of the Council's Lords licensing him to preach'. Giles' brother Francis was curate of Collingtree and had been schoolmaster at the adjacent parish of Blisworth where, on the same day, Wigginton had interrupted the curate, whose intention to preach was disturbed when Giles rushed up into the pulpit to give a sermon of his own.[18] The context of the presentments suggest that the authorities were sensitive about Wigginton, who appears to have lost none of his impetuosity, and that the parochial officers in both places, where the congregations included puritan sympathizers, had a somewhat ambivalent attitude to the man. It would be unfair to characterize an area from the idiosyncratic activities of Giles Wigginton, and the presentment from Wollaston, further east, provides a better introduction to the problems of recording puritan activity in the 1590s. The churchwardens there were presented in 1597 for failure to inform on their nonconformist minister, who had served there since 1582. The minister, Thomas Sutton, may have been protected by the squire George Carleton until the latter's death in 1591. Although conclusions can only be tentative it may be that the puritan control of the parish only began to fragment after Carleton's death, and that opponents of the puritans began to speak out in the years after 1590.[19] Tentative as this conclusion must be, the charge against the churchwardens, who subsequently allowed Francis Foster of Whiston to preach there, does underline the deficiencies of the visitation system.[20] These deficiencies and the paucity of information can be gauged in part by comparing information from this period with that from the crisis years after the accession of James I which led to the disappointment of puritan hopes and the imposition by Bancroft, by that time Archbishop of Canterbury, of the Canons of 1604.

[15]P.D.R., X611/29, f. 5; 31, ff. 5v., 93.

[16]Bancroft, *Daungerous Positions*, 159–164, 171–172.

[17]B.L., Harl. Ms. 7042, f. 12, but see L. Carlson and R. Paulson, *English Satire* (Los Angeles, 1972), 16–36.

[18]B.L., Lansd. Ms. 84, f. 238; P.D.R., X610/26, ff. 203v., 245.

[19]B.L. Lansd. Ms. 443, f. 311v; P.D.R., X610/26, f. 264 and v. For Carleton see *Eliz. Puritan Movt.* 142–145, 394–396.

[20]P.D.R., Archd. Ct. Bk. 20, f. 149v.

*The accession of James I*

The death of Elizabeth and the accession of a Scottish monarch with some theological interests was the signal for puritans to organize themselves once again in order to seek the help of the Crown in the cause of further reformation. On 16 May 1603 the following petition was forthcoming from Northampton-shire:

> We whose names are subscribed do agree to make a humble petition to the King's Majesty that the present state of our church may be further reformed in all things needfull and according to the rule of God's holy word, and agree-ably to the example of other reformed churches which have restored both the doctrine and discipline as it was delivered by our saviour Christ and his apostles.[21]

It is not clear whether the discipline referred to followed the strict presbyterian model; such lack of precision was probably deliberate, but we do know that the diocese was in the forefront of the revived puritan campaign. Stephen Egerton, a leading London puritan wrote 'that only county of Northampton is sufficient to stop the mouths of them that say there are not above some 10 or 12 factious persons that desire reformation of these things; we do with patience expect the confirmation of our gracious King's coronation, after we hope he will hearken to our motions in the behalf of the church'.[22] The events of Eliza-beth's reign would naturally lead one to expect that the diocese would be among the most forward areas of the country in their anticipation of a favourable re-ception to puritan demands. That this was the case is proved by the survival of a letter-book compiled by one of the survivors of the 1580s, Robert Smart. In his book he gives details of the meetings and correspondence of a group of puritan ministers meeting at Northampton in 1603 and 1604. The first impres-sion to be gained from the book is one of continuity; of sixteen signatories to one petition, five were veterans of earlier battles; and two of them, Thomas Stone and John Barebone, were among the leaders of the group. The sense of continuity is emphasized by the instructions sent out by Egerton from London, 'Besides it will be very fit that a true survey of the state of the parishes be taken, and that his majesty be not abused with a deceitful show of sufficient provision and, as much as in them lieth, good men are to be encouraged to accept places in parliament . . .' Clearly the precedents of the 1580s were to be relied upon again; the local gentry were to be primed to provide vocal support in parliament for the puritans, the local deficiencies of the church were to be highlighted by a survey of the ministry, and two delegates were to be sent from the diocese to further the puritan cause at Parliament, their expenses and pastoral obligations to be supplied by the remaining puritan clergy.[23]

The general appeal for reform referred to above was followed by a more detailed plan of campaign decided upon at a meeting in the county town on 21 July. Egerton's suggestions were followed and Christopher Yelverton, re-corder of Northampton, was singled out to organize a petition among the gentry

---

[21]B.L., Sloane Ms. 271, f. 20. Similar meetings took place elsewhere and several petitions were organized, *Eliz. Puritan Movt.*, 453–454.

[22]B. L. Sloane Ms. 271, f. 20 and v.

[23]The others were Daniel Wight, Robert Smart, and Thomas London; *ibid.*, ff. 20v–21v. The organization of the arrangements was to be in the hands of Stone, Barebone, and Robert Catelin, vicar of All Saints, Northampton.

in support of the puritan ministers. Arrangements were made for the survey of the diocese, which was to be the responsibility of Barebone and Robert Binks, a newcomer who had been serving the Isham living at Pytchley since 1597. They were to carry out the survey in consultation with the godly laity and the findings were to be communicated to Barebone, Stone, and Robert Catelin, vicar of All Saints Northampton. The survey followed those of the mid 1580s, concentrating on the dumb ministry, their congregations and incomes; cases of non-residence and pluralism; the moral and pastoral failings of the clergy; simonical transactions between ministers and patrons; and the effect of impropiate rectories upon clerical incomes. Catelin, Stone, and Barebone were to supervise the work and were also responsible for keeping registers of the letters and activities of the group.[24]

The sense of continuity was seized upon by R. G. Usher in his book, *The Reconstruction of the English Church*, where the document was printed with a misleading title, 'Action of the Northampton Classis, July 1603.'[25] Despite the personnel and the plan of campaign, the group meeting in Northampton in 1603 was very different from the *classes*. Nowhere was there any mention of subscription or submission to discipline; the ultimate ambition, whilst tending towards presbyterianism, concentrated more on the eradication of abuses in the church than on the establishment of a particular ecclesiology, and the laity were considered to have an integral part to play in the petition. Not only were the gentry to be involved, but the advice of the godly was also sought, and any sense of clerical exclusiveness and conspiracy was deliberately avoided. The London ministers went so far as to send out a cautionary directive to other local churches, suggesting that, where petitions of a particular nature were drawn up, only a few signatories should be appended in order to avoid likely charges of conspiracy.[26] Not only had the puritans made tactical advances since the *classes*, but they were also designing a much more widely-based lobby involving the laity at all levels of society. That they could embark on this is indicative of both the success of their evangelization in the last two decades of the 16th century and of a less dogmatic approach to the problems of reform, there was no alternative liturgy to set against the *Book of Common Prayer*. To be less dogmatic did not imply that the puritan campaign was any less organized; as the plans mentioned above suggest the local petitions were part of a coherent strategy. At London the secretariat was being organized by two survivors of earlier trials, Stephen Egerton and Edmund Snape, formerly a 'chief man' of the Northampton *classis* and now partially restored to his calling after some years of imprisonment.[27] Smart's letter-book, with its copies of similar petitions from Oxford, London, and elsewhere, emphasizes that local activity was to be placed in the context of a national campaign. This had also been the case in the 1580s, but it is important to underline the point that, despite the continuity in personnel and tactics, the later campaign differed from its predecessor in overall strategy and

[24]*Ibid.* The text of the petition with these details has been printed, R. G. Usher, *The Reconstruction of the English Church*, ii. 361–362, though he wrongly identifies the local leadership. In S. B. Babbage, *Puritanism and Richard Bancroft* (1962), 49, the petition is wrongly dated to 16 May.

[25]R. G. Usher, *op. cit.*, ii. 361, see also i. 297 where he also uses the term in the same context.          [26]B.L., Sloane Ms. 271, f. 20v.

[27]Snape's sentence had been commuted to 10 years' suspension from orders, and he remained in London keeping contacts with his old county and with Devon. Two other local puritans who had fallen foul of authority had earlier found refuge in Devon, Eusebius Paget and William Jennings.

was less dogmatic in its demands. This change in emphasis resulted from the declining position of the Oxford presbyterians within the broader puritan movement. Though their experience and seniority gave them considerable influence, the leadership of the puritans was passing to men bred in the Cambridge tradition of Emmanuel College, itself the creation of an *alumnus* of Christ's. That college in the later 16th-century established a puritan tradition more moderate in its reactions to matters of church order 'but passionately indignant against the practical inadequacies of the Elizabethan Church and above all against its pastoral deficiencies'. The success of that tradition in the 17th century owed much to two Christ's men, Laurence Chaderton and William Perkins, who were to supersede the Oxford divines, Thomas Sampson and Laurence Humphrey, as the major educational influences on puritan policy. It was during the twenty years between 1590 and 1610 that this transition began to take place.[28]

Concern with pastoral deficiencies once again drew attention to that central issue between the puritans and their opponents, the ministry. A survey was intended and attention was to be drawn to the life and doctrines of all churchmen. This was carried out in 1603 amid optimistic reports from the London puritans about their contacts with the new King. The survey was completed and turned attention to the local situation once more, most particularly to the activities of Richard Butler, rector of Aston le Walls. Butler was a protégé of the Arminian John Neile and was given responsibility within the diocese by the new bishop, Thomas Dove, who appointed him a surrogate in the diocesan courts. Butler's Arminian views and his defence of ceremonial led to a revival of activity against the puritans and, most particularly, against Robert Catelin, vicar of All Saints, Northampton. Butler's activities were reported by the local puritans to Stephen Egerton, in much the same way as the earlier generation had sent material on their sufferings to John Field. It deserves quotation in full for the detailed description it gives of the local situation. The obstruction and harassment of the local puritans at the hands of the diocesan authorities contrasted nicely with the optimistic reports they were receiving from their London contacts. The details were provided on 9 December in 'A Copy of Certain advertisements given to Mr Catelin, minister at Northampton, by Mr B(arebone), Mr Chalenor, Mr Wood, and Mr Smart' and were as follows:

  1 Imprimis, that whereas Mr Butler hath broached, as Mr Catelin knoweth under his hand, certain points of false doctrine and the matter is spread far and wide and is become public, and he vaunteth it himself, and vaunteth that he will maintain it, and his disgrace will be a shrewd check unto them. It is thought good, of some of us, that Mr Catelin draw a letter to the Bishop, Chancellor, and Official to require of them that he [Butler] may recant of those doctrines except they be of this mind; that they are justifiable. And if so be they judge so, the ministers that are of another mind and judgement do require indifferent hearing and conference, nothing doubting but that they shall prove them to be erronious. And if they may not be in this respect, they may justly conceive that they are exceeding partial and standing upon ceremonies, suffer the doctrine of the truth freely to be impugned and may justly proceed further to the displaying of their corrupt dealing.

[28]Curtis, *Oxford and Cambridge in Transition*, 191–196, 208; P. Collinson, *A Mirror of Elizabethan Puritanism, The Life and Letters of 'Godly Master Dering'* (1964), 6–12.

2 Also they conceive that if he shall be convinced to be erronious in doctrine and hold popish doctrine, he is unfit to have the charge of souls and to sit in court, and manage the discipline of the Church.

3 That Mr Catelin make choice (because the matter especially concerneth him) of such as shall joyne with him in the conference, offering to the adversary that within the diocese he may make his choice number for number, excepting none, the place and the hearers and moderators being indifferently chosen and agreed upon. And if they refuse this, be it known to all they suspect their cause.

4 Further, if Mr Catelin do think it unfit that he be alone in the letter, that he require the handes of those that are like minded and hold this judgement to be erronious.[29]

So it was that, against the background of preparation for the Hampton Court Conference which was to take place between the national leaders of the established church and the puritans, the puritan clergy of the diocese were proposing to engage in a local disputation with their adversaries; appealing to their own authority in much the same way as John Sibthorpe had done 30 years previously when his sermon at the Northampton exercise had been challenged. The situation in Peterborough clearly gave less cause for optimism than was apparent at London, for Butler's attempts to revive the vigour of the local courts in harassing nonconformity undermined the uneasy truce between the puritans and the diocesan authorities that had existed since 1590. Stephen Egerton asked for further details of the dealings with Butler and a letter from eight of the ministers at the end of 1603 showed clearly that the recent tranquillity of the diocese had depended to a large extent on the willingness of the authorities to overlook nonconformist practices. In their reply they wrote

So it is that upon pretence of his Majesty's letters against novelties etc., whereof we are no ways guilty continuing still in the same course (some of us) for the space of 20 years and upwards. We have been extraordinarily, in place unfit and unaccustomed, in extremity of weather to the hazarding of some men's lives and limbs, convented and charged by a surrogate holding and preaching popish positions, more than we have been for this 45 years concerning the strict observation of all the ceremonies, in particular and namely, crossing in baptism, kneeling at the communion both minister and people, wearing the surplice both on the holy days and sundays (to use the Surrogate his words), the asking of the questions and answers in baptism as 'Tis in the Common Prayer Book, the churching of women and, in conclusion, using all that is in The Book of Common Prayer upon the penalty of suspension *ab officio et beneficio* within one month, viz. the 17 January next.

Clearly others, probably the eight signatories, were also under threat from the church courts, but attention was focused on Catelin's case.[30]

The attempt by the revitalized diocesan authorities to enforce conformity through the church courts was hampered not only by the strength of the puritans in the region but by the previous history of the courts themselves. The local conflict was soon to be swallowed up by the widespread confrontation provoked

[29]B. L., Sloane Ms. 271, f. 23 and v.

[30]*Ibid.*, f. 25 and v. This was couched in the form of a petition and signed by Thomas Stone, John Barebone, Sampson Sheffield, Daniel Wight, Sampson Wood, Robert Smart, Robert Binks, and John Rogers. For Sibthorpe see above p. 30.

by the failure of the puritans at the Hampton Court Conference and by Bancroft's attempt to impose uniformity through subscription to the Canons. The events in the diocese during the two years after James' accession illustrated the kind of problems Bancroft would have to face. The troubled career of Robert Smart has already been noticed and other veterans of the 1580s were to renew their acquaintance with local officialdom during these years. Daniel Wight, who had been serving the cure at Norton Davy from 1602, was presented for preaching without licence and for not bidding the holy days. He had also invited Sampson Wood of Fawsley, who also attended the meetings at Northampton, to administer the communion in the parish and Wood was presented for refusing the sacrament to a parishioner who desired to receive the same whilst kneeling.[31] Another ex-*classis* member presented at this time was John Barebone who neglected to follow the *Book of Common Prayer*. Other clerics with long service in the diocese were also presented, including Thomas Gibson of Ridlington for not wearing the surplice, not using the cross in baptism or the ring in marriage, and Giles Whiting the rector of Etton, who objected to much of the ceremonial of the prescribed services.[32] Among the clergy who had entered livings in the diocese since the break up of the *classes* was the ex-separatist Robert Browne who was presented for not wearing the surplice by his churchwardens at Thorpe Achurch. Parishes where nonconformity was a long established tradition continued to be served by puritan clerics and at Manton in Rutland the curate, Mr Mellers, was neglecting to wear the surplice, as was Jonas Chalenor of Byfield.[33]

At Weston Favell the incumbent Robert Travell was suspended for nonconformity in 1604, but the parish was served during his suspension by a variety of ministers who neglected to wear the surplice, among their number were Francis Smith, the curate of Great Houghton, and John Drakeford of Little Houghton, both presented by the churchwardens of their own parishes for nonconformity. Travell was apparently reinstated at Weston Favell by the autumn when he was again presented for disregarding the order of service as established.[34] Henry Bourne of East Haddon had entered the diocese in the 1590s as had Travell, and was also one of the Northampton group. Early in 1604 he was presented for not wearing the surplice, for not using the sign of the cross in baptism, and for administering the communion to the congregation whilst they were standing. In the same year Henry Beck, curate at Everdon, and another member of the Northampton group exhibited an aggressive attitude by not only neglecting to follow the *Book of Common Prayer*, but also in his determination to 'publicly preach against the orders and ceremonies of the Church of England'.[35]

A number of clerics had their only brush with authority at this date, otherwise remaining fairly shadowy figures. At Little Billing, an early puritan centre, the curate, William Elliott, was presented for administering the sacraments without the surplice on 27 February 1604, thereby coming into conflict with authority less than one week after his ordination. Two weeks later he was excommunicated.[36] Three other curates, John Green of Market Overton, Thomas Foxe of Syresham, and a Mr Warren of Denton, were all presented for nonconformity

[31]P.D.R., X612/35, f. 84v.; X613/37, f. 149v.

[32]*Ibid.*, X613/36, f. 163v.; 37, f. 124; X3588/15, f. 7.

[33]*Ibid.*, X612/35, f. 157v.; X613/36, f. 163v.; X3588/15, f. 7v.

[34]*Ibid.*, X612/34, f. 209; X614/38, ff. 89v., 94v., 95; X613/37, f. 135v.

[35]They both signed the petitions of 21 July, B.L. Sloane Ms. 271, f. 21v.; P.D.R., X613/37, f. 76v.; X614/38, f. 55v.

[36]P.D.R., X614/38, ff. 56v., 65.

in 1604, as was Thomas Courte, who had been appointed vicar of Sulgrave in 1601.[37]

None of these clerics reappeared before the diocesan courts for nonconformity during our period, and they may have been simply concerned about the surplice or ceremonies. However, two other recent additions to the ranks of the parochial clergy exhibited more positive puritan sympathies. William Dale had been instituted to Moulton in 1597 and was presented on a number of occasions in the early years of the 17th century for nonconformist practices. In July 1600 he was presented for not reading the Injunctions, not wearing the surplice, not using the sign of the cross in baptism, for refusing to church women after child-birth, and for administering the communion whilst his parishioners were stand-ing or sitting. Almost exactly two years later Dale was presented for similar offences and for inviting his fellow puritan Henry Beck to preach in the parish. In 1604 he continued in his nonconforming way, despite being suspended on 13 February that year.[38] Also in 1604 John Hawkins, recently admitted to the living of Woodford Halse, was presented for administering the communion to his congregation after the puritan fashion, and also for refusing to admit those of his parishioners who asked to receive in a kneeling position.[39] Neither Hawkins nor Dale were otherwise well-known for their views, but their activi-ties in 1604 are an indication that obscurity was not necessarily the fate of the anti-ceremonial puritans alone. A number of thoroughgoing puritan pastors could escape detection for long periods of time and might only appear, as did Thomas Gibson, in the context of ceremonial trifles such as the surplice. The foregoing examples give some indication of the extent of clerical nonconformity uncovered in the diocese by 1605, but even this list is not complete. Appearances before the court were also made by two puritan veterans, Simon Rogers of Barby and John Rogers of Chacombe though the issues at this date were not made clear.[40]

Despite their local difficulties the puritan clergy of the diocese continued to take an active interest in the national campaign. They had already determined to send representatives up to lobby parliament and the prospect of the Hampton Court Conference, at which the hierarchy and the puritans were supposed to debate the future of the established church, was good cause for optimism. As 1603 wore on the optimism began to diminish. Some puritans, including the Northamptonshire contingent, were prepared to support an overtly presby-terian reform at least as a bargaining point, others wanted to concentrate on the abuses within the church and not to tackle the structural problems. Late in the year, although the counties had nominated delegates to represent them and to lobby the puritan party at the conference, it became clear that the official puritan representatives were to be government nominees rather than local delegates. Notwithstanding this the four delegates from Northamptonshire proceeded to London to meet with their colleagues from other shires, including that old *classis* leader Edmund Snape who was then representing Devon. The local representa-tives were Knightley's veteran protégé, John Barebone of Charwelton, Samp-son Sheffield, another long serving cleric from Rutland, and two more recent recruits to the diocese, Robert Binks and Sampson Wood.[41] Their meetings

[37]P.D.R., X613/36, f. 163; 37, f. 48v.; X614/38, ff. 48v., 156.
[38]H.I.L. xvi. 49; P.D.R., X612/34, f. 89; 35, f. 99v.; X613/37, f. 57v.; X614/38, ff. 43, 54.
[39]*Ibid.*, Inst. Bk. IV, f. 8.; X613/37, f. 71v.
[40]*Ibid.*, X612/35, f. 83v.; X613/37, f. 52v.
[41]Hist. Mss. Com., *Montague Mss.*, 32–34; *Eliz. Puritan Movt.*, 455–456.

continued alongside the official sessions of the conference early in 1604, but it was clear that the conference itself was no more going to win general acceptance than had the Act of Uniformity, the Injunctions, and the 39 articles at the beginning of Elizabeth's reign. For the radicals and for the presbyterians the conference was a failure, for more moderate puritans a few successes were achieved and many of James' subsequent episcopal appointments were to be sympathetic to their aims. The aims of the moderates were to focus on the creation of a nation of godly households and godly congregations, rather than upon the vision of a godly commonwealth imposed from above by the magistracy that had been so vivid to many returning exiles in 1559. There remained the disappointed radicals, but many of these were veterans by now well-used to furthering their quiet reformations beneath the open eye of an indulgent bishop or the closed one of an inefficient bureaucracy. If the peace of the Jacobean church was to be disturbed, as indeed it was, it was not due to the unreasonable demands of the presbyterian faction, but to the rashness of the government in attempting to impose a level of uniformity unprecedented in the post-reformation church.[42] Behind this move lay Richard Bancroft, Whitgift's policeman in uncovering the *classes* and in October 1604 his successor as Archbishop of Canterbury.

## The enforcement of the Canons

The promulgation and enforcement of the Canons of 1604 took place against a background of local confrontation and national disappointment of puritan hopes. The Canons were to turn that disappointment to anger and frustration. The national campaign leading up to the establishment of the Canons, and the legal precedents for what was essentially a legislative device of the pre-reformation church, has been the subject of a recent monograph and the text of the 141 articles has long been in print.[43] That they were an attempt to end the puritan challenge is undeniable, but they also set out to reform visitation and disciplinary procedures and to reduce the abuses of pluralism and non-residence. Uniformity was the principle concern, however, as the precedence given to canons dealing with that problem made clear. Canon 4 ordered the censuring of those who impugned the established forms of worship; article 6 made the same point about ceremonies; 7 and 8 defended episcopacy; canon 10 was directed against schismatics in the Church of England; and canon 11 ordered excommunication for those who maintained conventicles. Later on a lengthy defence of the use of the sign of the cross in baptism was made in canon 30 and canon 72 was directed against private fasts and prophesyings.[44] Clearly these were to prove unacceptable to the many puritans, who not only objected to the content of the canons but also to their legal validity. The legality of enforcing the canons as far as deprivation was challenged by puritans who were supported by the common lawyers, but the right of the bishops and the Ecclesiastical Commissioners to proceed was upheld. The ensuing conflict between the common and civil lawyers and the constitutional aspects of the problem need not detain us, but formed another chapter in the long struggle which the common lawyers were ultimately

[42]*Eliz. Puritan Movt.*, 460–463; N. R. N. Tyacke, 'Puritanism, Arminianism and Counter Revolution', 138–140, for subsequent attempts.

[43]S. B. Babbage, *Puritanism and Richard Bancroft* (1962), 74–102; E. Cardwell, *Synodalia* (Oxford, 1842, repr. 1966), i. 245–329. For a contentious view of the Canons see R. G. Usher, *The Reconstruction of the English Church*, i. 359–402.

[44]Cardwell, *Synodalia*, i. 249–252, 260–264, 287–288.

to win.[45] More important for the story of puritanism was Bancroft's determination to act vigorously and thoroughly. There was to be no compromise as had been the case in 1584, and the bishops were not to content themselves with making examples of the most notorious offenders but were to root out all nonconformists. A survey of the conflict between puritans and the bishops in a number of dioceses has recently been provided, and events in the dioceses of London, Lincoln, and Chichester have been chronicled most thoroughly, but the conclusion that 'Information about individual puritans in the diocese of Peterborough is tantalizingly meagre' needs to be modified considerably. Only three of the parochial clergy said to have been deprived were identified; Robert Catelin of Northampton, Richard Baldock, and Robert Travell, whereas the institution books reveal the names of most of those deprived.[46]

Despite attempts in parliament to block the publication of the Canons, the bishops went ahead, after a royal proclamation of 16 July 1604 gave the nonconforming clergy a period of grace until the last day of November before action was to be taken against them. In Peterborough the bishop undertook the onerous task of public disputation with his puritan clergy, and at first deprived one and suspended nine or ten with a warning that continued resistance would result in similar action being taken against them. Their obstinacy resulted in a further 15 deprivations, possibly before 16 January 1605, certainly by 4 February and Dove recalled the long history of puritanism in the diocese when explaining the high numbers involved. Appeals were registered against the sentence of the bishop by the puritan clergy.[47] The one member deprived early on as the ringleader was probably Richard Baldock of Brigstock, who was succeeded as early as 15 February 1605 by George Sharpe, who wrote to Cranborne nine days later about the problems posed by the strength of the puritans in the parish.[48]

Sharpe's letter indicates that Baldock had accepted his deprivation quietly, possibly because he retained his other living of Little Oakley where he remained for a while. The letter further suggests a recurring theme of the ecclesiastical history of the period; that enthusiasm was found amongst puritans and papists but that there was no real evidence of vigorous support for the establishment. It may have been that Sharpe's good reception in the parish stemmed from confidence that he would bend a little to the scruples of his puritan charges, at any rate on 13 June 1605 he was himself before the court for not wearing the surplice at the administration of the communion.[49] Whether the environment in which he found himself influenced him, or whether he was a moderate nonconformist with scruples about ceremonies but not about the Canons cannot be known. Nevertheless Sharpe's appearance before the court does illustrate the ability of puritans to preserve some measure of continuity in many of those parishes in which clergy were deprived. The influential support of the gentry, who organized a petitition on behalf of the puritan clergy, no doubt helped to explain this, and the extent of that support must be borne in mind throughout the discussion of the crisis of 1605. Full details of the gentry involvement are reserved for a later chapter.[50]

[45]Babbage, *Puritanism and Richard Bancroft*, 98–102.

[46]*Ibid.*, 206, 209–211. In fact of these three only Baldock was deprived outright for the others were restored to their livings.

[47]Hist. Mss. Com., *Salisbury Mss.*, xvii. 17, 46–47.          [48]P.D.R., Inst. Bk. IV, f. 12.

[49]Hist. Mss. Com., *Salisbury Mss.*, xvii. 67; P.D.R., X613/36, f. 227. Baldock was named as rector of Little Oakley later in the year, P.D.R., Vis. Bk. 7, ff. 47v.–58.

[50]See Chapter 7; Baldock had the support of the Montague family when entering the living of Little Oakley, see above p. 40.

In all 16 clergymen were deprived of their livings as a result of the Canons, but not all were removed at the same time and their appeals must have been heard separately. Edmund Rideout of Moreton Pinkney was the only other cleric deprived at an early stage like Baldock, possibly because he also held a living in the Crown's gift, and by the end of January 1605 his successor had been appointed.[51] By the end of April Edward Rudyard of Culworth had also been deprived, but Robert Travell of Weston Favell was reinstated to his living, perhaps as a result of his appeal or because of his local family connections. Rudyard, Rideout, and Travell had all entered their livings during the 1590s, for the most part soon after the Star Chamber trial of the *classis* members and, although they had come to the notice of the courts for their nonconformity, they are not known to have played a vigorous part in diocesan puritan activity, none of them belonged to the Northampton group recorded in Smart's letter-book.[52] There were, however, some among those deprived who had long-standing reputations for vigorous and outspoken puritan opinions; the most senior of all was Thomas Gibson of Ridlington whom the establishment finally removed after a ministry of over twenty years, and others were two ex-*classis* members, Robert Smart and John Barebone, both of whom played central roles in the petitions organized in the diocese after the accession of James I.[53] None of these, however, had served in the diocese for as long as Timothy Raffe, the vicar of Lilbourne who, after spending over thirty years in his living without ever attracting the attention of the authorities or displaying strong puritan opinions, was suddenly deprived for opposition to the Canons.[54] This example is an instructive reminder of the deficiencies and bias of surviving records.

Five parishes with long established puritan traditions were affected by the deprivations. At Cawdry's old parish of South Luffenham the incumbent Robert Milward, who had spent some time in the Channel Islands in company with other puritans in the diocese, was deprived five years after being presented to the living by Thomas Cecil, Lord Burghley, and at Little Casterton, another Rutland parish, Philip Browne, brother of the former separatist leader Robert, was deprived.[55] In western Northamptonshire Sampson Wood of Fawsley and Jonas Chalenor of Byfield were deprived, and the important puritan centre of Whiston to the east of Northampton town lost its incumbent Francis Foster, after a career which had caused considerable trouble to the authorities.[56] The three remaining clergymen deprived were Henry Bridger of Hemington, who had already come to the notice of the authorities for his nonconformity, Thomas Greenwood of Clipsham and Robert Cuthbert, vicar of Exton, the home parish of the Harrington family.[57]

The list of deprivations emphasizes the continuity of puritan tradition in the west of Northamptonshire and in Rutland, but few of the parishes in the vicinity of Northampton town were affected although Robert Catelin, vicar of All Saints, was suspended. Peterborough was said to be one of the dioceses most affected by deprivation, but a quick comparison with the list of signatories to

[51]P.D.R., Inst. Bk. IV, f. 12.

[52]*Ibid.*, f. 12v.; *H.I.L.*, xi. 201; xii. 11; xiv. 11.

[53]P.D.R., Inst. Bk. IV, ff. 13, 14, 15.

[54]*Ibid.*, f. 14.

[55]*Ibid.*, ff. 3, 13v., 18; X950/16g a testimonial from his congregation when he was minister at Guernsey Castle. Snape, Wiburn, and Arthur Wake had also been there, A. F. Scott-Pearson, *Thomas Cartwright and Elizabethan Puritanism* (Cambridge, 1925), 161–164.

[56]P.D.R., Inst. Bk. IV, ff. 13v., 14, 16.

[57]*Ibid.*, ff. 13v., 15.

the letters recorded in Robert Smart's letter-book and the list of the deprived ministers indicates that, despite Bancroft's wishes, a number of prominent non-conformists were not removed from their livings; among them were Thomas London, Robert Binks, Henry Bourne, and Sampson Sheffield, all of whom had played an active part in the petitions of the previous two years.[58] The reasons for this are not entirely due to administrative inefficiency or puritan evasiveness. By his own account Dove had made strenuous efforts to meet puritan objections and engaged in a public disputation lasting for two whole days, before a sizeable congregation gathered in the cathedral, as well as in private conferences. He claimed to have won more to his side than he deprived, and appears to have used a former *classis* member Robert Williamson as a principal assistant in this work.[59]

Despite this many of those who escaped deprivation may have been able to do so by offering a casuistical form of submission simply to obey the letter of the law. Some such documents were recorded at the end of a visitation call-book, and illustrate the compromise reached between the diocesan authorities and some of the puritan clergy. Richard Baldock, presumably wearing his alternative hat as rector of Little Oakley, having already been deprived of Brig-stock, offered the following submission: 'I Richard Baldock do promise to confer with Master Doctor Williamson touching the use of the sign of the cross in baptism, the wearing of the surplice etc., and that, simply as before the searcher of the heart, to the end he might yield to the truth of conformity herein so far forth as with the peace of the conscience may'; and thus had his suspension lifted. On 23 May Baldock went further and declared that he promised 'to confer with Mr Doctor Williamson in matters of ceremony and will never refuse to acknowledge and yield to any truth which I shall therein hear war-ranted from the holy scriptures'. Baldock remained in the diocese, living at Irthlingborough in 1607, and at his death in 1632 was described as a 'godly Old Minister'. A similar submission was made by Robert Binks of Pytchley on 16 May and his suspension was also lifted.[60]

In June of the same year Sampson Wood of Fawsley sought to be restored to his living, but, having refused to make submission in any form similar to that of Baldock, he was deprived. His near neighbour Jonas Chalenor made the following submission on 20 June: 'I Jonas Chalenor do promise to confer with Mr Bust, parson of Everdon, touching the use of the cross in baptism and the surplice in divine service and seeing clearer evidence (obstinacy not apart) I will willingly thereto yield so far as with the peace of my conscience I may in God's sight.' As a result Chalenor's suspension was lifted, and he was restored on con-dition that 'he do not preach against the ceremonies of the church now estab-lished. And that he do administer the sacraments according to the Book of Common Prayer.'[61]

These conditions proved to be his undoing, suggesting how specious such promises could be, for in July he was presented for refusing to publish the *Book of Canons*, for excluding the churchwardens from the church while communion was being administered in order to prevent them making a return of noncon-formists, for not using the surplice or the cross in baptism, and for preaching without licence. Clearly the visitation articles drew the attention of church-wardens to the Canons, and such a clear contravention of the conditions imposed

[58]B. L., Sloane Ms. 271, f. 21v.
[59]Hist. Mss. Com., *Salisbury Mss.*, xvii. 46, 58–59; P.D.R., Vis. Bk. 7, ff. 57v.–60.
[60]P.D.R., Vis. Bk. 7, f. 58; *H.I.L.*, i. 159.
[61]P.D.R., Vis. Bk. 7, f. 59v.

THOMAS DOVE, BISHOP OF PETERBOROUGH 1601–1630

LETTER FROM THE CORPORATION OF NORTHAMPTON TO ROBERT CECIL, 21 JANUARY 1604/5

upon him inevitably led to Chalenor's deprivation. A similar course of events occurred at Culworth where Edward Rudyard was temporarily restored prior to deprivation.[62]

Others were more successful in getting restored to their livings, David Thomson of Kettering, a former *classis* centre, was absolved and restored, as was an ex-*classis* member, John Rogers of Chacombe. Rogers submitted on the following terms:

> I, John Rogers, master of arts and vicar of the church of Chacombe do affirm and promise to confer with any learned man whosoever touching the matter of conformity, and namely in the matter of the cross and surplice, and if any such by learning or reasons shall convince my judgement and fully satisfy my conscience, or if by my own private study and industry I shall find better reasons to resell my former judgement to the conforming of myself, I promise (God aid me) not to be obstinate but in all duty and obedience to submit myself to the promises.

A submission it was, but there remained a note of challenge and defiance in its tone whilst little more than a willingness to listen to his opponents was promised. The authorities, *faute de mieux*, accepted it and Rogers was restored to his living on the same conditions as Jonas Chalenor, but with more success. An experienced campaigner on behalf of puritan demands, his survival was due more to his tact than to any change of mind.[63] Rogers was suspended again on 3 October 1605, and his parishioners remained uncertain of his status in September 1607 when he

[62]*Ibid.*, f. 60; X614/40, f. 82.
[63]*Ibid.*, Vis. Bk. 7, ff. 59v., 60; another old campaigner to be restored was Richard Lee of Kilsby, where the eldership had been erected in the 1580s, *ibid.*, see above p. 56.

---

Maye it please your good Lordship, recounting with singuler comfort the christian zeale of your right honourable father to the truthe of the ghospell, with his regardfull love to the sincere ministers and professors therof, and his noe small care of the afflicted members of god's churche, and in theis things, as otherwise, the semblable proportion of your Lordship (most admirable) to the multiplication of our comforts. Wee the maior of the towne of Northampton, and aldermen his brethren, late maiors, as well in this our deprivation of the spirituall blessings wee have long enioyed, by the godlie labours of Mr. Robert Catelin our minister, whoe hath peacablie and painfullie, to the great edificacion and comfort of the churche here, about fouretene yeares exercised his ministrie, as also in the particular losse and distres that befalleth our said minister's estate, his mouth being stopped, and himselfe deprived from his lyvinge, for not conforming himselfe to the use of the ceremonies (in this churche omitted and growne out of use, for almost fourtie yeares together), wee have adventured to become most humble suetors unto your good lordship, that it would please yow to stande soe good lorde to him and us as to become an honourable meanes of his restoring unto his former state and libertie in his ministrie, which he soe peacablie enioyed in her late Majestie's dayes of famous memorie, and whereof above fiftene hundred communicants in this churche have and doe feele the want, wherein your Lordship shall both performe a worke verie acceptable to god, and profitable to his churche, and shall also thereby most straightlie bynde him and us, as to all the humble dueties, which wee shall ever be able to performe, soe speciallie to praise god for your good Lordship, and praye unto him for all increase of happines, both concerning this lyfe and the lyfe to come.

Northampton this
21 Januarie 1604

Signed by Thomas Craswell, mayor; John Bryan; George Raynford; John Mercer; Thomas Humfrey; Thomas Cowper; Lawrence Ball; Edward Mercer; Edward Hensman; Thomas Judkyn.

was presented for saying service but refusing to show to the churchwardens any proof of his absolution and restitution. He was further presented

> for saying service not conformable to the Book of Common Prayer the 25 and 26 days, viz. the 25 being Saturday at morning prayer, it being St James day, & he did not read the litany and for the ordinary lessons, he made the first of Genesis and for the second lesson the first of Matthew, and on the 26th day of July, being Sunday, the surplice was offered to him by John Bennett, the churchwarden, and he would not wear it, neither did he read the litany, and for the lessons he read the 2 of Genesis and the second of Matthew.

No further action appears to have been taken and Rogers could have conceivably got through the whole of the Bible, if that was his intention, before his death in 1632, still as 'vicar of the church of Chacombe'.[64]

At Geddington Thomas Jones, a recent recruit to the ranks of the parochial clergy, subscribed but as early as 12 March 1605 it was presented 'that since his subscription he hath ommitted the sign of the cross in baptism'. He admitted the offence 'because he did take it to be used and to be left at his discretion'.[65] That this was a commonplace attitude to subscription can be taken as established; the tone of those subscriptions discussed above and the frequency with which puritans were again brought before the courts is ample testimony to this. Ambrose Hooke of Blakesley may well have been another of those suspended and later restored. His only previous brush with the diocesan authorities came in 1585, but on 18 February 1605 he was charged with keeping the *Book of Canons* from his churchwardens and, shortly afterwards, was presented for removing the surplice from the church and for saying divine service in his 'pied wrought cap'.[66]

The enforcement of the Canons was the most vigorous of the campaigns conducted against the puritans in the diocese during our period. Bancroft's determination to purge each diocese of puritans was far from successful as far as Peterborough was concerned. The 16 deprivations represented more than in any other diocese at the time, greater even than in the diocese of London where 13 ministers were deprived, or the diocese of Norwich from which nine clerics were removed from their livings.[67] Both of those dioceses had long traditions as centres of puritan activity and were larger than Peterborough yet more clergy were deprived in Peterborough. Dove might well complain that his diocese had been 'from time to time the nest and nursery of factious ministers'.[68] Some indication of the local deficiencies of the campaign can be found in the fact that 15 of the clergy who signed the letters from the meetings held at Northampton in 1603 were able to continue their ministry after 1605, although some action had been taken against two of their number, Robert Binks and Robert Catelin. Later that year another of the Northampton clergy, Thomas London of Bradden, appeared before the court for departing from the service prescribed in the *Book of Common Prayer* and for not wearing the surplice. Another of the signatories, Thomas Randleson, was presented in April 1605 for not wearing the surplice and in July of that year was charged with administering the communion after the puritan fashion to Francis Foster, the deprived minister of Whiston,

---

[64]*Ibid.*, X614/40, f. 82.
[65]*Ibid.*, Inst. Bk. IV, f. 50; X613/36, f. 209.
[66]*Ibid.*, X610/24, f. 32v.; X614/38, ff. 175, 187.
[67]Babbage, *Puritanism and Richard Bancroft*, 149–191.
[68]Hist. Mss. Com. *Salisbury Mss.*, xvii. 46–47.

and his wife.[69] Good relations remained between the deprived puritans and their subscribing colleagues in some quarters at least.

As always, the deficiencies of diocesan administration make it difficult to assess accurately the number of puritan clergy affected by the enforcement of the Canons. It is already clear that those deprived were only a percentage of the total involved, but the size of that percentage remains obscure. Two sources, one emanating from the puritans themselves and the other of an official nature, help to clarify the situation. In the light of Bancroft's policy, the puritans organized a petition by 'the ministers of Lincoln diocese' which was presented to the king at the end of 1605. The petition collected 746 signatures in all, from every part of the country, and, although no names are mentioned the numbers are given from each county. Suffolk was most heavily represented with 71 signatories, but Northamptonshire stood next in line, with Leicestershire and Essex, having 57 signatures each.[70] This figure, representing 20 per cent of the clergy working in the diocese, gives a clearer picture of active puritan commitment. The court records and Sharpe's letter-book help us to identify just over half of these by name, but we are left with 26 clergy prepared to sign the petition about whom we know nothing. We can be confident about a few of these; the long serving pastor of Crick, Giles Sharrocke, was likely to support a general petition, as was the ex-separatist Robert Browne, now rector of Thorpe Achurch but noted as being under suspension in June 1605. Both of them, in company with their puritan colleagues and other clergy of the diocese, were refusing to cooperate over one clause of the Canons, that covered by article 114. This article, paradoxically, was concerned with recusancy and required ministers to send up lists of popish recusants over the age of thirteen who were resident in their parish. Reporting on papists ought to have caused no problems for puritan or protestant clergy, but the position of the Canon, following as it did those concerned with schismatics, disturbers of divine service, and absentees from the Easter Communion (all of which could have embraced puritans as well as papists) may have aroused suspicions among the clergy. This specific fear, accompanied by general dissatisfaction with the proceedings set on foot by the Canons led to a widespread refusal to comply with the order. In seven deaneries of the diocese 163 ministers, well over half of the parish clergy, failed to send in a certificate when first asked but, on being pressed further, 91 of them complied with the order. Nevertheless this left a hard core of 72 who stood out against the order, and among that number were all the puritans known to be working in the deaneries covered by the report.[71]

The numbers involved in obstructing the enforcement of Canon 114, and these signing the Lincoln petition, indicate that between 20 and 28 per cent of the parochial clergy were unhappy about the enforcement of the Canons. The degree of opposition varied from individual to individual, but 12 per cent of all ministers either appeared before the local courts as nonconformists or attended the puritan gatherings at Northampton in 1603, whilst 6 per cent took their opposition as far as deprivation.

The impact which the crisis had in the diocese was not confined to the clergy

[69]P.D.R., X613/37, f. 210; X614/38, f. 254v., 263.

[70]*An Abridgement of that Booke which the Ministers of Lincoln Diocese delivered to his Maiestie upon the first of December last, 1605* (1605), 52.

[71]P.D.R., Vis. Bk. 7, sub. Achurch; Cardwell, *Synodalia*, ii. 309–311; P.D.R., X614/38, ff. 164v.–183v. For use of the term 'recusant' in talking of puritans see B.L., Harl. Ms. 594, ff. 254–264. The names of those puritans refusing to comply are noted in Sheils, 'Thesis', 164.

alone, and the support which puritan ministers received from the gentry and the godly laity far exceeded that given previously. The petition on behalf of the deprived ministers was signed by 44 of the landowners of Northamptonshire, and individual puritans received similar support from the godly among their congregations. The crisis itself was concerned not only with religion, but with local opposition to the interference of central government in matters of local concern. As such it belongs not only to the history of the English reformation but also to the general administrative history of the Tudor state and this aspect is treated in more detail elsewhere.[72] Nevertheless, Bancroft's policy brought together the puritan clergy and their patrons once more, in much the same way that Whitgift's Three Articles had done, in the defence of local custom and tradition. This inadvertent consequence of the enforcement of the Canons was of more lasting effect than were the deprivations.

The casuistical submission of John Rogers did not inhibit him from continuing to disregard the *Book of Common Prayer* when he felt that it infringed his conscience, but even in parishes deprived of their ministers some continuity of practice was maintained. We know that Richard Baldock, Robert Smart, Francis Foster, and Sampson Wood remained nearby to continue their ministries in an unofficial and private capacity. In Rutland Thomas Gibson was succeeded at Ridlington by his son, also Thomas, a graduate of the puritan Emmanuel College, and a fellow of Sidney Sussex, another new college which shared the same inspiration. Two other Emmanuel graduates, Timothy and John Whiting, sons of the puritan Giles, also succeeded deprived ministers at Lilbourne and South Luffenham respectively.[73] In Northamptonshire some of the gentry patrons refused to acknowledge the deprivations and left it to the bishop to re-appoint, but even Dove was forced to provide the puritan Christopher Spicer to Sir Richard Knightley's parish at Fawsley. Nearby, at Charwelton, John Barebone was replaced by Samuel Denton whose nonconformity had first attracted the attention of the diocesan authorities in 1589.[74]

Bishop Dove, following Bancroft's lead, had shown more determination than his predecessors in facing up to the puritans but like them he was defeated by the obduracy of a provincial society led by men jealous of their local rights. The puritans had always respected and recognized the importance of their local connections, and were again able to avoid the worst consequences of persistent nonconformity. Such local contacts made the diocese an attractive location for deprived ministers of other dioceses in the early 17th century. The celebrated John Dod, deprived of his living at Hanwell in Oxfordshire, continued to enjoy the support of the Cope family and, in 1607, was invited to preach at Moreton Pinkney where Edward Cope was farmer of the rectory. Cope, the vicar, and the churchwardens were presented for not reporting the event and, on the same day, a similar warning was given to the churchwardens of Sulgrave for permitting Dod's illustrious collaborator Robert Cleaver to preach in their parish.[75] Dod and Cleaver were giants of early 17th-century puritanism and their publications, most notably *A Plain and Familiar Exposition of the Ten Commandments*,

[72]See Chapter 7.

[73]See above pp. 47–51; for Wood at Fawsley see P.R.O., S.P. Dom. Chas. 1/308/52; for Foster see P.D.R., Archd. Ct. Bk. 16, f. 146; 20, ff. 149v., 176 for preaching activity in his own house, at Wollaston and at Weston Favell between 1606 and 1611. For the Whitings and Gibson see *H.I.L.*, v. 221; xv. 51, 53.

[74]P.D.R., Inst. Bk. IV, ff. 15, 16v., Vis. Bk. 7, f. 57; X609/23, f. 113. Barebone was preaching at Charwelton in 1611, P.R.O., SP 14/68/58.

[75]P.D.R., X614/40, ff. 62v., 72, 82.

went to many editions, providing the stuff of puritan sermons and common places for the godly laity. Their stress on personal discipline and social responsibility within a Calvinist framework became the central concerns of English life and letters for a generation or more in circles outside the royal courts.[76] The nature of the presentments suggests that in 1607 they were conducting a joint mission in the western part of the diocese with the agreement of the local clergy and the support of the gentry.

As with other crises that of 1605 was followed by a period of calm, and the years after 1605 are barren ones for the historian tracking puritans through the church courts. Despite regular articles at visitation against clergy who openly opposed the *Book of Common Prayer*, against the godly who attended 'conventicles or private congregations', or other authors or maintainers of schism, the rate of detection remained pitifully low.[77] Dove himself was forced to come to terms with his puritan subordinates and the early decades of the 17th century were probably the most hopeful years for the puritans since the heady days of the 1570s. The death of Bancroft in 1610 removed the last of the Elizabethan bishops to place ceremonial uniformity before Calvinist theology, and his successor Abbot, himself a London preacher of the 1590s, was to prove to be a benign bishop as far as puritanism was concerned over the next two decades.[78] On the puritan side the deprivations of 1605 had removed most, if not quite all, of the 'presbyterian faction' of the 1580s from the ministry of the established church. They had had the respect of their younger colleagues and successors, but most of these had been educated in a less dogmatic climate characterized by the preaching of William Perkins, the teaching of Laurence Chaderton, and the homilectic writings of Dod and Cleaver. This tradition hoped no less for the reform of the commonwealth, but sought to bring it about through the hearts and minds of men rather than by insitutional reform. Its adherents were more willing to accept the institutional impurities of the church, as long as its pastoral responsibilities were provided for in the localities.[79]

In this period of tranquillity which followed the elevation of Abbot to Canterbury, Calvinism remained the prevailing theological orthodoxy. There was, however, an intellectual movement in the process of organizing a coup within the established church, and this had already made its appearance in the diocese. The Arminians, who departed from Calvinism, were at this date largely confined to the universities and to protégés of Richard Neile, but they had already made an appearance in the diocese in the person of Richard Butler. He was soon joined by other sympathizers, among whom John Buckeridge, Archdeacon of Northampton from 1604 to 1611, and John Lambe, diocesan chancellor from 1615, were most prominent. Under these men the diocesan courts became

[76]C. Hill, *Society and Puritanism*, 18, 243–244, 274; W. Haller, *The Rise of Puritanism*, 122–123.

[77]A series of 10 printed sets of Visitation articles issued by Dove for the years, 1600, 1602, 1605, 1608, 1611, 1614, 1617, 1620, 1623, and 1626 are bound together with Metropolitan visitation articles for 1607 and 1613 at Lambeth Palace Library, call mark 1599. 18 (7a); see in particular articles 15 (1602), 9, 12, 21, 29, 31, 42, 43, and 74 (1607), and 11 (1608). Concern over private conventicles, many of which must have been held by or attended by clergy deprived in 1605, increased greatly in the years between 1602 and 1626, if the articles are used as a guideline.

[78]N. R. N. Tyacke, 'Puritanism, Arminianism, and Counter Revolution', 123, 125–126.

[79]For Perkins and Chaderton see P. Collinson, *A Mirror of Elizabethan Puritanism*, 6–8; for Dod and Cleaver see C. Hill, *Society and Puritanism*, 17–18, 244, 279; W. Haller, *The Rise of Puritanism* (1957 edn. New York), 120–123.

instruments of a vigorous partisan policy uncaring of local prejudices and tradition, and it was not to be long before the puritans joined battle once again.[80] The confrontations of the 1620s and 1630s were largely brought about by the puritan response to the aggressive leadership of the Arminian minority. Although that struggle was conducted with similar tactics over familiar terrain the premisses had changed in a way that would have been unrecognizable to an earlier generation. To the puritans it was almost as if the worst fear of the returning exiles in the 1560s, that of a backsliding towards popery, were about to be fulfilled. Thus the future of Calvinism itself became the cause of the puritans.

[80]Sheils, 'Some problems', *Continuity and Change*, 173–174, 181, 185–186.

# 6 THE MINISTRY

*Abilities and responsibilities*

THE position of the puritan clergy in the diocese needs to be set against that of the parochial ministry as a whole. Nobody disagreed with the biblical exhortation to the clergy to be both teachers and shepherds to their flocks. The practical application of these roles in the reformed church led to much discussion which turned progressively to disagreement between the puritans and their opponents. Even the greatest intellectual apologist for the established church, Richard Hooker, could write in 1594 of 'that threefold blot or blemish of notable ignorance, inconscionable absence from the cures whereof men have taken charge, and insatiable hunting after spiritual preferments' which still disfigured the church. Disputes arose about the extent of the pastoral deficiencies of the church, and about the causes and remedies for the same. Such disputes had, in turn, their roots in differing views as to the function of the ministry, in particular about the level of priority to be given to preaching. Reformed churches were, of course, preaching churches, but early protestant confidence that continual exposition of the Bible would inevitably lead to acceptance of the reformation was to be disappointed. More than mere preaching was needed and by the end of the century Hooker had provided for the hierarchy a judicious defence for the importance of the pastoral side of the ministry. Attention on the pastoral ministry grew, particularly as preaching itself became increasingly a source of disruption. All parties agreed that it was desirable to preach the reformation, but was it to be a presbyterian or an episcopal one?[1]

The value of the sermon as a vehicle of instruction and propaganda was not lost on government, but preaching activity needed to be strictly controlled. The character of the Queen, who considered that the *Book of Common Prayer, The Homilies,* and the quarterly sermon required in parish churches provided a sufficient spiritual diet rather than a mere survival kit for salvation, reinforced this distrust of preaching. Her attitude was not shared by the first generation of Elizabethan bishops but, as the reign drew on, bishops like Aylmer and local clergy like Simon Gibbs of Boddington could go so far as to suggest that there was something unwholesome in seeking after sermons when the word of God was available in the liturgy. Theirs was an extreme position, but it emerged in response to the rigorous insistence of the puritans that the ability to preach was a minimum requirement in a minister. As a result not only were the contents of sermons themselves sources of controversy, but preaching activity itself was suspect.[2]

This had not always been the case. In the years before the suppression of the exercises in 1577, the necessity of improving clerical standards, particularly in

[1]See above pp. 44–45; R. Hooker, *The Laws of Ecclesiastical Polity* (Everyman edn.) ii. 466.
[2]See above p. 45.

understanding of the Bible, was generally accepted as a major priority. So it was that the exercises, designed as local extra-mural means of improving the preaching ability of the local clergy, emerged in the 1570s with a large measure of episcopal support. Among a number of bishops they were only abandoned with reluctance. The ambivalent attitude of the hierarchy is illustrated by the case of Thomas Bentham, bishop of Coventry and Lichfield, who was apparently unaware of the activities at the puritan exercise at Southam in his own diocese whilst, at the same time, he was contributing towards the maintenance of a lecturer at Towcester.[3]

After the suppression of the exercises the attitudes of both puritans and bishops hardened. The latter accused the puritans of exaggerating the deficiencies of the clergy, whilst they in turn made the bishops responsible for the ills of the church. Hauled before the High Commission in 1578, the Northampton puritan Francis Merbury could turn on his prosecutors with the following accusation, 'I say that the bishops of London and Peterborough, and the bishops of England are guilty of the death of as many souls as have perished by the ignorance of the

**Table 2**  Pluralism

|  | Parishes[a] | Clergy | Pluralists University | Pluralists Non-University | Parishes affected[b] |
|---|---|---|---|---|---|
| 1560 | 287 | 229 | 16 | 32 | 86 |
| 1576 | 296 | 264 | 24 | 34 | 90 |
| 1585 | 296 | 268 | 23 | 19 | 67 |
| 1589 | 297 | 273 | 21 | 15 | 58 |
| 1600 | 296 | 278 | 27 | 6 | 51 |
| 1610 | 292 | 279 | 25 | 3 | 41 |

a. This refers to the total of parishes for which details can be established.

b. This figure is not double the number of pluralists because some held livings in this diocese in conjunction with others elsewhere.

*Sources*
H.I.L. supplemented by P.D.R., Vis. Bks. 1, 2, 4, 7 and Lamb. Pal. Lib., Carte Miscellanee, xiii. 56.

ministers of their making whom they knew to be unable.'[4] Merbury's views may in part reflect his disappointment at the recent suppression of the exercises, but there is no doubt that at the time of his trial he was not exaggerating the problem even if his causal explanation was too glib. Scambler inherited an almost intractable problem, as Table 2 suggests. In 1560 there were 48 pluralists in the diocese serving a total of 86 livings; at best, assuming each man lived on one of his benefices, this left 38 parishes, or 12.7 per cent of the total, dependent on the services of a curate or neighbouring cleric. A survey drawn up in that year confirms this view; dealing with 257 parishes it found that 21 were vacant and 27 held by non-resident incumbents. The upheavals of the 1550s had left over one-sixth of the parishes surveyed bereft of a pastor in 1560. Unfortunately the problem was not resolved quickly despite the efforts of the bishop to restrict plural-

[3]P.R.O., SP. 12/150/42 (1); see also R. B. Manning, *Religion and Society*, 190–191 for Sussex examples.
[4]Hist. Mss. Com., *Various Collections*, iii. 3.

ism and non-residence in 1566.[5] However praiseworthy his intentions, they met with little success, as became obvious at the visitation of 1573. Not only did this visitation first uncover the details of puritan support in and around the county town, it also provided depressing news about pastoral provision. Of the 288 parishes making returns, 51 had non-resident incumbents, a figure worse than that for 1560. At Barton Seagrave not only was there no incumbent but no Bible or *Book of Common Prayer*, and the churchwardens of Apethorpe complained that they had 'never a curate, nor have no service said, nor any sermons according to the Queen's Injunctions and, for want of a priest, they have been compelled to bury the dead bodies themselves.'[6]

By 1576, when the next survey was made, the number of pluralists in the diocese had increased to 58 and, most damaging, the majority of them had not attended university. It was the problem of ill-qualified clergy that Merbury referred to in his accusation; the shortage of ministers at the beginning of the reign had necessitated ordaining candidates in considerable numbers and without close scrutiny of their qualifications. Many of the bishops were unhappy about this, but could see no alternative in the short term until the universities, under the new regime, began to supply candidates trained and taught in a reformed climate. How long this situation took varied from diocese to diocese, but at Peterborough things had not progressed far by the mid 1570s, and of the clergy working in the diocese in 1576 only 25 per cent are known to have attended university. The puritans, with the priority they gave to preaching, put a high premium on academic quality and on the university experience which many of them shared. The hierarchy placed attention on the other aspects of the minister's work and took a more benign view of the learning of the parish clergy. There is clearly no ultimate test of clerical fitness; the preaching activity of Richard Lively led to complaint being made against him for neglecting his parish duties in 1570. At the same time the wardens of Denton complained about their non-resident graduate for neglecting his duties and not providing a deputy. Learning was no guarantee of the provision of pastoral care, but ignorance ensured that it would be lacking. The insufficiency of Nicholas Walker, curate of Cransley, so exasperated the godly squire Edward Dallyson, that he offered in 1570 to guarantee a salary of £12 or £13 'if an honest man be there appointed'; it was to take 15 years to find one.[7]

From an examination of court records, it is the deficiencies that strike one. The honest, conscientious, non-graduate priest leaves little trace to posterity whatever impact he had on his contemporaries. With the more articulate puritans the historian often finds that he has to rely upon the confident preacher's view of his own worth. It is important not to take this at face value. In the absence of other criteria any survey of the fitness of the ministry for its task must consider the academic quality of the membership and the assessments made either by the hierarchy or their opponents. The details of these are set out in Tables 3 and 4, but the implications are not immediately obvious. It is clear that between 1560 and 1576 little improvement was made in the intellectual quality of the clergy; the number that had attended university had increased from 38 to 66 but,

[5]Corpus Christi College, Cambridge, Ms. 122, ff. 195–265; P.D.R., ML 559 contains several actions against non-resident clergy. Scambler also tried to enforce residence at his cathedral, B.L., Lansd. Ms. 71, f. 178 and v; W. M. Kennedy (ed.) *Elizabethan Episcopal Administration* (1924), ii. 39–40; iii. 159–160; 235–236.

[6]P.D.R., Vis. Bk. 3, unfoliated, see parish heading, for specific references.

[7]Lamb. Pal. Lib., Carte Miscellanee, xiii. 56; Irons, 'An Episcopal Visitation in 1570', 178, 204.

even so, this only represented one-quarter of the parish priests of the diocese. Progress still remained slow, but a better guide may be found in the surveys compiled by diocesan and metropolitan authority in 1560 and 1576. In assessing the clergy of the diocese the officials used vague phrases such as *Doctus* or *eruditus*, which were open to subjective interpretation. Nevertheless it is clear that the information from 1576 is much more in line with what we know of the academic qualifications than that of 1560. The implication is that officialdom was responding to the more stringent demands which the returning exiles made on the ministry, and the hand of Archbishop Grindal may have been behind the 1576 survey. The first generation of Elizabethan bishops may not have been able

**Table 3**  Academic Qualifications

|      | Parishes | Clergy | No academic record | BA or less | MA | BD×DD | Other | % |
|------|----------|--------|---------------------|------------|-----|-------|-------|------|
| 1560 | 285 | 229 | 191 | 9 | 14 | 7 | 8 | 16.5 |
| 1576 | 296 | 264 | 198 | 29 | 25 | 8 | 4 | 25.0 |
| 1585 | 296 | 268 | 188 | 31 | 35 | 13 | 2 | 29.8 |
| 1590 | 297 | 273 | 178 | 33 | 44 | 16 | 2 | 34.8 |
| 1600 | 296 | 278 | 137 | 50 | 65 | 23 | 3 | 50.7 |
| 1610 | 292 | 279 | 101 | 53 | 90 | 34 | 1 | 63.8 |

*Sources*
H.I.L.; Venn & Venn, *Al. Cant.*; Foster, *Al. Oxon.*

**Table 4**  Official Surveys

|      | Clergy | |
|------|--------|--|
| 1560 | 166 | 94 *Doctus*, 54 *Doctus mediocritus*, 18 *Indoctus*, 9 preachers |
| 1576 | 230 | 56 *Bene eruditus*, 38 *Competenter eruditus*, 144 *mediocritur eruditus*, 3 *Parum eruditus*, 19 *Exigue eruditus*, 40 preachers |
| 1603 | | 293 parishes, 144 preachers of which 5 were DD, 23 were BD, 74 were MA, 31 were BA, 1 had a law degree, 9 were non graduates. |

*Sources*
Corpus Christi College, Cambridge Ms. 122; Lamb. Pal. Lib., Carte Miscellanee, xiii. 56; B. L. Harl. Ms. 280, f. 157.

to find learned men for the parishes, but they were beginning to set higher standards for those men they did find. It was this concern which led to the early alliance with many puritans.

Clearly the survey of 1560 offered only the most cursory guide to clerical standards, in a church emerging from five years of sacramental catholicism there were only nine preachers and 38 graduates, yet the visitors found 32 per cent of the clergy sufficiently learned and a further 56.6 per cent were said to be learned, a phrase which must have had the widest of interpretations. The survey of 1576 found about the same proportion (90 per cent) to be sufficient or above, but by this date the emphasis had changed. Of the total in the survey 50 per cent were merely 'sufficient', 16 per cent were 'competent', and 24 per cent were said to be 'able'. The proportion of 'able' clerics was close to the proportion of graduates in the diocese, though the lists were by no means identical, and some confidence can therefore be placed in the objectivity of the survey. That being so it is clear that by 1576 the standards of learning in the ministry had improved rather more than a strict analysis of the number of graduates would lead one to believe.[8]

The diocesan authorities may have responded to the reformed view of the ministry by setting higher standards, but could they claim the credit for the improvement? It has been said that the list of these described as *bene eruditus* included some non-graduates, and consideration of this group suggests that credit for the improvement lay elsewhere. There were eight clergy in this category and six of them, John Tymms of Whiston, Hugh Okes of Weekley, William Wood of Plumpton, John Sibthorpe of Ashton and Roade, John Smeton of Overstone, and John Ringrose of Weedon Bec were known puritans or associated with vigorous puritan centres. Almost certainly they had been in attendance at the exercises or at preaching centres like Overstone, and the coincidence is too strong to escape notice. It was surely at the exercises that these men had acquired the skills which were to impress their examiners. This accounted for the uncompromising nature of Merbury's accusation. Not only had the bishops ordained unfit men, but they had also suppressed the exercises which did so much to make such men fit for the ministry. Merbury must have been aware of this during his stay at Northampton, and his impression was supported by the examiners in 1576, who found some nongraduates to be learned and only one nonconformist, Robert Morris of Brafield on the Green, who dropped into the category of *mediocritur eruditus*.[9]

The years following 1576 were difficult ones for bishop Scambler. He had fallen out with his patron Leicester because of his opposition to the puritans, and a group of young confident puritans was entering the diocese under gentry patronage. From then until his translation to Norwich in 1585, Scambler presided over a diocese in which the puritan ministers and their orthodox colleagues were increasingly at loggerheads. Details of puritan sermons against non-preaching ministers, and of counter attack by the authorities have already been given and it is clear from Thomas Gibson's comments that local relationships were acrimonious at times.[10] Some small improvements were made in coping with pluralism and non-residence and by 1585 pluralists who had not been to university were in a minority. The number of double beneficed clergy was only six fewer than in 1560, but the situation had eased considerably because by the mid 1580s there were a number of able curates available to serve in the place of absentee incumbents. Puritans such as Daniel Wight at Daventry or Edmund Snape at St Peter's in Northampton were only too ready to accept curacies if they provided a pulpit in an advantageous place. That such eminent men survived on the pittance provided for curates testifies to the support they received from their congregations or gentry patrons. It was not only puritans who filled such posts, at Evenley the non-graduate, non-resident incumbent found a curate in Henry Walden who had an M.A. from Oxford. The small increase in university men working in the parishes was little comfort to the bishop for they included a vociferous group of puritans whose uncompromising attitudes were to find expression in the *classes*. This group, mainly from Oxford, has already been discussed and accounted for many of the puritans at odds with Scambler

[8]See Table 4.
[9]Lamb. Pal. Lib., Carte Miscellanee xiii. 56.
[10]See above pp. 44–45.

over Whitgift's Three Articles. A confrontation which was ended by the bishop's removal to Norwich and the arrival of Richard Howland in 1585.[11]

Howland was previously head of a Cambridge college, St John's, a post which he continued to hold for the first eighteen months of his episcopate because of the difficulties involved in the election of his successor. He had evidently been at home in university circles, and when he finally removed himself to his cathedral city he took some of his university friends with him. At his death the bishop owned over 1,000 books, but their titles suggest that Howland's interests were donnish rather than evangelical or pastoral and few of the titles reflected contemporary theological debate. Those which did, such as Whitgift's writings in the debate with Thomas Cartwright, suggest that his sympathies were firmly on the side of authority.[12] Nevertheless he had, whilst at St John's College, been instrumental in finding a compromise between the puritans and their opponents in the college, and his respect for learning remained with him. Very little is known of his views or his career, but he did permit an exercise to continue in the diocese long after they were illegal in the southern province. The circumstances of the exercise were peculiar. It was located at Oundle, a town situated on the edge of Rockingham Forest and close to the extensive estates of the recusant families of Vaux and Tresham. The influence of the catholics in the locality probably persuaded the diocesan authorities to continue the exercise but there was also a challenge from the left. A group of radicals had emerged in the town around the persons of William Hackett and Giles Wigginton, and the puritan curate Hugh Clark 'had many bickerings and disputations with some of the chief of them, whom he mightily confuted and through God's grace reclaimed some of them'. Attacked from the right and the left, the church needed some defence in the area and the exercise, even if still puritan inspired, provided that. Howland not only ordered the less able clergy of the region to attend the exercise and perform the tasks allotted to them, but also insisted that the laity attended. These orders were backed up in the diocesan courts in 1590 when the rectors of Wadenhoe and King's Cliffe were ordered to appear at the exercise, with several of the separatists who were also commanded to attend.[13]

Exceptional circumstances required unorthodox methods and the bishop appeared to support this exercise at the very time that the activities of the *classes* were preoccupying his superiors at London. Elsewhere Howland proved more orthodox; at the visitation of 1588 he chose Bancroft's appointee John Beatniffe to preach the sermon at Towcester. Although Beatniffe's later career was to disappoint his patron, the cleric prepared a lengthy attack on those who preferred sermons to the reading of the word of God, which was published as part of the campaign against the puritans.[14] During Howland's years at Peterborough the flow of graduate clergy into the diocese increased so that, by 1600, just over half of the parish clergy had attended university. For the first half of this period, the years up to 1592, the puritan clergy continued to represent an academic élite among the parish clergy, but in the later years the policy of Whitgift in encouraging young defenders of the establishment, and the great increase in the supply of graduates to the ministry, altered the relationship. By 1600 the academic achievement of the puritan clergy was matched by the orthodox clergy. The introduction of statutes in Oxford in 1581 requiring subscription to the 39

[11]P.D.R., Vis. Bk. 4, *passim*; H.I.L. xii. 265; xiv. 121; xv. 69; xvi. 140.
[12]*D.N.B.*, Howland, Richard; P.R.O., E178/1703.
[13]P.D.R., X610/24, f. 283; Irons, 'A Calendar of a Court Book', 222.
[14]J. Beatniffe, *A Sermon Preached at Towcester.*

Articles meant that the character of puritanism was also altered and attention switched to Cambridge. The debate over the preaching ministry was no longer conducted with the acrimony that characterized the 1580s and, as general standards improved, it ceased to be so central an issue.[15]

The improvement at Peterborough also took place elsewhere and owed as much to what has been termed 'the educational revolution' as to the example of the bishop.[16] Where Howland can perhaps claim more credit is in the reduction of pluralism and non-residence. In 1600 there were still 33 pluralists in the diocese, but only six were non-graduates and only one of these, the puritan William Cherington, was a recent appointment. Even he had to serve an apprenticeship of 12 years as a curate before getting his second living of Cotterstock in 1597. The visitation of 1591 brought to light only seven cases of non-residence in which the incumbent made no provision for a curate, and presentments concerned with the moral or pastoral failings of the clergy were reduced to a trickle.[17] It would be fair to say that, by the time of bishop Dove's consecration, the struggle between the puritans and the authorities over the quality of the ministry was no longer conducted on the same terms. When the puritans set out to survey the ministry in 1604 their criteria must surely have been different from those employed in the 1580s and more concerned with doctrine and conscientiousness than mere ability.

The new bishop was no friend to the puritans, but he shared the concern for rooting out the 'threefold blot or blemish' on the church. His first visitation articles were headed by one concerned with the residence of incumbents whilst the third asked if pluralists provided curates on their livings. Sandwiched between these was an article stressing the importance of instructing the laity and requiring regular catechizing and weekly instruction, for half an hour before Evening Prayer, in the Lord's Prayer, the Ten Commandments, and the Creed.[18] A concern with lay evangelization which was later echoed by the puritan Robert Cawdry who wrote 'it cannot be shewed that God, his religion, hath taken any good effect in any town . . . but where catechizing is practised both by ministers publicly, and by householders privately'. He went on to provide examples of easy catechisms for the 'meanest sort' and pointed out that 'the neglect of this duty in those ministers that be preachers is in very deed the cause why their preaching taketh so little effect amongst their parishioners'. This represented a dramatic change from the claims he had made in 1583 and 1584.[19] This concern with evangelization did not blind the bishop to the pockets of clerical ignorance that still existed, and he apparently set his clergy to their books. At his visitation in 1602 he enquired 'whether the exercises heretofore prescribed and enjoyed to the clergy of this diocese, for the increase of their knowledge in the Holy Scriptures, be accordingly observed; and if not, in whose default the same hath been or is so omitted or neglected'. Following that instruction Dove issued many preaching licences in 1603 so that, in the return made to Whitgift, he could claim that there were 144 preachers in the diocese. This sudden increase reflected

[15]See Table 3; M. H. Curtis, *Oxford and Cambridge in Transition*, 170.

[16]L. Stone, 'The Educational Revolution in England 1560–1640', *Past and Present*, no. 28 (1964), 41–80.

[17]H.I.L., iii. 101; xvi. 41; the others included three nonconformists Henry Hargreaves, Robert Morris, and Giles Sharrocke. P.D.R., Vis. Bk. 5, unfoliated, only four clerics were presented at this date for not providing the required services.

[18]*Articles to be Enquired of Within the Dioces of Peterborough . . . 1600* (unpublished) printed copy of 1600 at Lamb. Pal. Lib., call mark 1599. 18 (7a).

[19]R. Cawdry, *A Short and Fruitfull Treatise* (1604), sigs. A, Biiij.

the bishop's concern with preaching and did not entail the licensing of unsuitable candidates merely to make the returns look impressive. Of the licensed preachers in the diocese in 1603 only nine had not attended a university.[20]

Some deficiencies remained, notably in the poorer livings, but presentment for failure to provide statutory sermons or services were very rare after 1590, and the morality of individual clergy was hardly called into question. There is no doubt that in the years prior to 1590 the puritans could claim the credit for such improvements as were made and could rightly accuse the bishop of suppressing the instruments through which that improvement had been brought about. After 1590 the situation reflected less the influence of a particular individual or group, and was really part of a general trend with parallels elsewhere. In 1603 the puritans were no longer the intellectual élite they had been in 1584 and because of the stricter control of conformity at the universities, they had begun to fall behind in terms of paper qualifications. Fewer of the puritans progressed beyond the degree of B.A. These changes had important consequences for the puritans, for it shifted the area of debate on the ministry from preaching abilities to pastoral conscientiousness. No longer vastly superior to their colleagues in learning the puritans did not enjoy immunity from the courts because of their academic attainments, but rather because they had established close connections with the leaders of local society.[21]

*University background*

The diocese enjoyed relatively easy access to both universities. The south-west of the diocese was only 30 miles from Oxford and the eastern borders about the same distance from Cambridge; a situation reflected in the geographical distribution of the graduate clergy. Oxford men rarely found livings in the eastern part of the diocese but Cambridge men, numerically greater, were less restricted. There were 247 men known to have been at Cambridge working in the diocese between 1558 and 1610 whilst Oxford provided 134 clerics. The total number was made up of 52 men noted as having degrees at ordination or institution but who left no record of their university, and two Scottish graduates one of whom, Thomas Randleson, was an active puritan.[22]

The importance of the experience gained at university in shaping religious attitudes was recognized by contemporaries like Sir Walter Mildmay, who founded Emmanuel College to supply a learned and godly ministry. Increasing numbers of laymen attended university, but the colleges still remained chiefly as training grounds for the ministry and teaching was solely in the hands of clerics. Traditions varied from college to college and this was reflected in the history of puritanism. The diocesan officials were all drawn from Cambridge except for archdeacon John Buckeridge, an Oxford man. He may have known bishop Dove there for the bishop had close links with both universities, having been one of the original fellows of Jesus College, Oxford in 1575. Among the Cambridge men the great majority came from Burghley's old college, St John's.

[20]*Articles to be Inquired of by the Churchwardens and Sworne men of the Dioces and Jurisdiction of Peterborough . . . 1602* (1602), article 12; P.D.R., Misc. Bk. ix, ff. 13v–20; B.L. Harl. Ms. 280, f. 157 printed in R. G. Usher, *The Reconstruction of the English Church,* i. 241.

[21]See M. R. O'Day, 'The Reformation of the Ministry', *Continuity and Change,* 66–68, 70, 73–75; Sheils, 'Some Problems', *Continuity and Change,* 182–184; see below pp. 99–101.

[22]Compiled from details in *H.I.L.,* supplemented by J. & J. A. Venn, *Alumni Cantabridgienses, part one* (Cambridge 1922–1927) and J. Foster, *Alumni Oxonienses, 1500–1714* (repr. 1968).

The college had been the scene of a power struggle between Whitgift and the puritans during the 1570s and that experience may have hardened the views of diocesan officials against the puritans during the 1580s. Certainly during Howland's episcopate almost all the diocesan officials would have been close to men involved in the conflict at the college.[23]

The puritan clergy of the diocese were of a more diverse academic background. If the diocese attracted the establishment men from St John's as its administrators, their puritan opponents in the college moved off in great numbers to Suffolk livings and few St John's men were found among the Peterborough puritans, though Percival Wiburn was a notable exception.[24] The pattern of puritan recruitment to the diocese was fragmentary and reflected the general trend of graduate recruitment. The largest colleges at both universities supplied the greatest number of recruits, but the evidence from Peterborough suggests that no college could be considered a puritan seminary until Emmanuel College in the latter half of the period. In the large colleges of Trinity, Cambridge, and Christ Church, Oxford the puritans represented about 25 per cent of the clergy supplied by each to the diocese and for other colleges the proportion was lower. The great congregations of Cambridge puritans from Christ's and St John's who did so much to characterize the religious temper of Essex and East Anglia were not found at Peterborough.[25]

Nevertheless it was Cambridge men who provided the first wave of puritan missionaries to the diocese. Wiburn has already been mentioned and among those deprived in 1574 were George Gilderd, a graduate of Pembroke College, and Eusebius Paget of Christ's. Another prominent puritan from Christ's was Francis Merbury and further support during the 1570s came from Trinity men like William Fludd and Robert Johnson. Paget had also spent some time at Christ Church where the former exile Thomas Sampson was Dean. Another Christ Church graduate, Arthur Wake, was among those deprived in 1574, but he was the only Oxford man of note in this first stage of puritan growth.[26]

Many of the early generation had moved on by the later 1580s and, although both Fludd and Johnson remained active, the leadership passed to a younger group of scholars, most of whom had been at Oxford. It was these men who assumed the leadership and provided the organizational needs of the *classes*. Edmund Snape, the leader of the Northampton *classis*, had graduated from Magdalen College, Oxford, from where John Barebone, the leader at Daventry had gained his degrees. The leader of the third *classis*, that of Kettering side, was another Oxford man, Thomas Stone, rector of Warkton, who had been at Christ Church. In addition to these leaders Andrew King of Culworth, John Spicer, Daniel Wight, and William Fleshware were all members who had attended Oxford University. The movement, however, was not exclusive to Oxford men and Nicholas Edwards, a graduate of King's College and significantly a man of an earlier generation, and Edward Sharpe were both Cambridge men. It was the Kettering *classis* in which Cambridge men predominated and among its members were two Christ's *alumni*, Robert Williamson and Leonard Pattinson, a Peterhouse man, Edmund Massey, and Ralph Fosbrooke from St John's

[23]For more detailed discussion of diocesan officials see Sheils, 'Some Problems', *Continuity and Change*, 173–178, 181–183, 185–186; details on individuals are in *H.I.L.* For Cecil's links with the college see Conyers Read, *Mr. Secretary Cecil and Queen Elizabeth* (1955), 24–28.

[24]*Eliz. Puritan Movt.*, 128; Venn, *Alumni Cant.*, iv. 481.

[25]At Cambridge Trinity provided 43 clerics and St John's 42; at Oxford 20 came from Christ Church and 18 from Magdalen.

[26]*H.I.L.*, v. 71, 243; viii. 31; ix. 121; x. 105, 141; xiv. 113.

College. Most interestingly this group appeared to be the less committed, and met erratically so that its leader, the Oxford man Thomas Stone, often attended the Northampton *classis* with Robert Williamson.[27] The lack of commitment to the organizational ambitions of the *classes* was evident among other Cambridge men who remained aloof including Giles Wigginton and his brother Francis, who had been at Peterhouse with Giles Whiting, the puritan rector of Etton.[28]

By the earlier years of James' reign the Oxford men were veteran campaigners who still provided local leadership but found themselves at the head of a younger generation of Cambridge graduates. The statutes of 1581 had made life harder for puritans at Oxford and by the end of the century the university had been infected by the anti-Calvinist Arminian churchmen. It is not surprising therefore to find that the younger generation of puritans came from 'the other place'. Thomas Greenwood had been at Corpus Christi College and Christopher Sanderson continued to represent Christ's among his puritan brethren. Two *alumni* of Queens' were among those deprived in 1605; one of these, Sampson Wood, had also been at Emmanuel College and it was here, among men like John Gibson and Timothy and John Whiting, that the future of local puritanism lay.[29]

The university background of the puritans displayed a pattern; a wave of Cambridge men was followed by one of Oxford graduates, this in turn was succeeded by another Cambridge wave. The importance of this for an understanding of the character of puritan activity in the diocese cannot be underestimated for the Oxford men, mostly presbyterians, fell into a more limited range of nonconformity than did their Cambridge counterparts. Over and above this, the shared experience of university was crucial in creating what has recently been called a 'common brotherhood' among the preachers. That sense of collegiality could only be sustained if it was nourished by the local contacts made by the preachers during their respective ministries in the diocese.[30]

*Brethren and friends*

The strength of the local contacts made by the puritan clergy was clear by 1605. Those contacts were founded on a common outlook and furthered by a shared educational experience and by the patronage system. Like all professional men the puritan clergy enjoyed each other's company and were keen to establish links with the leaders of local society. Initial contacts may have come through the patronage system or through the mechanics of entering a living, which required that a new incumbent be inducted by a fellow clergyman. The exercises of the 1570s and subsequent experiments provided puritans with the opportunity to meet with friends over and above the usual contacts involved in yearly attendance at visitation and the occasional need to substitute for each other during absences or sickness. They were members of the landholding class with glebe to work or farm and so regular attendance at market to buy and sell as well as to preach was likely. The clergy were not as yet a class apart and their life need not have been isolated. From such opportunities for meeting, enduring friendships were made and often recalled when clergy made their wills. So it was that

[27]*H.I.L.*, iv. 201; v. 57, 91; viii. 75; ix. 165; x. 197; xii. 265; xiii. 17, 85; xv. 69, 111; Venn, *Alumni Cant.*, iv. 49; Foster, *Alumni Oxon.*, i. 68.

[28]*H.I.L.*, xv. 49, 69; xvi. 140.

[29]*Ibid.*, vi. 57; xii. 65; xv. 53, 167; *Alumni Cant.*, i. 73; B.L., Sloane Ms. 271, f. 21v.

[30]*Eliz. Puritan Movt.*, 122–130.

Ralph Smith of Braunston asked his old friend Daniel Wight, formerly of the Daventry *classis*, to provide his funeral service for him in 1611, leaving him 10s. for his pains. Another member of that group, Edward Sharpe of Fawsley, left several bequests of books to his family; he left his youngest child in the care of his squire, Valentine Knightley, and his old friend John Barebone, who also received 20s. and Sharpe's Hebrew Bible as memorials.[31]

The puritans in the west were a close-knit group, but similar friendships are noted elsewhere. When making his will in 1590 John Sibthorpe chose as his overseers two old friends, Thomas London of Bradden and Nicholas Edwards of Courteenhall, who had defended Sibthorpe's sermon at the Northampton exercise sixteen years earlier. The moderator of the Kettering *classis*, Thomas Stone of Warkton, retained links with several of the members and in 1614 was left a copy of a puritan classic, Thomas Wilcox's *A Right Godly and Learned Exposition upon the whole booke of the Psalmes*, by Hugh Okes of Weekley.[32] Such examples could be multiplied, but even closer links were formed by marriage between members of clerical families. When Richard Lively resigned his living of Maxey, he did so in favour of his son-in-law Robert Buddle.[33] John Spicer of Cogenhoe married one of his daughters to Jonas Chalenor and his clerical son Christopher to Rachel, a daughter of the puritan patriarch Percival Wiburn who was still residing at Whiston in 1599 when the ceremony took place. Another son and daughter married into the Isham branch of the Pickering family, cousins of the puritan family of Titchmarsh.[34] Of similar status to these was the Fosbrooke family of Cranford, two of whom were puritan clergy in the 1580s. Ralph, the elder, had married into the family of Robert Cawdry and, although the relationship is uncertain, Robert was witness to Ralph's will in 1591, in company with Thomas Stone of Warkton. Ralph's younger half-brother, John married a Lynne of Southwick, a family of similar status which was a minor patron to puritan clergy and also provided younger sons for the ministry itself.[35]

When puritans used the word brethren of each other, they may have been doing nothing more sinister than commenting on the cousinage that was emerging between clerical families and like-minded laity. Indeed a sizeable minority of puritans working in the diocese were sons of local households. Among the most well connected was Robert Johnson, the son of a Stamford alderman from a family which included Marian exiles. Johnson remained on close terms throughout his life with Sir Walter Mildmay, who was also an early patron of the less well-born Giles Wigginton of Oundle, though that friendship cooled with Wigginton's increasingly radical stance.[36] Another local man of humble origin to receive gentry patronage was Francis Foster, a Northampton man who served as chaplain for six years in the household of Sir Thomas Catesby before receiving the family living of Whiston. A similar career structure was followed

[31]P.D.R., Will Volume W 627; H.I.L., xv. 69.
[32]P.D.R., Will Volume V 798; H.I.L., xiii. 85; and see the wills of Francis Battie of Aston le Walls; P.R.O., P.C.C. wills, Montagu 36, and William Woodcrofte of Peakirk, P.D.R., will volume V 146.
[33]H.I.L., ix. 9.
[34]*Ibid.*, xiii. 17; xv. 65.
[35]*Visitations of Northants, 1564, 1618–19*, 89–90; P.D.R., will volume Y 1; H.I.L., ix. 71; xi. 6–7; Irons 'A paper on Sir Robert Cawdrie', 24.
[36]G. T. Armytage (ed.), *Visitation of Rutland, 1618–19* (Harleian Soc. iii, 1870), 14. His will is in P.R.O., P.C.C. wills, Clarke 131, abstracted in H.I.L., viii. 31; C. Garrett, *The Marian Exiles* (Cambridge, 1938), 199–200.

by Henry Hargreaves, who spent eight years as chaplain to Sir James Harrington at Ridlington.[37] For the sons of clergy or the humble an apprenticeship as a schoolmaster often served as another means to attract the attention of godly patrons or puritan clergy. Robert Catelin of Raunds served as a schoolmaster at Oundle before moving to the vicarage of All Saints Northampton on the recommendation of a local puritan minister, Thomas Deacon of Stoke Doyle, and Henry Bourne taught school at Courteenhall where his energy was noted by Sir Richard Knightley and William Tate of Delapré who put Bourne in touch with the patron of East Haddon, a vacant benefice.[38] Higher up the social scale several puritans, such as Arthur Wake of Great Billing, Philip Browne of Casterton, Sampson Sheffield of Seaton, and the Fosbrooke brothers could use their own family contacts to secure livings in the diocese.[39]

There emerged a godly brotherhood among the puritan clergy and the godly magistracy of the two counties which was in stark contrast to the poor relations that existed between the bishops and diocesan officials and the gentry of the diocese. Howland complained, shortly after his promotion to the see, that the gentry had in fact wilfully excluded him from the bench of magistrates because the patent had incorrectly given the christian name of his predecessor as bishop.[40] The puritans, for the most part, enjoyed more support from that quarter and though the patronage system was the hinge on which that relationship turned, family friendships and other local contacts did much to sustain the clergy. During his troubles at Preston Capes Robert Smart may have derived some small comfort, and perhaps some financial assistance, from the fact that various members of the Knightley family were godparents to his children. Nor in fairness, was the relationship between the puritan clergy and the gentry always a dependent one, though that was a danger. For example, John Ford of Barby found himself in trouble with his congregation because he sided 'with the rich against the poor.'[41]

Not all the puritan gentry were solely concerned with the social teaching of the puritans with its stress on personal discipline and social orderliness. Neither were they always dominated by political considerations. Regular attendance by the gentry at the exercises, and the careful note-taking by Toby Houghton at the Stamford fast, suggests that the puritan clergy were also looked to as spiritual guides and leaders. None more so than the chief men, Wiburn, Snape, and Fludd.[42] A nice example of the effect that puritan preaching could have on the spiritual formation of a godly gentleman comes from a letter to William Fludd written by Thomas the heir to the Isham estate in 1585. Thomas, who had been plagued by poor eyesight since birth, was at that time 30 years of age and had recently lost two married sisters. The shock of the sudden loss caused Thomas to ponder on the transitoriness of life and of earthly possessions and to turn his thoughts, like Simeon, to his own destiny. From a study of the Bible and other writings Thomas composed a small book which he sent to Fludd for comment, help, and criticism for 'In this you shall find neither eloquent speech, nor excellent matter, yet the truth as I trust rudely disclosed. And for as much as I have heard of your great learning and judgement (though I have some familiarity with other good

[37]P.D.R., Misc. Bk. ix, f. 89v.; H.I.L., v. 43.
[38]P.D.R., Misc. Bk. ix, ff. 92v., 103v.; P.R.O., E134/36 Eliz. H. 10.
[39]V.C.H. Rutland, ii. 215, 237; H.I.L., xiv. 113.
[40]B.L., Lansd. Ms. 52/68, f. 197.
[41]Ibid., Sloane Ms. 271, f. 72v.; P.D.R., Archd. Vis. 7, f. 130v.
[42]See above pp. 45–47.

men) yet I have made a special choice of you before the rest to peruse this my labour, knowing your diligent pains in such things . . .' He finished by comending his 'bungerly' work to Fludd and others 'of great skill to judge thereof' with regrets that 'though the professing of the word of God belongeth to all men, I am not one of those that are called to teach in God's church, but of the idle sort of people (the more is the pity) nowadays termed gentlemen.'[43] Isham's piety was not unique, nor was his respect for the learning of his clerical leaders. The preachers could influence the lay magistracy and their advice was often sought and sometimes heeded. Their power would never be as great as that of the squire who sought to hold sway over the opinions of his subordinates, but the success of puritan evangelization depended on a sharing of responsibility between minister and gentleman. Such sharing was at the centre of Calvin's consistory at Geneva and constantly referred to in puritan literature. There were of course ambiguities and disagreements as to the precise role of each partner, and these remained unresolved as long as the puritans were denied executive power. The godly magistrates, however, did accept their responsibilities within their own communities, and it is their contribution in this sphere which now requires examination.

[43]N.R.O., Isham Correspondence, 3480; Finch, *Five Northants. Families*, 25 and pedigree at end.

# 7 THE PURITAN GENTRY

THE landowning class in the diocese have hitherto occupied the background of the story and readers might be forgiven for seeing puritanism as an essentially clerical movement. Indeed, during the *classis* experiment it threatened to become so among the presbyterians, but the social and political ramifications of puritanism and the social structure of England ensured that the gentry would be involved. Assessment of the impact of puritanism on the governing classes in the region depends upon a study of local office-holding and faction, and of the personal relationships of the puritan gentry. As has been suggested the diocese, and in particular the county of Northampton, was 'favoured or embarrassed with eminent men' who sought to take part in local affairs, as well as in national politics. Apart from government service, the principal national platform for the gentry was in parliament and the representation of the county and borough seats in the diocese reflects the growing strength of puritanism in the area. At the pinnacle were the county seats which in Northampton were dominated by puritan supporters; Sir Walter Mildmay was often returned for the county and in 1588 was joined as member by Sir Richard Knightley. In that parliament the county had a representative of the moderate reforming wing of puritanism and also, in Knightley, an aggressive and politically active radical closely connected to the presbyterian *classes* and soon to be involved in the production of the Marprelate tracts, one of which was printed at his home in Fawsley. Other puritans to represent the county were more of Mildmay's stamp and included Thomas Cecil. The only anti-puritan to be elected during the period was Sir Christopher Hatton member for the county in 1572, 1584, and 1586 and he, despite his views, remained on close terms with Sir Richard Knightley and is known to have entertained an unimpressed John Dod at his palatial home at Holdenby.[1] In Rutland the Harrington family dominated local politics and its members were regularly returned for one of the county seats, usually in the company of Sir Andrew Noel, the only other gentlemen of comparable status in the county and brother-in-law to Sir John Harrington. That these men were returned to parliament was not due to their puritanism, but their pre-eminent social position. The puritans were keen to ensure that good men entered parliament to support their attempts at reform, but there is no suggestion that they needed to lobby for the county seats. The only evidence we have for a disputed election comes from Rutland in 1601 when Sir Andrew Noel, who was unfortunately sheriff and thereby barred from parliament, tried to secure the election of his nineteen-year-old son as second member. The Harrington family would not tolerate this and proposed that Sir John be accompanied by his brother, Sir James Harrington of Ridlington, as county member. This was not an attempt at a puritan coup, but in the lengthy law suits that followed it was

[1] J. E. Neale, *The Elizabethan House of Commons* (1963), 30. Details of particular elections here and below come from the files of the History of Parliament Trust; I am grateful to the former secretary Mr E. L. C. Mullins for allowing me access to them.

claimed by the Harringtons that Noel had sought the support of the catholics among the freeholders to elect his son. That sort of canvassing merely aggravated the situation. Religion may have been totally absent at the beginning of the dispute, but once litigation started parties often did align on religious grounds, and puritans quickly reacted against any attempt at consorting with the recusants.[2]

The borough seats were more open to influence by individuals or groups, and in the diocese that influence was puritan. At Northampton, where the two members were elected by the mayor, burgesses and common council, a succession of puritan champions were returned. Those in the earlier part of the period were associated with the politically active group around the Earl of Leicester, and included Sir Richard Knightley, Thomas Catesby of Whiston, and Peter Wentworth. Later on the most influential member was Sir Christopher Yelverton, who had recently settled his family at Easton Mauduit.[3] At Peterborough the bishops held some sway and their relations or diocesan officials were often returned for one seat. The other seat was usually in the gift of the Cecils whose kinsmen were often returned. Among them was Sir William Fitzwilliam, related to the Cecils through marriage into the puritan Cooke family of Essex, a family with ramifications which included several of the lay puritan leaders in the early part of Elizabeth's reign. At Brackley and at Higham Ferrers the influences at work are not so clear, though at the latter the Mildmay and Montague families seemed to dominate by the end of the century.[4] Puritan activism in the matter of parliamentary elections was most in evidence in the county town, but the strength of the puritans ensured that their presence was felt elsewhere. Another test of the determination of the puritans to use parliament is the extent to which local puritan gentry sought out seats elsewhere. The election of William Lane and William Tate to distant boroughs in 1593 has already been noted, but other puritans were equally active. Two Dorset livings in the gift of the Earl of Bedford, Poole and Dorchester, were held in succession by George Carleton of Wollaston in 1570 and 1571. Thomas Andrews of Charwelton and George Cope of Canons Ashby were members for Sudbury (Suffolk) and Ludgershall (Wilts) in 1563. All of these men were later associated with the Earl of Leicester and with Sir Richard Knightley and represent the more political wing of puritanism. Sir Richard's son, Valentine, represented boroughs as far apart as Tavistock (Devon) in 1584 and Dunwich (Suffolk) in 1601. At the latter date Sir Richard himself had to suffer the indignity of seeking another Suffolk borough, Orford, being unable to find a more local place.[5]

This group represented the parliamentary champions of the puritans in the years up to 1590. Wentworth and Knightley were among the leaders of the puritan choir which regularly asked for far-reaching reforms of the church at successive parliaments. The vigour with which they pursued their aims led Peter Wentworth to imprisonment in 1587, 1591, and 1593 and to a place in the history of liberty and free speech. Their insistence on the rightness of their cause antagonized the Queen and they also encountered opposition from otherwise sympathetic figures such as Mildmay and Burghley who, however much

[2]Neale, *op. cit.*, 122–132.
[3]Sir Gyles Isham, *Easton Mauduit and the Yelvertons* (1962); *The Borough Records*, ii. 494–495.
[4]Neale, *op. cit.*, 218–219; Finch, *Five Northants. Families*, 105; both Sir William Cecil and Sir Nicholas Bacon married daughters of Sir Anthony Cooke.
[5]History of Parliament Trust.

they might support puritan ministers, defended government action and helped to maintain that uneasy alliance between Crown, parliament, and the local community. Once in parliament the puritan gentry did not let their ministers down, but that history has already been recounted and does not really apertain to the local narrative.[6]

*County society and office-holding*

The parliamentary gentry shared the government of the county with the local aristocracy, but puritans were few in number among this last group. The diocese was not dominated, as were Leicestershire and Norfolk for much of the period, by a particular aristocratic family. The Vaux family of Harrowden remained catholic throughout the period and the Mordaunts of Drayton and Turvey (Beds) were associated with recusancy for most of the period. The Vaux family took no part in local affairs after the 1570s.[7] Henry, Lord Compton, was no friend to the puritans either and took great pains to remove the puritan Nicholas Williamson from the benefice at Castle Ashby. Elsewhere Compton's chaplain at Oakham was at loggerheads with his parishioners over the exercise located in the town.[8] Puritans did of course receive support from two families ennobled during the period, the Cecils and the Harringtons, but aristocratic support also came from two other sources, one resident the other not. The latter was of course Robert Dudley, Earl of Leicester, whose activities as a puritan patron have recently been recorded at length. His links with the parliamentary gentry have already been discussed, and his influence was most strongly felt at Northampton and at Towcester where he helped to establish a lectureship.[9] The resident aristocrat was Edward, Lord Zouche of Harringworth. His family had secured a puritan centre at nearby Warmington and he himself had taken the lead in supporting the fast held at Stamford in 1580. Zouche had been to Gray's Inn where a number of the gentry of the county had also made early contact with puritanism, but puritan hopes in him were to be disappointed. His matrimonial difficulties after 1582 were a set-back to his career, and his local influence was reduced by a six-year period abroad after 1587 and by five years as President of the Council of the Marches between 1602 and 1607. Zouche did still intervene on the side of the puritans in local disputes and in 1594 took the lead in demanding the removal of Walter Baker, incumbent of Barby, for simony. Baker was deprived and the congregation provided with a puritan incumbent, Simon Rogers, presented by William Hinton of Coventry, who had received a grant *pro hac vice* from Lord Zouche. Such help was very valuable, but it was not of the same sort of order as that associated with puritan magnates elsewhere, such as the Earl of Huntingdon or the Earl of Bedford, who were able to use their influence to dominate the religious temper of the counties where they lived and had estates.[10]

[6]Neale, *Elizabeth I and her Parliaments*.

[7]G. Anstruther, *Vaux of Harrowden, passim;* G.E.C. ix. 195–197. Lewis, Lord Mordaunt remained active on a number of local commissions until his death in 1601, but his son Henry was implicated in the Gunpowder Plot. For Lewis's activities see SP. 12/112/7; 118/4; 148/33 and Hist. Mss. Com., *Buccleuch Mss.* iii. 51, 55. For Leicestershire see M. C. Cross, *The Puritan Earl*, 122–142, for Norfolk see A. Hassell Smith, *County and Court, Government and Politics in Norfolk, 1558–1603* (Oxford, 1974), 24–25.

[8]G.E.C., ix. 197, he was father-in-law to Henry, Lord Mordant. Peel, *The Seconde Parte*, i. 241; P.D.R., Misc. Bk. viii, f. 75; X648/1, f. 109.

[9]See above p. 26 and below p. 121.

[10]G.E.C., xii (pt. 2), 949–952; Hist. Mss. Com., *Salisbury Mss.*, ii. 332; Sheils, 'Some Problems', *Continuity and Change*, 182.

It was the group of gentlemen associated with the Earl of Leicester that were responsible for the invitation to Percival Wiburn in 1570 which began what has been described as the 'religious revolution' which swept through the area in the following five years. Yet what is known of the aristocracy and from the report of Bishop Scambler on the justices of the county in 1564, religious conservation was the chief characteristic of the local leadership in the years following Elizabeth's accession.[11] There were in fact several prominent families attached to the old religion whose catholicism was revived by the missionary activities of the 1580s. Most notable among them were the Treshams of Rushton, the Griffins of Dingley, and the Digbys of Stoke Dry in Rutland. The religious affiliations of these families prevented them from playing a full part in local politics and other families of equivalent status, such as the Brudenells of Deene, the Catesbys of Ashby St Ledgers, and the Fermors of Easton Neston, included catholic members. Indeed several of them were implicated in the Gunpowder Plot of 1605.[12] In addition to the more substantial families there were minor gentry like the Prices of Tansor, the Charnocks of Wellingborough, and the Pultons of Desborough, who remained catholic for much of the period. Most of these families resided in the eastern part of the diocese, and it is important to see that the connections between the puritan gentry of the county, from magnates like Knightley to lesser men like John Fosbrooke, were paralleled by a similar set of relationships among the recusants.[13]

Proximity to recusant families may account for the vigour with which some puritan gentry pursued their aims. The diocese was not a puritan country estate where men like Sir Richard Knightley met no opposition. The gentry inviting puritans into their midst in 1570 were indeed trying to bring about a religious revolution in the area, for the power of popery and superstition was all too obvious to them. George Carleton could write to Burghley in 1572 dividing the population of the realm into three types of subject; the papist, the atheist, and the protestant. The first two were not only to be misliked, but had to be removed from the commonwealth by a government which would 'join with the good to tread the bad under foot or else to yield when that shall end, that the wicked shall devour the godly'. Carleton pointed out that there were a 'great people daily increasing which are professors of the gospel' and suggested that these should be planted in Ulster with grants of lands, in order that they might provide a bulwark against popery. He even named a leader for this group, his servant Robert Smith, and they set off together for Ireland to spy out the land. How far this was Carleton's private brainchild it is hard to say, but other Northamptonshire puritans appear to have been privy to the plan, and, when Smith made a will before setting out on the journey, his overseers were the puritan ministers Percival Wiburn and Arthur Wake.[14] To this little group at any rate, popery was a powerful enemy and one that was clearly in their midst.

[11]*Eliz. Puritan Movt.*, 141–145; M. E. Bateson, 'Original Letters from the Bishops to the Privy Council, 1564', *Camden Miscellany*, ix (Camden Society, New Series, iii), 35–36.

[12]Finch, *Five Northants. Families*, 76–92, 151, 163; J. Wake, *The Brudenells of Deene* (1953) 66, 94–98; *Miscellanea* xii (Catholic Record Society, xxii), 121–125; *Recusant Roll no. 2* (ed.) H. Bowler (Cath. Rec. Soc. lvii), 116–118; J. Strype, *Annals of the Reformation ... during Queen Elizabeth's reign* (Oxford, 1824), iii (pt. 2), 452; Hist. Mss. Com., *Salisbury Mss.*, xvii. 539, 569.

[13]See the list in J. Wake (ed.) *The Montagu Musters Book* (N.R.S., viii. 1935), 225 and also P.D.R. X613/37, f. 5; X612/35, f. 201; X614/38, f. 252v.; X648/1, f. 13v. for examples.

[14]P.R.O., SP. 15/21/121; P.C.C. wills Martyn 23; discussed in *Eliz. Puritan Movt.* 144–145.

Its progress was to be halted by a militia of the 'meetest in godliness and religion, to be framed to the defence of the gospel and preservation of the state'. Clearly feelings were running high in the south of Northamptonshire in the early 1570s, and the reformation still had a long way to go. There were no seasoned protestants of Edward VI's vintage, as there were in Kent, to lend support to this younger generation of puritan gentry or to curb their enthusiasm by reference to practicalities. The crisis years of 1574–1576 did that.[15]

One important foundation of the puritan state in the writings of the 1570s was the godly magistrate who, in company with the ministers, ruled the commonwealth. The stress on the magistrates' role placed a responsibility on the puritan gentleman which may have predisposed him to play a part in local government.[16] One practical way of ensuring the continuation of the reformation was to place local affairs in the hands of the puritans and to remove catholics from the bench. The commission of peace in Northamptonshire was relatively stable throughout the period. The catholics in the county were mostly removed from the commission by the middle of Elizabeth's reign, Vaux and Tresham made no appearance on the list between 1578 and 1603 but Edward Griffin of Dingley remained a little longer and was even pricked as sheriff in 1582.[17] In Rutland the catholics retained their places for longer periods, Kenelm Digby, George Mackworth, and Henry Herenden were all magistrates in 1580 and, despite their catholicism, all were subsequently sheriffs of the county. Their ability to remain on the bench may have been due, as in Sussex and Cheshire, to the valuable experience they had in local government and the shortage of suitable candidates able to take their place.[18] In Northamptonshire there was no such shortage and the puritan gentry seized the opportunity to take a leading part in local affairs. This they had achieved by 1584.

Among the 30 local commissioners of the peace in 1584 were the following known puritan sympathizers; Lord Zouche, Sir Thomas Cecil, Sir William Fitzwilliam and his son, Sir Robert Lane, Sir Richard Knightley and his son, Sir Edward Montague, Anthony Mildmay, Christopher Yelverton, Bartholomew Tate, Edward Cope, John Wake, George Lynne, and John Isham. Their commitment to puritanism varied but their numbers suggest that the gentry had already brought about something of a revolution among their peers at least. The proportion of puritans on this bench was significantly higher than elsewhere. This was of course the year of Whitgift's translation to Canterbury and one of crisis for the puritan clergy of the diocese.[19]

The extent to which the puritans dominated the commission was emphasized by Bishop Howland's report on the justices, made in 1587. In contrast to the return of Scambler in 1564, when religious conservatism was the chief problem,

[15]P. Clark, English Provincial Society from the Reformation to the Revolution (1977), 88–98, 151–152, 169.

[16]See the comments by Hassell Smith, County and Court, 231, 338.

[17]P.R.O., SP 12/121, f. 22. In 1605 Tresham was reported as saying 'he had been kept from the face of his country, and had not been in any commission there these xxiiij years . . .' SP 14/14, examination of William Cayworth. P.R.O. Lists and Indexes no. ix, List of Sheriffs (repr. 1963), 94.

[18]P.R.O. Lists and Indexes no. ix, 113–114; P.R.O., SP 12/133/10; B.L., Lansd. Ms. 54/75, f. 179. For Sussex see R. B. Manning, Religion and Society in Elizabethan Sussex, 241–253, esp. his assessment of affairs in 1587, 259; for Cheshire see R. B. Manning, 'The Making of a Protestant aristocracy; the ecclesiastical commissioners of the diocese of Chester, 1550–98', B.I.H.R. xlix, 60–80.

[19]List printed in J. H. Gleason, The Justices of the Peace in England 1558–1640 (Oxford, 1969), 168.

Howland reported *a propos* Edward Cope of Canons Ashby that he was 'an honest gentleman, but that he doth over greatly countenance such preachers as do impugn all orders established. Which some others also in this commission do.' He named no names, but as the commission had changed little since 1584, one need not look far. Cope was removed from the commission for a while as were other puritans such as Valentine Knightley and William Fitzwilliam. Both of them lost their place following Burghley's directive that fathers and sons should not both sit on the commission, an order re-enforcing an earlier decision of the Privy Council which had remained something of a dead letter.[20] Despite the uncovering of the *classes* and the Marprelate scandal the puritans remained on the commission, and those removed in 1587 soon returned. They remained because it was among the puritans that the local expertise in county government was to be found; eight of the puritan J.P.s in 1584 had attended one of the Inns of Court, and nine of them had had experience in parliament. They were among the élite of the commission.[21]

It was not until the reign of James that puritans found themselves removed from the commission for their religious views. After the petition on behalf of the deprived ministers in 1605, the ringleaders were put out of the commission for a while. Sir Richard and Sir Valentine Knightley, Sir Edward Montague, Sir William Lane, and Erasmus Dryden, were removed but were soon restored. The puritan justices were again threatened in 1608, by which time their opponents were gaining in representation on the bench. By 1610 the Northamptonshire commission had grown in size, but the attempt to counter the influence of the puritans had not yet created the huge, divided bench which was at the centre of county faction in the 1620s.[22]

The magistracy was the traditional vehicle of local government, and membership of the bench was an ambition of most gentlemen, but it is difficult to determine which of the justices were the most involved and influential in its affairs. Wealth and experience were important factors in this, but the determination of an individual to play a full part could give him influence over and above his station. It has already been suggested that, by the mid 1580s, the puritan gentry formed an élite among local officials, and this is borne out by examining the other commissions and offices related to the governance of the shire. In these commissions, most notably these concerned with subsidies and musters, a group of 10 or 12 gentlemen emerge as the leaders of local society. The commissioners for musters were responsible for the local militia until the appointment of a lord lieutenant for Northamptonshire in 1585. During the 1570s, the commissioners numbered as many as 15 but from 1580 there were only seven commissioners, Lord Mordaunt, Sir Walter Mildmay, Sir Thomas Cecil, Sir William Fitzwilliam, Sir John Spencer, Sir Richard Knightley, and Sir Edward Montague. All of them, with the exception of Mordaunt and Spencer, were puritans and most of the work devolved on Knightley, Montague, and Spencer. With the appointment of Hatton as Lord Lieutenant these three were made his deputies. After Spencer's death in 1586 Sir Thomas Cecil was made third deputy and in 1590 a fourth was added when Sir George Fermor was appointed. The work however was carried out for the most part by Knightley and Montague who,

[20]Strype, *Annals of the Reformation*, iii (pt. 2), 452; Hassell Smith, *County and Court*, 84.
[21]Gleason, *Justices of the Peace*, 168; the emergence of a small influential group of J.P.s was also noticeable on the Norfolk bench, Hassell Smith, *op. cit.* 114–116.
[22]Hist. Mss. Com., *Montague Mss.*, 45–46; P.R.O., SP 14/12/95; Gleason, *op. cit.*, 174–179.

until the latter's death in 1601, were rarely far from the centre of local affairs.[23] They were the very essence of the puritan godly magistrates and the career of Knightley illustrates the contribution one man could make. An early convert to puritanism he was one of the governors of the property of the ministers of the gospel in Warwickshire in the late 1560s. His early association with the Earl of Leicester has been noted and his alliance with the puritan party in parliament remained throughout the period, in 1586–1587 he sat on a commons' committee for the redress of grievances of ministers of religion who were required to subscribe to offensive articles of religion. A patron of *classis* members, a host to the Marprelate press, and one of the organizers of the petition of 1605, his commitment to puritanism was radical and open. Moreover, his marriage to the widow of Protector Somerset involved him in that most sensitive of Elizabethan issues, the succession. Nevertheless, associated with this was a long career of local service; he was sheriff of the county on three occasions, 1568, 1581, and 1589, was M.P. for the county twice and for the county town on two further occasions. A regular member of the bench he was a J.P. of the *quorum* from 1580, was deputy-lieutenant of the county from 1586, a regular fixture of the musters' commission and on several other commissions for specific local causes. His zeal led to a fine for his part in the Marprelate tracts and in the 17th century he was removed from the commission of peace for a short time, but for the most part his opposition to government ecclesiastical policy did not prevent an outstanding record of public service to his county for half a century before his death in 1615 at the age of 82.[24]

Knightley's activities as muster commissioner and deputy-lieutenant have been the subject of a recent publication by the Northamptonshire Record Society. He and Montague were given considerable latitude by the Lord Lieutenant Hatton, whose career at court did not give him much time to attend to local matters. It was work which, despite the problems of raising the necessary levies from his fellow gentry, was congenial to the puritans, for much of their time was concerned with the need to prepare against threatened Spanish invasions in support of the Counter-Reformation. After 20 years or so at the helm of county government the puritans were jealous of their rights and privileges. In East Anglia it has been suggested that puritanism influenced the attitude of the local justices against innovations in local administration and the puritans were generally found to be in opposition to government patentees. In Northamptonshire the problem was not so clear cut, but some issues revealed deep-rooted tensions. The attempt to impose on the county a relative newcomer, Arthur Throckmorton, as supervisor of militia at the muster of 1601 was greeted locally with vociferous opposition. Not only did they object to Throckmorton but they accepted Robert Cecil's challenge to find someone more suitable, recommending the puritan Sir William Lane in his place. The argument was, of course, not about religion, but about the right of the provinces to safeguard their traditional privileges against encroachment from central government. From the 1590s government, by the use of patents of monopolies and other prerogative devices, tried to circumvent traditional privileges. Financial need

[23]J. Goring and J. Wake (eds.), *Northants. Lieutenancy Papers, 1580–1614* (N.R.S. xxvii, 1975), pp. xviii–xix; P.R.O., SP 12/118/4; 96/12.
[24]Goring and Wake, *op. cit., passim*; P.R.O., SP 12/44/72; 19 f. 12; 121 f. 22; 150/42. Hist. of Parliament Trust, files; O. Barron, *VCH Northamptonshire Families*, pedigree of Knightley; W. Pierce, *An Historical Introduction to the Marprelate Tracts*, 167–173;*A.P.C.* xiv. 224, 293, xxi. 422; xxiii. 252–258.

**Map 2**  Principal Residences of the Puritan Gentry.

and the faction at court provoked by the Earl of Essex were the principal motives behind this, and the puritans remained its chief opponents. As leaders of local society they saw themselves as the protectors of its privileges.[25] When central government chose to use its prerogative in the ecclesiastical sphere, it was the threat to local custom in addition to the religious consequences which roused the gentry to action. This is what happened in 1605.

The attempt to enforce the Canons took no account of the religious temper of the diocese, and the gentry were moved to solid opposition. Previously when puritan clergy were under attack individuals found support from their gentry patrons or their associates, but their interests had not previously been identified with those of the whole community.[26] In 1574 the puritans were still too few for this to have occurred; in 1584 compromise on the part of the government averted such a confrontation, and in 1589 the exclusively clerical nature of the *classes* and the scurrilous sequel of Marprelate made the gentry wary of open support. In 1605, however, there was no doubt among the leaders of local society that 'the good of the church and the country [*sic* county] in which we serve' was at stake and the unity of the county threatened. The decision was taken to petition the King. The petition was drawn up by a long-standing puritan champion Sir Francis Hastings. Hastings was a brother of the puritan third Earl of Huntingdon, the apostle of Leicestershire, and had served with Knightley on parliamentary committees. The petition is couched in pious phrases, but clearly expressed local fears.

> We your Majesty's loyal and true-hearted subjects, Justices of the peace and gentlemen within your highness' county of Northampton, finding just cause to fear the loss of many a learned painful and profitable minister, if the execution of this late decree for subscription and conformity should proceed (as in part it is begun) to the deprivation and suspension of many of our most learned and profitable teachers, do not (pressed thereunto) but of ourselves most willingly in regard of the good of the Church of God (the comfort of your subjects there) with all reverence upon our knees prostrate ourselves at your Majesty's feet, and most humbly beg and crave of your highness that the hand of your kingly favour may be stretched out to moderate the extremity of this decree, which otherwise is like to deprive us and thousands of your local and true hearted people of the labours of many faithful preachers... that these men for whom we sue have laboured long amongst us, with great pains and faithfulness profitted us and many of your subjects, by their conscionable and sincere teaching confuted papisme, repressed Brownism and all other schismatical and heretical opinions carefully, beaten down sin and impiety powerfully, and have proved lights of great comfort and furtherance to us and all others your Majesty's subjects within their several charges both by their doctrine and example.

Moreover some had been workers 'in this part of the Lord's harvest' for upwards of 20 years, undisturbed in their valuable ministry. The petition was signed by 45 gentlemen, who also put their names to a letter authorizing Sir Edward Montague, Sir Richard Knightley and his son Sir Valentine, who were all attending parliament, to present the petition to the Privy Council and King

[25]Goring and Wake, *op. cit.* pp. xvii, xxii–xxvii; Hassell Smith, *County and Court*, 231; Hist. Mss. Com., *Salisbury Mss.*, xi. 224–225, 257, 464–465. For an earlier dispute in 1599 see J. Wake (ed.) *Musters, Beacons, and Subsidies, 1586–1623* (N.R.S. iii. 1926), p. lxxxvii.
[26]See above pp. 28–32, 48–51.

on behalf of all of them.[27] This they did in the company of Sir William Lane. It went to the council first, on Sunday 17 February 1605, who demanded that the wording be altered in some respects and required two petitioners to sign a submission of their fault to the King. Sir Edward Montague objected to this but his account of the affair shows that the deputation was divided. He wrote

> the next morning we attended the Lords' again, where I submitted myself to his Majesty's mercy and their lordships good pleasure. The rest did the like. Then the Lords asked if we would not do as much as we had done yesterday. I denied it for my part, some or most of the rest yielding, yet at the length, by the persuasion of my companions, and because I would not be singular, and could not tell how it might be taken, I yielded likewise to that. Then the Lords asked for it [a submission] but we told them it was defaced, but Sir William Lane had a copy fair wherein certain words were added, which he acquainted us withall, and then the Lords demanded of us if we would subscribe to that, which I refused. Sir Richard and Sir William subscribed. Sir Valentine had respite given him till Sunday following. Then I was censured to be put out of all commissions for his Majesty's service and to depart into the country . . . Sir Valentine at the time, refusing to subscribe, was censured as I was.[28]

The strong reaction of the Council, which dealt with Sir Francis Hastings in the same way as Montague and also committed Sir Erasmus Dryden to Fleet prison, took the petitioners unawares. The puritans, confident of their local support, underestimated the determination of the government to force the Canons through to deprivation. The affair was further complicated by the so-called Bywater plot in which Thomas Bywater, a clerical associate of the London puritan Stephen Egerton, distributed a broadsheet critical of government policy and was imprisoned. He was assisted by a minor Northamptonshire gentleman, Lewis Pickering of Irthlingborough who provided the link with the petition from the county for he implicated in the plot the veteran minister Thomas Stone of Warkton, describing him as 'preacher' to Sir Edward Montague (d. 1601), father of the petitioner.[29]

The long-term consequences of the petition were, as usual, less drastic; the gentlemen were soon restored to their commissions, Sir Richard Knightley continued as Deputy Lieutenant, and Sir Edward Montague was chosen by parliament at the end of 1605 to move the speech of thanksgiving for delivery from the Gunpowder Plot.[30] The signatories of the petition, which displayed a bias towards the south and west of the county, were not eclipsed in local politics. Eleven of them were on the commission of the peace for 1608 and four,

[27]P.R.O., SP 14/12/96, quoted in full in M. C. Cross, The Letters of Sir Francis Hastings (Somerset Record Society, 1969), 88–89.

[28]Hist. Mss. Com., Montague Mss. 45–46.

[29]R. Winwood, Memorials of affairs of state in the reigns of Queen Elizabeth and King James I (1725), ii. 48; P.R.O., SP 14/12/95; Hist. Mss. Com., Salisbury Mss. xvii. 114–115, 124–126, 270–271, 619–623; Bridges, ii. 388. Pickering deserves some attention as one of the minor or parish gentry who did much to keep the differing puritan communities in touch with one another. He may have been sent by the local puritans as an unofficial representative to Edinburgh after the death of Elizabeth. At that time the local puritans were fearful that the catholics would seize the initiative with the new king; Usher, Reconstruction of the English Church, i. 294. Whether he was used wittingly or not by the gentry he represents a point of contact between the respectable and more radical wings of puritanism similar to that represented by Robert Welford, see below pp. 128–129.

[30]Hist. Mss. Com., Buccleuch Mss. iii. 121; Montague Mss. 49.

William Samwell, Thomas Elmes, John Isham, and Euseby Andrews served as sheriff of the county before 1620.[31] Many of them were linked to Knightley, Montague, or Lord Zouche by marriage. The petition marked both an end and a beginning. It showed the strength of puritan support among the county governors and it also marked the first public declaration by hitherto unknown families of their support for puritanism and provincial privilege; William Samwell, William and Robert Pargiter, Nicholas Woodhall, Thomas Elmes, and John Blencowe were all members of families later to be involved in the disputes of the 1620s and 1630s.[32]

## Faction

One of the concerns of the petitioners was for the 'unity' of the county, but faction was an ever present feature of local politics in Elizabethan England. Disputes over enclosures, land settlements, the rights of various office-holders and a variety of other contingencies were heard before the local sessions, at the assizes, and before the equity courts of Star Chamber and Chancery. The reasons for the disputes were several and it is difficult to disentangle religion from the other forces at work in society. There are two main problems; firstly, was religion itself a divisive force in local society? Secondly, when other issues arose, such as disputes over land, did the protagonists divide on religious lines, as was suggested by Harrington when referring to the role of the catholics in the Rutland parliamentary election of 1601? The presence of a hard core of recusant families in the diocese was itself a source of faction. It has already been suggested that it may have coloured the views of the puritan gentry, but even allowing for this it created problems. During the years following 1581 the local justices were continually asked to make returns of catholic sympathizers, and this task involved them in a variety of disputes. In 1581 Sir Walter Mildmay, Sir Edward Montague, and Sir Henry D'Arcy were ordered to search the homes of Lord Vaux, Sir Thomas Tresham, Sir Edward Griffin, Sir William Catesby, and Mr Price for priests, and a similar request was made to Montague in 1586. At that time Sir James Harrington and Sir Andrew Noel were to make search in Rutland, with the help of those justices 'well affected in religion'. The Northamptonshire justices complained of lack of cooperation from the recusants at that time and good relations were difficult to maintain.[33] The attempted assassination of the Queen by Anthony Babington and his associates aggravated the situation, and Sir Richard Knightley was responsible for arresting some of the conspirators living in the south-west of the county.[34]

The leading gentry of the county may have been unwilling to act against their peers, but the enforcement of the recusancy laws among the minor gentry resulted in considerable friction. As deputy lieutenants and J.P.s the leading gentry were involved in these disputes and in 1591 and 1592 Knightley and Montague, together with Euseby Isham, Thomas Mulsho, Sir John Spencer, William Lane, and Bartholomew Tate, were required to adjudicate or bring to

[31]P.R.O., *Lists and Indexes no. ix*, 94; P.R.O., SP 14/12/69; Gleason, *Justices of the Peace*, 170–171.

[32]See A. Everitt, *The Local Community and the Great Rebellion* (1969), 17–18 and the recently completed D.Phil. thesis by J. Burgess for the University of York. I am grateful to Dr Burgess for his comments here. See also *Cabala sive scrinia sacra* (1691) i. 198, for an indication of the extent of religious antipathy in the 1620s.

[33]*A.P.C.*, xiii. 153, 155; xiv. 140; P.R.O., SP 12/189/47.

[34]*A.P.C.*, xiv. 224, 293.

the assizes a number of cases of assault resulting from the implementation of the recusancy laws.[35] At that time the government was equally concerned with the threat posed by the puritans and their alleged involvement in discussions concerning the succession of the Crown. While puritans were searching out recusants, the Privy Council sought the assistance of Sir George Fermor, whose wife was a catholic, to search out the houses of notable puritans like Sir Peter Wentworth at Lillingstone Lovell and Sir Anthony Cope at Hanbury for all books and papers concerning the succession; if resisted he was 'not to fail to break open doors, locks, and such other places'. Cope and Wentworth were long-standing friends of Sir Richard Knightley and Fermor's actions would hardly endear him to his godly colleagues. In the following year a violent quarrel broke out between Fermor and his puritan neighbour, John Wake.[36]

In a letter to Bishop Howland, Sir Richard Knightley, Sir Edward Montague, and Sir John Spencer on 12 November 1592 the Privy Council remarked upon the 'foul outrage betwixt Sir George Fermor and Mr John Wake' committed in the presence of the justices at quarter sessions. They had disturbed the sessions 'with open violence at dinner time' and both were ordered to be removed from the bench. Clearly those present at the affray took sides, for three weeks later the Council wrote to those justices who had not attended the dinner requesting them to adjudicate. The dispute may have arisen from a simple case of assault and both parties were soon restored to the bench, though Fermor was reprimanded for ignoring the prohibition originally made against him. The influence of religion in this dispute was probably minor, but set against recent events and other contemporaneous disputes between puritans and recusants, such as that between Castle Carleton, the son of George, and the Price family of Washingley over the rectory of Wollaston, it is clear that in the early years of the 1590s the county was divided and that religion was a contributory factor.[37]

The divisions may have been of long standing, for a lengthy dispute had erupted in the 1570s which split the county into rival religious camps. The issue itself had little to do with religion and concerned the lands of Sir Thomas Tresham in Houghton, Abington, and Piddington near to the county town. Tresham claimed to have been illegally ousted from these lands by one of his tenants John Robyns. After Robyns' death Tresham re-entered the lands but was faced with an action by Robyns' heir, his son George, at the assizes held in Trinity term 1575, but this was not proceeded with. Tresham started a counter action in Chancery, claiming that he could not get satisfaction from the ordinary processes of the common law and, indeed, the subsequent stages of the case, mostly heard in Star Chamber, involved accusations by each party of attempts by the other to interfere in the procedure of the local courts.[38] In Trinity term 1576 Robyns renewed his action at the assizes but the decision went against him, whereupon he claimed that the jury had been bribed by a recusant tenant of Tresham's, Gilbert Hussey of Oundle. Another writ of *novel disseisin* was sued by Robyns in the summer assizes held at Wellingborough in 1576. On this occasion the writ was issued to one of the coroners, the puritan John Fosbrooke of Cranford. According to one of Tresham's tenants who gave evidence in Star Chamber Fosbrooke exceeded his brief

[35]*Ibid.*, xxi. 311, 354, 360, 368–9, 384, 386, 422, 467; xxii. 190, 546.
[36]*Ibid.*, xxi. 392.
[37]*Ibid.*, xxiii. 286, 333, 367; xxiv. 41, 85, 102–103; 137; P.R.O., STAC 5/C 10/10; 28/23; 50/30.
[38]P.R.O., STAC 5/T 24/20; 14/39; C3/175/11.

for those of the jury which were at the view of Houghton aforesaid were so bent on Robyns side by the persuasion of the said John Fosbrooke, coroner, who did only read and explain the evidences of the said Robyns, as well those that were in Latin and expounded them in English, as also such as were in English, unto to the jury, but did further tell unto the said jury that they had need to have great regard and care to restore the said Robyns to his land again.

Not surprisingly Tresham objected to the coroner's proceedings and brought another action in Star Chamber against Fosbrooke. He further objected to seven of the jurors, among whom were prominent puritans from the lesser gentry such as John Dryden of Canons Ashby, William Matthew of Bradden, and Alexander Travell. Thus Tresham prevented the case from proceeding further, but another attempt was made by Robyns at the assizes in the following year. On this occasion Tresham had taken care to ensure that his supporters acted, and his tenant and neighbour Thomas Vavasour of Rushton issued a writ of *venire facias* empowering the crypto-catholic Sir Thomas Brudenell to empanel a jury. Such a jury was likely to favour Tresham and Robyns realistically chose not to to proceed with the case. Eventually on 11 November 1579 the Star Chamber took the matter out of the hands of the minor gentry of the area and commissioned Tresham's puritan neighbours, Lord Zouche, Sir Edward Montague, John Wake, and Thomas Mulsho to hear the case. This they did, deciding in favour of Tresham. The case had dragged on for more than four years by then and, although the more substantial landowners appear to have remained aloof, progress had been impeded by the tendency of the lesser gentry to align on religious lines, regardless of the issue. Certainly Tresham suspected a conspiracy and claimed that 'the judges of that circuit, also all the puritans and preachers, combined therein against me'.[39]

Contemporaneous with that dispute were a number of other actions in Star Chamber between puritans and their recusant neighbours. John Isham of Lamport was involved in a dispute over the ownership of Lamport rectory with Robert Mallory of Litchborough, gentleman. Mallory was suspected of having catholic sympathies and was a notable absentee from his parish church.[40] Edward Dallyson, the godly squire of Cransley who paid his curate's wages, was also at odds with his catholic neighbours over property. He had sold an estate at Cransley, Marston's Manor, to Giles Barnewell. Barnewell, who lived in the parish, never attended the church and was also involved, as a witness on Sir Thomas Tresham's behalf, in the case against Robyns. Dallyson claimed that he, Barnewell, and a catholic accomplice, Roger Charnock of Wellingborough, had forged documents in order to bring a writ of usury against Dallyson. The outcome of the case is unknown, but Charnock was a notorious litigant, later involved in another land dispute with the puritan Dryden family.[41] Although none of these cases involved matters of religious principle it is clear that, be-

[39]P.R.O., STAC 5/T 24/20; SP 12/96 f. 12; Hist. Mss. Com. *Various Collections*, iii. 98; Finch, *Five Northants. Families*, 73 n. 1.
[40]P.R.O., STAC 5/J 12/28; 16/38; for Mallory's absence from church see P.D.R. X609/21, f. 190; X610/24, f. 159.
[41]P.R.O., STAC 5/D 16/11. Barnewell had given evidence on Tresham's behalf in the case against Robyns, *ibid.* T 24/20, and refrained from attendance at Cransley, his parish church, during the incumbency of the *classis* member Leonard Pattinson, e.g. P.D.R. Archd. Vis. Bk. 7, ff. 10, 99v. For Charnock's refusal to attend church see P.D.R., X609/21, f. 192; X611/31, f. 81v; X612/35, f. 78. He was subsequently party to a Star Chamber case against another puritan George Dryden, P.R.O., STAC 5/D 19/13.

tween 1575 and 1580, in the area in the central and eastern part of the county, where catholics and puritans existed in almost equal numbers among the gentry, there was considerable friction among the rival groups.

In 1584 an attempt by the puritans to secure the appointment of a minister to their liking at Little Oakley added religious commitment to these rivalries. The living was a poor one and had been empty for some time when Robert Norbury was instituted in 1576. His institution was contested locally, and although inducted, he had been unable to take up residence in the parish, living instead with a brother at Bozeat. Oakley was a Crown living and its neglect gave the puritans the opportunity to seek letters of presentation for Richard Baldock. They may have been prompted to do this because of Norbury's undoubtedly catholic associates, one of whom, Owen Ragsdale, was a defendant with him in an exchequer case brought by Baldock. Ragsdale, who styled himself gentleman, lived at Rothwell, and was a friend of Sir Thomas Tresham, whom he named as trustee of a school he endowed there.[42] Whatever the reason for the suit, the puritans were on doubtful legal grounds and Baldock was somewhat irregularly inducted to his new living by Christopher Green, schoolmaster in the household of Sir Edward Montague, on Easter Tuesday 1584. When Baldock attempted to read the articles they were snatched from him by Ragsdale and so started the first of several brawls between rival parties. Baldock's cause was supported at one stage by a company armed with staves from Brigstock, Boughton, and Weekley, including among the gentry William and Thomas Montague, and a Mr Mulsho. Later, the more rational tactic of challenging Norbury's fitness for the office of minister was adopted, and the opinion of a neighbouring cleric, John Backhouse of Thorpe Achurch, was canvassed. Norbury was interviewed by the bishop and, after conference, he left the diocese. The initiative taken by the puritans was of doubtful legality, but once the process was set in motion they successfully removed a clergyman friendly with the catholic gentry of the area.[43]

These cases involved for the most part the minor landowners of the area or younger sons of more substantial households, but the implementation of the recusancy laws sometimes led to friction between puritans and catholics among the county leaders. This was particularly marked in the period between 1586 and 1592, but the success of the leading puritan gentry in controlling local government meant that they could adopt a fairly benevolent attitude towards their catholic neighbours, if not towards their religion. Towards the end of Elizabeth's reign the succession occupied the attention of both puritans and catholics and, as in the election of 1601, religion again cropped up in the background of local disputes. Each hoped for some favours from the new king and were keen to appear as loyal subjects. On the death of the Queen the catholics attempted to sieze the initiative in proclaiming the new monarch, and Lord Mordaunt was successful at Daventry. Sir Thomas Tresham met with sterner opposition when he tried to do the same at Northampton where the puritan governors would have none of it, and one puritan gentleman, Lewis Pickering, rode hot-foot to Edinburgh to greet the new King. In the early years of James' reign the catholics had some success in regaining their position in local affairs, and the puritans were punished for their zeal on behalf of their ministers in 1605. The Gunpowder Plot later that year, in which a number of local recusant families were implicated, put paid to catholic hopes and there was no real threat to the

[42]P.R.O., E 134/27 Eliz. T6; P.C.C. wills, Harrington 4.
[43]Ibid., E 134/27 Eliz. T6; E 8.

position of the puritans in the community after that date.[44] The puritan gentry dominated local society, but to their less exalted brethren, the presence of a wealthy recusant magnate like Sir Thomas Tresham was a constant reminder of the potential threat from popery and he became a focus for the fears of the commonalty. Scaremongering by puritans in Northampton had him leading an armed catholic revolt in 1604, and in 1607 it was on his estates that a celebrated, if ill-fated, agrarian rising took place.[45]

Local disputes were often an opportunity for religious loyalties to harden in the period up to 1590, when the puritans were still in the process of securing their position in local society and when fear of invasion led the government to take vigorous action against recusants. Once that fear receded, and the puritan ascendancy in local affairs was confirmed, the role of religion in local politics is more difficult to trace. That is not to say that it had ceased to be of importance, but rather that the puritans had achieved their aims. When the civil war divided county society a generation later there was a marked tendency to divide once again along religious lines.[46] The level of commitment of the puritan gentry in the diocese to the protestant reformation owed something to the frequent contact that they had with popery as well as to the preaching of their ministers.

## Background and kinship

The universities provided the aspiring clergyman with his education, but for most young country gentlemen a stay at university was less important than time spent in London at one of the Inns of Court. It was there that they met their peers from other counties and acquired that knowledge of the law needed by a local magistrate. They also made their first contact with the varied diversions of the capital and of the court itself, if they had a patron who could gain them entry. The puritan gentry of the diocese were associated in particular with Gray's Inn. In this they followed the lead of the two great local magnates, Lord Burghley and Sir Walter Mildmay, who both went to Gray's Inn and subsequently sent members of their families to attend there. Among the leading county families passing through Gray's were several members of the Knightley family, admitted between 1582 and 1613, the Yelverton family, two generations of the Fitzwilliams, and Edward, Lord Zouche, who was admitted in 1575.[47] Primarily concerned with the study of the law, men did not go to the Inns solely for religion. However, during the 1570s and 1580s the importance of the lectureships and pulpits established in the various Inns was not lost to the puritans; here was an opportunity to meet and influence the leaders of provincial society and the clergy seized their opportunities. At Gray's Inn the students would hear lectures from men like William Charke, preacher in 1574, and Thomas Crooke, preacher in 1581, both of them prominent puritan clerics.[48] Indeed when Fitzwilliam wanted a minister for his living at Etton he took the advice of

[44]G.E.C., ix. 197; Hist. Mss. Com., *Various Collections*, iii. 118–123. See above p. 107.

[45]P.R.O., SP 14/12/96; E. F. Gay, 'The Midland Revolt and Inquisitions of Depopulation of 1607', *Transactions of the Royal Historical Society* (new series, xvii, 1906). For other examples of popular unrest on Tresham estates see Finch, *Five Northants. Families*, 88–89.

[46]Everitt, *The Local Community and the Great Rebellion* (1969), 17–18.

[47]J. Foster (ed.), *Gray's Inn Admission Registers, 1521–1887*, cols. 18, 23, 28, 38, 45, 53, 57, 58, 61, 62, 74, 77, 78, 85, 91, 92, 101, 114, 115, 133.

[48]W. Prest, *The Inns of Court under Elizabeth I and the Early Stuarts, 1590–1640* (1972), 191–192; S. J. Knox, *Walter Travers* (1962), 54–88 discusses the importance puritans attached to lectureships at the inns.

Crooke and placed there Giles Whiting, who had recently been deprived of his Essex living.[49] The contact between the Inn and local puritan leadership was close, but what really clinches the importance of the connection is the extent to which the lesser gentry of the shire were associated with Gray's. The list reads like a litany of those names which have regularly cropped up in the narrative and includes successive generations of the Cope family of Canons Ashby; John Travell, admitted in 1578; William Fosbrooke in 1588; Lewis Pickering of Titchmarsh in 1592; and Joseph Bryan, son of a former puritan mayor of Northampton, who was admitted in 1607. In addition to these were members of the Cleypoole family of Northborough, one of the few fenland parishes with a puritan tradition. The connection with Gray's Inn was marked among the petitioners of 1605, and may have been reflected among puritans in other mid-land shires. Associates of Sir Richard Knightley such as John Hales of Coventry and Francis Hastings, who phrased the petition of 1605, had also been students at the Inn.[50]

The influence of Gray's in guiding and reinforcing the attitudes of the puritan gentry was often strengthened by the kinship ties that emerged between puritan families. These ties could of course be a source of friction too, over a disputed marriage settlement or the terms of a family bequest, and it would be quite wrong to suggest that the puritans deliberately set out to create an infra-structure of family relationships within county society. Several marriage alliances cut right across religious divisions. Isabel Catesby of Whiston, the patroness of Percival Wiburn, was an aunt of Sir Thomas Tresham and the Ashby St Ledgers branch of the Catesby family produced a son who was involved in the Gun-powder Plot with Sir Thomas's son, Francis.[51] Sir Richard Knightley had as his first wife the sister of Sir George Fermor, who was himself on the fringes of the Gunpowder Plot.[52] Marriage among county society usually involved a choice from a fairly limited circle of one's peers in one's own or neighbouring counties. Considerations of economic advantage were often paramount, with religious sympathies not playing a large part in what was essentially a dynastic contract. Marriage into recusant families was ill-advised more because of the economic and social implications of recusancy rather than because of the fear of spiritual contamination. Having said this, it cannot be denied that there were family ties between puritan households, and that these were of importance. Both Sir John and Sir James Harrington were brothers-in-law to Sir Edward Montague (d. 1601), and Sir James' son married a daughter of William Samwell, a signatory of the 1605 petition. Two sisters of Samwell had married Thomas Mulsho of Finedon and Robert Pargiter of Greatworth, both of whom signed the petition of 1605.[53]

Another signatory of the petition, Euseby Andrews of Charwelton, was a son-in-law of Sir Richard Knightley. Euseby's mother was an Isham, and his sister Mary was married to Sir William Lane. Lane's aunt was the wife of the puritan champion, Peter Wentworth of Lillingstone Lovell in Buckinghamshire. It was not surprising to find such families represented in the petition.[54] Also

[49]See above p. 40.
[50]Foster, *Gray's Inn Registers*, cols. 46, 53, 69, 73, 81, 115, 125.
[51]Finch, *Five Northants. Families*, pedigree of Tresham; D.N.B., *sub*. Catesby, Robert; see above p. 26.
[52]Barron, *V.C.H. Northants. Families*, pedigree of Knightley; see above p. 107.
[53]*Visitation of Rutland 1618–19*, 38–39; *Visitations of Northants, 1564, 1618–19*, 115, 194.
[54]*Visitations of Northants, 1564, 1618–19*, 64, 186; T. Blore, *The History and Antiquities of Rutland* (1811), 169.

from that area were Edward Cope and his cousin Erasmus Dryden, whilst from the east of the county were Anthony Palmer of Stoke Doyle, a kinsman of Knightley, and his father-in-law William Watts of Blakesley. The links between other minor gentry in that area, and between them and the puritan clergy, have already been explored.[55]

The ramifications of the puritan families in the county were considerable, but that is not to say that they always displayed a united front in their support for puritanism. The regional differences in puritan activity throughout the diocese have already been noticed, and this was no less true of the gentry than the clergy. Mildmay and Fitzwilliam could never be said to have taken their puritanism into the political arena in opposition to the government, but this was not true of Knightley. He was prepared to oppose government policy vigorously, and with other friends in Leicester's group was involved in discussions about the succession in 1579 which disturbed the government. Marriage to the widow of protector Somerset made Knightley a party to the Hertford–Grey claim to the succession and, although this was never pursued seriously, the catholics attempted to use this against him in 1603. How far Knightley and his friends were moved by political ambition in their support of the puritans has been a problem for several generations of historians. It seems unlikely that they would have kept the trust of both Cecils and of Hatton if there were serious doubts about their loyalty. They retained a vision of a godly commonwealth beyond their immediate locality, and with men like George Carleton they were anxious to ensure its defence. Despite setbacks and disappointments from government their loyalty was never put to the final test and, at the end of the century, Sir William Fitzwilliam was quick to point out that although many puritans had close connections with the Earl of Essex they had remained aloof from his ill-fated revolt. They might remind each other and the government, as did Robert Smith in his will, that 'both prince and people shall give an account to god of their obedience to him and duty to his church' but, for the most part they worked to forward and defend the reformation in their localities.[56] This they did through direct patronage, through the exercise of local office, and through the social and personal influence they could bring to bear on their peers and their inferiors in the community. They were so successful that by the end of the period the puritans could legitimately claim to prepresent the wishes of local society on a wide range of issues. They did indeed form a godly magistracy.

[55]*Visitations of Northants, 1564, 1618–19*, 15, 123, 178, 203.
[56]See Hist. Mss. Com., *Salisbury Mss.*, xv. 223; P.R.O., P.C.C. wills, Martyn, 23.

# 8   A GODLY TOWN: NORTHAMPTON

*Internal history*

THE county town was by far the most important urban centre in the diocese, being approximately half the size again of Stamford on the northern boundary of the diocese. The population of Northampton was close to 3,000 in the early 16th century and the 1524 subsidy assessment listed 63 trades. The most important occupation was shoemaking but other leather trades and textile crafts figured prominently in the economy of the town, which was chiefly an important market centre for the produce of the surrounding countryside and had a cattle fair of national importance.[1] Its government was like that of comparable towns, being oligarchical in structure. Power resided with the mayor and ex-mayors, known as the Twenty-Four or the assembly, and the company of 48 representing the commonalty of the town. The charter of 1599 increased the control of the senior body over the town affairs and appointed J.P.s consisting of the mayor, two burgesses, and the recorder. The office of recorder, requiring as it did legal skills, was held by outsiders and from 1568 was filled by Christopher Yelverton and later by his son Henry. They settled at Easton Mauduit and their sympathy for the puritan cause made them popular with the town and with the ministers in the country.[2]

For most of the period there were four parishes in the town, the most important being All Saints, situated at the market-place. St Peter's served the populous west end of the town near the old castle site; St Sepulchre's the northern area and St Giles' the eastern suburbs of the town. The first stage of the reformation reduced the number of parish churches and removed a number of religious houses, but one survivor, the hospital of St John, situated by the bridge at the southern end of the town, continued to play an important part in the religious life of the community. The control which the oligarchy exercised over the town did not extend to religious life at the start of our period, for three of the urban parishes were in the patronage of the Crown and the advowson of St Peter's was owned by the Morgan family of Heyford.[3] The corporation could not hope to alter the formal structure of ecclesiastical patronage, but the religious history of the community is characterized by their attempts to control local church affairs. In this way they were no different from several other corporations, and their motives were a mixture of religious zeal, urban pride, and a determination to influence all aspects of town life from regulation of trade to the provision of education and the administration of poor relief.

Church affairs became a contentious matter because of the success of puritan

[1]W. G. Hoskins, *Provincial England* (1963), 79; A. Rogers (ed.) *The Making of Stamford*, 60.
[2]*V.C.H. Northants*, iii. 9, 14; *The Borough Records*, i. 119-125; Christopher Yelverton was asked by the puritans to intervene on their behalf in 1603, B.L., Sloane Ms. 271, f. 20v.
[3]*V.C.H. Northants*, ii. 236; iii. 55; *The Borough Records* ii. 335-336, 383; R. M. Serjeantson, *All Saints, Northampton*, 97.

evangelism in the town. The evidence for early protestantism is fragmentary, but the story really began in 1570 with the arrival of Percival Wiburn. The general implications of the order of Northampton, established on 5 June 1571 by the bishop, the mayor, and other justices of the town and country, have already been discussed, but its impact on the town requires some elaboration. The services in the town churches were reorganized to ensure that preaching was an integral part of proceedings and, although the *Book of Common Prayer* was adhered to, psalm singing was to precede and follow the main service. Sunday services in the parish churches were timed to finish by 9 a.m. so that the population could gather at one church to hear a sermon. Attendance at this sermon was compulsory unless the congregation had already heard a sermon in their parish churches. Further lectures were provided at All Saints Church on Tuesdays and Thursdays, the latter being followed by disciplining of faults, for which elaborate instructions were compiled:

> there is also a weekly assembly every Thursday, after the lecture, by the mayor and his brethren, assisted with the preacher, minister, and other gentlemen, appointed to them by the bishop, for the correction of discords made in the town as for notorious blasphemy, whoredom, drunkeness, railing against religion or the preachers thereof, scolds, ribauld, and such like, which faults are each Thursday presented unto them in writing by certain sworn men, appointed for that service in each parish, so the bishop's authority and the mayor's joined together, ill life is corrected, God's glory set forth, and the people brought in good obedience.

The model was clearly Calvin's Geneva and the order was intended to replace the ecclesiastical courts with a more regular and vigorous local discipline involving secular officials also. The association made between preaching the word, glorifying God, and the obedience of 'the people' was a recurring theme in puritan history. The towns of Kent, faced with growing numbers of poor and vagrants, were also conscious of the usefulness of locally administered discipline, and puritanism, with its emphasis on the role of local elders and deacons, provided an ecclesiology which suited those needs.[4]

Whether the order was even put into practice remains unclear, for within six months it had been suppressed by the bishop. Nevertheless the Mayor and assembly continued to take an interest in the moral and religious life of the town. Bye-laws enforcing strict observance of the Sabbath were issued, and on 7 June 1582 an order was made forbidding anyone to open a shop on Sunday during sermon time on pain of a fine of 3s. 4d. Refusal to pay the fine led to committal to the town jail for three days, and this also applied to any inhabitants found in the offending shop who were liable to a fine of 12d. At least one innkeeper was fined for illegal opening and his money donated to poor relief. When the matter came to imprisonment the assembly was on more difficult ground. On one occasion their right to commit offenders was challenged at law by one Owen Jackson, who had been imprisoned for not attending church and for disturbing the preacher. Jackson brought an action against the mayor at the assizes of 1584 and was successful. The assembly undertook to pay the mayor's costs and sought advice from the recorder, Christopher Yelverton, about an appeal. Unfortunately the outcome is not known, but the episode does show that suppression of

---

[4] A copy of the order is in P.R.O., SP 12/38/138 and they have been printed on several occasions, *V.C.H. Northants*, ii. 38–39; *The Borough Records*, ii. 386–390; Serjeantson, *op. cit.* 104–108.

the order did not prevent the town governors from continuing to enforce a Sabbatarian code on the inhabitants over and above the normal requirements of the law.[5]

The Thursday court also had responsibility for supervising the conduct of the quarterly communions. Notice of a general communion had to be given in the parish church one month in advance, and a fortnight later the clergy and church-wardens were empowered to go from house to house to examine the lives of the communicants. Any discord among neighbours was to be reported to the mayor and his fellow justices who could refuse the sacrament to the offending parties. On the day appointed for the communion two separate services were held, each with a sermon; the first was to last from 5 a.m. to 8 a.m. and was for servants and officers, the other, for the higher ranks in society, began at 9 a.m. and lasted until noon. The communion was to involve four clergy, three to administer the sacrament and another to read from the scriptures. Those who absented themselves from the communion, as did Owen Jackson in 1583, were to be reported to the mayor and justices.[6]

The arrangements were elaborate, and the community was to be divided into its social hierarchy. The order reveals religious fervour and an attention to discipline and orderliness in about equal proportions. Membership was not voluntary and embraced all of the community. Northampton was to become an English Geneva. The bishop realized this quickly and may have had his suspicions aroused by a group of opponents of the order who circulated a scurrilous broadsheet in the town attacking Percival Wiburn. Despite the inter-vention of the Earl of Leicester, Scambler suppressed the order and Wiburn was forced to withdraw to Whiston where Isabel Catesby provided hospitality for him.[7] Within a year the scheme had come to nothing but, although formally disbanded, the order provided a precedent which was not ignored. A tradition whereby the corporation took an active part in the religious life of the com-munity had begun. It is not difficult to see in the order of 1571 an embryonic system of pastors, elders, and deacons. Indeed it was possible to graft the presby-terian model on to the normal offices of churchwarden and remain technically within the law. During the heyday of the *classes* in the later 1580s, this was planned and, although the information is ambiguous, may have been carried out in St Peter's parish at least. One witness before the Star Chamber, a shoe-maker called Richard Holmes, claimed that the election of elders and deacons had been organized in the parish, but was prevented by the arrest of Edmund Snape in 1590. John Johnson, however, gave an example of the discipline in use as early as 1587 when Snape took it upon himself to discipline the daughter of one of his congregation, John Nelson. Johnson did not refer directly to the presbyterian forms, but in the course of the narrative he described Nelson as a deacon, thereby implying that the discipline was established. Like most issues which are on the fringes of the law, it is difficult to establish the truth. It would have been rash to have formally established a presbytery in any parish, but the spirit could exist without the form. Certainly Snape was accustomed to confide in four or five of his more trusted parishioners on matters of wider implication

[5]N.R.O., Minutes of the Town Assembly, 1549–1627, ff. 210v., 218; *The Borough Records*, ii. 552.

[6]P.R.O., SP 12/38/128.

[7]N.R.A., Baskerville Transcripts, De L'isle and Dudley Papers, ii. no. 60; Magdalene College, Cambridge, Pepys Ms., Papers of State, ii. 389–390; 647–648; *An Answer at Large. to a most hereticall, traytorous, and papisticall bill* (Northampton, 1881); *Eliz. Puritan Movt.*, 141–143.

for the puritans, and this parochial élite may have looked upon themselves as a
*de facto* eldership. In this way they would remain within the letter of the law.[8]

The order was thus the first and most comprehensive of a series of experiments
in which the respectable godly set about regulating the moral and religious life
of their inferiors, and the search for a locally based form of discipline continued
among the puritans. The suppression of the order in 1571 was a setback to the
puritans, but within a year they had reasserted their position. The assembly
appointed seven 'cessors for the wage of a minister in All Hallows to teach and
to preach', including two ex-Mayors, Mr Bryan and Mr Manley.[9] In the mean-
time, however, the puritans in the town had been deprived of their spiritual
guide and withdrew from their parishes. It was at the visitation of 1573 that the
authorities got to hear of this. Simon Smith was presented because he 'went to
Whiston on Easter Day last to receive the communion, and despiseth the communion at Northampton'. He was accompanied by parishioners from St
Sepulchre's, where another member of the congregation was refused the communion because he insisted on receiving it while standing. The removal of some
puritan clergy from rural parishes in the neighbourhood following the dis-
coveries in the visitation of 1573 further weakened the position of the puritans
in the town.[10] The assessors were apparently unsuccessful in their attempt to
secure a preacher, and the institution of William Smith to All Saints church in
1574 faced them with a determined opponent, who also acted as a surrogate in
the ecclesiastical courts. The puritans at this time depended on the ministration
of William Dawson, the deprived minister of Weston Favell, who continued
in his puritanism and gathered a group of adherents to services at St James's, a
former house of Austin Canons in the southern part of the town. It was close
by St John's hospital where another puritan, Arthur Wake the deprived minister
of Great Billing, was master.[11]

Smith's ministry at All Saints met with opposition in the town from a number
of puritans later to be involved in the Marprelate tracts and other radical departures. Henry Sharpe, the bookbinder who distributed the tracts in 1589,
appeared before the local ecclesiastical commission because 'he rageth against
Mr Smith and speaketh evil of his doctrine, commenteth upon his sermons and
libelled him'. He also challenged the right of the commission to 'persecute God's
church'. Sharpe may have already been involved in the distribution of puritan
literature, for Thomas Cartwright's *Replye* to Whitgift was said to have been
printed in the county in 1573. This, and his combative nature, probably explains
why Sharpe and one accomplice, Henry Capper, were singled out for the attention of the commission.[12] Other opponents of Smith, including Sharpe's wife,
an ex-mayor called John Balguy, and Henry Godly (later the brother-in-law of
the separatist martyr John Penry) were dealt with by the normal church courts
in 1576. Godly and some others were excommunicated for publicly declaring
their opposition to the *Book of Common Prayer*, but Mistress Sharpe and John
Balguy were merely suspended *ab ingressu ecclesiam*.[13]

The assessors for the wage of a preacher or teacher in the town may have

[8]P.R.O., STAC 5/A 27/33.

[9]*The Borough Records*, ii. 397, 551.

[10]P.D.R., Vis. Bk. 3, unfoliated.

[11]B.L., Lansd. Ms. 443, f. 42v.; Peel, *The Seconde Parte*, i. 121; P.D.R., X607/9, f. 12v.;
*V.C.H. Northants*, iii. 57–58.

[12]P.D.R., X607/9, ff. 6, 14; E. Arber, *An Introductory Sketch to the Martin Marprelate
Controversy* (1879), 94–104; *A.P.C.*, viii. 93.

[13]P.D.R., X608/13, ff. 5, 16, 60v.; P.R.O., SP14/12/96; *The Borough Records*, ii. 139, 551.

acquired the services of Edmund Snape for a short period in the 1570s, and certainly had Francis Merbury as their preacher before 1578, but another tactic open to them was to try and influence Crown appointments to the parish churches. In this they had their first success in 1575 when they secured the services of a former London puritan, Martin Clipsham, as vicar of St Giles.[14] Almost at once defections from St Giles by the congregation ceased and, during his three years there, puritan ideas spread to the neighbouring parish of Abington. Little is known of the details of his ministry, but Clipsham was obviously in contact with the gentry associated with Leicester's group. Soon after his departure, perhaps following deprivation, the Privy Council asked the bishop, with the assistance of William Smith, to examine the disorders in the town. Scambler prevaricated but another letter followed asking him and some of the local justices to take firm action. On the same day, 29 May 1579, the Council asked the mayor John Bryan to send up for examination a certain Mr Flower who had made some inflammatory remarks about the Queen. It was clear that fear of a marriage alliance with the catholic French royal house was behind the trouble, for negotiations with the Duke of Anjou had recently been revived by the government. The threat this posed to the protestant succession aroused the opposition of Leicester's faction and Peter Wentworth was under suspicion. A letter to Wentworth and a reference to Clipsham's 'lewd and heinous words touching her Majesty' indicates the Council's concern. It is clear that there were wild rumours in the town which the Council wanted to stop.[15]

Some puritans in the town may have been made more radical by the suppression of the exercise in 1576, and the fears over the succession would confirm that trend. In addition the arrival of plague in the town in 1578 created an atmosphere of uncertainty which disturbed the unity of the puritans among the town government and the commonalty.[16] A local row sprang up, turning on the attempt by Edward Manley, a former mayor of the town, to disinherit his son of the impropriate rectory of Spratton. Manley had the support of the puritan William Jennings who had succeeded William Smith as vicar of All Saints, possibly on the recommendation of Sir Richard Knightley, but the meddlesome figure of Henry Sharpe appeared on the side of the son. The issue was itself a trifling one, but the confused state of affairs in the town led a sensitive Privy Council to ask Burghley and Sir Walter Mildmay to interrupt a visit to Sir Christopher Hatton at Holdenby in order to sort things out. This was heavy armoury indeed. Jennings had put the High Commission on to Sharpe, already a known radical, but when the messenger came from the court Sharpe diverted attention back to Jennings, claiming that the vicar had in his possession some of the writings of the separatist leader Robert Harrison. On this issue the government was very sensitive and sent down an order prohibiting further action agsinst Sharpe and demanding the removal of Jennings to a more distant and tranquil living in Devon. The vicar was deprived, but did not leave the town at once, being granted a lease of corporation property in 1582.[17]

Clearly the personalities of both Sharpe and Jennings aggravated local ten-

[14]Hist. Mss. Com., *Various Collections*, iii. 3; R. M. Serjeantson, *A History of the Church of St Peter's Northampton* (Northampton, 1904), 25; B.L., Lansd. Ms. 443, f. 223; *H.I.L.* iii. 161.

[15]*A.P.C.*, xi. 93, 132–133, 159, 218–219; for a discussion of puritan reactions to the proposed marriage see *Eliz. Puritan Movt.*, 199–200.

[16]*The Borough Records*, ii. 238, where there is also reference to another coincidence of plague and the attempt to suppress puritan activity in 1638.

[17]*A.P.C.*, xi. 182, 218–219; xii. 194; P.R.O., SP 15/27A/9, f. 14; 15/27A/10 esp. f. 22v; Serjeantson, *All Saints Northampton*, 114; N.R.O., Assembly Minutes, f. 210.

sions. Sharpe is well-known for his involvement in Marprelate, but Jennings was also said to be 'a very busy man, and a medler in many men's matters'. They were both puritans however and although Sharpe claimed that Jennings was 'in points unfit for the profession he is of, being a minister of God's holy word' he added the qualification that he was not 'altogether unfit for the profession thereof'. The concern expressed by the Privy Council suggested that there was more to the matter than two irreconcilable temperaments, and illustrated its sensitivity to the political ambitions of Leicester's faction. Puritan propaganda against government foreign policy had disturbed the unity of the town and. once that had been done, a situation was created in which radical ideas thrived, Unlikely as it seems when discussing the fortunes of a provincial town, it was the failure of the royal marriage negotiations which helped to restore calm to the community. Nevertheless a split had occurred in puritan ranks between the moderates and the radicals which was to reappear in times of stress.[18]

In contrast the years from 1580 to 1588 were ones of relative calm. After the deprivation of Jennings three aldermen of the town visited London 'touching the getting of a minister' and secured as their vicar the puritan John Johnson. A small group of puritans had been regularly presented during the 1570s for attending services at Whiston and objecting to their non-preaching minister. One of their number, Thomas Waylesbie, was acting as an unlicensed school-master and, after Clipsham's departure, he and his friends were joined once more by some dissidents at St Giles' parish. In 1590 one of this group, Magdalene Gybbins, was presented for being married by Francis Foster, vicar of Whiston, in his own home. These small groups of puritans, which included the household of John Kirtland, a prominent townsman and lessee of St George's Hall, are important in that, at a time when All Saints had a puritan incumbent and St Peter's was served by Edmund Snape, they continued to travel the eight miles or so to Whiston where Percival Wiburn had settled. Whether this represented a conscious rejection of the puritan ministers in the town, or a sentimental attachment to the first apostle of the area is difficult to say. Some of them may have objected to the more rigorous clerical presbyterianism of the town ministers, both of whom belonged to the *classis*.[19]

Within the town both Johnson and Snape soon established followings. Johnson had very close links with the corporation and, soon after his arrival, was granted the same rights 'as other freemen'. In November 1585 he was granted an extra ½d. over and above the usual dues paid by those who received the communion at his church and, on 27 June 1588, the assembly redeemed his debts to the sum of £30. The money was paid to his creditors by the chamberlain in yearly instalments of £10 raised by a subscription among 20 of the leading townsmen.[20]

This eloquent testimony to Johnson's standing among the ruling oligarchy came at the time when a rift developed between him and his fellow presbyterians. How far this affected their congregations is difficult to say and, in giving evidence before the Star Chamber, Johnson was probably keen to exaggerate the extent of his estrangement from the *classis*. Snape too was one of the more radical pres-

[18]P.R.O., SP 15/27A/10, f. 15v.

[19]N.R.O., Assembly Minutes, ff. 207v.; 216v.; P.D.R., Archd. Ct. Bk. 4, ff. 2v., 25v.; s. f. 14, 114; ix. f. 9; Archd. Vis. Bk. 7 ff. 6, 94; X648/1, ff. 8v., 20; X608/18, f. 18v.; X609/21, ff. 204v.–05; X609/23, f. 105v.; X610/24, ff. 28v-9. Edmund Skinner joined Snape and Johnson in membership of the *classis*.

[20]N.R.O., Assembly Minutes, ff. 224, 225v.

byterians, and given to forecasting the success of presbyterianism in inflammatory words. He stressed the exclusive tendencies of puritanism, calling the godly a select minority picked out from the 'rude and common multitude'. When he refused to baptize the child of a parishioner because it had a non-biblical name, it was to Johnson at All Saints that the outraged parents went.[21] The uncovering of the *classes* effectively ended the ministries of both men in the town; Snape was removed to London and to prison, and Johnson to a rural parish at Yelvertoft. Johnson's living was secured with the assistance of the townsmen of Northampton, from whom Snape also got support. While in prison he appealed to members of his congregation to join with those of his imprisoned colleagues in organizing petitions on their behalf. This was done at Coventry, Stretton and Wolston in Warwickshire and the inhabitants were summoned to the Privy Council for their trouble. The townsmen of Northampton were not summoned, but they also acted on behalf of their minister. The evidence comes from 17 years later when, on 10 February 1607, Richard Ridge, a mercer, was granted a lease from the corporation 'in response of his time lost and money spent, and trouble that he had by reason of a petition delivered on the behalf of Master Snape in the late Lord Chancellor Hatton, his time'.[22]

The effect of the estrangement between Johnson and Snape, and the subsequent removal of both, on the morale of the puritans in the town was uneven. The petition for the freedom of the town from one Richard Awner suggests that the commonalty reacted more strongly than their superiors. Awner's nominees included Richard Bancroft, the chief prosecutor of the presbyterians, and the commonalty were not prepared, under the circumstances, to allow Awner to be discharged from the customary payment of £10 for the privilege of freedom. The assembly, more cautious in the face of the request from powerful patrons, decided to write to each of Awner's referees, three in all, making it quite clear who was obstructing Awner's request. Whether the caution of the assembly was merely a tactful gesture, or whether the commonalty were prepared to act in a more radical way is difficult to decide.[23] Snape's support was not confined to the burgesses alone but included members of the assembly. John Hopkins a former mayor of the town, left 40s. each to Snape, Francis Merbury, and William Fludd in his will made on 1 July 1588. Over six years later his widow Agnes again remembered Snape in her will and also left 20s. a year for the maintenance of a preacher at All Saints.[24] It would be an oversimplification to suggest that the town was led by a cautious puritan oligarchy and contained a radical commonalty, but it is important to stress that there were puritans of widely differing views in the town among all levels of society. At times of crisis their differences might surface, but for much of the time they were of course in close sympathy with one another.

The effect of the events of 1589–1590 on parochial life in the town can be traced in the church courts. On 16 June 1590 21 parishioners of All Saints were presented for a variety of offences including absenting themselves from the Easter Communion, refusing the same because the schoolmaster Christopher Sanderson (who tended the vacant living) was a dumb minister, for not baptizing their children in the parish, and accusing Johnson's successor, Philip Favor, of preaching false doctrine. Among those so presented were two of

[21]P.R.O., STAC 5/A 49/34, Johnson; A 27/33; B.L. Lansd. Ms. 64, f. 53.
[22]*A.P.C.*, xx. 313–314; *Eliz. Puritan Movt.*, 414; N.R.O., Assembly Minutes, f. 313.
[23]N.R.O., Assembly Minutes, f. 241v.
[24]P.R.O., P.C.C. wills Rutland 58, Dixy 13.

Snape's congregation who had testified against him in Star Chamber John Holmes and Robert Vicars, Richard Ridge and his wife, and two men, Edward Mercer and John Fryer, who were shortly to be elected mayor of the town.[25] The strength of the opposition made Favor glad to seek a living elsewhere, and the puritans soon found a minister to their liking when on 4 October 1591 Robert Catelin 'at the request of the townsmen of Northampton' came as vicar of All Saints.[26] So began a long series of confrontations with the diocesan authorities. He was presented in 1593, 1597, and 1598, for minor offences like breaking the sequestration of the living, not wearing the surplice, and more critically, for allowing a layman to read the service unlicensed. At the accession of James, when Northampton again became a regular meeting place for the puritan clergy, Catelin assumed a major part in their discussions and on 5 November 1603 he was suspended for preaching about certain prohibited matters. A year later some of his opponents in the parish reported him for 'preaching schismatical doctrine' and also presented the churchwardens, the parish clerk, and Simon Wastell, the schoolmaster of the town, for aiding and abetting him.[27] The enforcement of the Canons resulted in Catelin's suspension and he retaliated by locking his church in order to deprive his opponents of access to the pulpit. In 1605 a national crisis in the church again coincided with local unrest brought about by a visitation of plague in the town, only two years after an earlier outbreak. The tensions in the town led to rumours of a general massacre by the catholics, who were to mark the doors of their intended victims, the godly. The leader of the local rising was said to be Sir Thomas Tresham, and the long-suffering conformist vicar of St Giles was also implicated. The source of the rumour was Henry Godly, Penry's former brother-in-law, who was quickly imprisoned by the mayor and justices of the town. A hostile observer, John Lambe, saw in this the reaction of the 'rude multitude' to the campaign against the ministers, 'whereby the simple puritan hath his humour of fear filled up and directed from the right object, and so is the more strengthened in his obstinacy conceiving that he standeth only against the cruelty of the papist for God, for religion, and for his own life'. In his analysis Lambe was shrewd in linking the radical reaction to the Canons' dispute, but was wrong in suggesting that 'the greatest number and strength of the puritans is in the rude multitude'.[28]

The corporation had little sympathy with Godly's scaremongering, but set about restoring their puritan minister in a more practical fashion. During Catelin's suspension they enjoyed the services of a sympathetic minister in William Dale of Moulton, son of the vicar of Montague's parish at Boughton. He was assisted by the schoolmaster Simon Wastell, another local man. The mayor and other leading townsmen wrote to Robert Cecil on 21 January 1605 asking for Catelin's reinstatement. In it they claimed that his suspension had deprived 1,500 communicants of services and complained that the ceremonies being enforced on Catelin had been omitted at All Saints ever since 1570. Clearly it was Bancroft and his assistants who wanted to force innovations on the town and not the puritans. The appeal was successful and Catelin continued

[25]P.R.O., STAC 5/A 27/33; P.D.R., X 610/24, f.38 and v.; B.L., Lansd. Ms. 444, f. 32v.; *The Borough Records*, ii. 552.
[26]P.D.R., Misc. Bk. viii, f. 92v.
[27]*Ibid.*, X610/25, f. 40; 26, f. 246; X611/31, ff. 13, 78, 100, X612/35, f. 248; X613/37, f. 163.
[28]Hist. Mss. Com., *Salisbury Mss.*, xvii, 58; P.R.O., SP 14/12/96; P.D.R., X612/34, ff. 28, 184; X613/37, ff. 70, 149; X614/38, f. 23.

at All Saints until 1613, during which time he was supported in his endeavours by Simon Wastell, who was granted the freedom of the borough in 1607 in recognition of his services.[29] Well might Martin Marprelate challenge the Bishop in 1590 to 'send Mr Wiburn to Northampton that he may see some fruit of the seed he sowed there 16 or 18 years ago' and John Lambe was right to describe the town in 1605 as 'the chief fountain of that humour' when talking of the puritans.[30]

## The hinterland

The economic impact of Northampton on its hinterland has been mentioned, and the influence of the exercise established in the town has been discussed in terms of the clergy of the area. It remains to consider the spiritual influence of such an important puritan centre on the laity of the surrounding countryside accustomed to use its markets for their more material needs. It was the visitation of 1573 which first showed the extent to which puritanism had disrupted the normal parochial structure of services. Bishop Scambler described events at Overstone, $4\frac{1}{2}$ miles north of the county town, where there was

> no divine service upon most Sundays and holydays, according to the Book of Common Prayer, but instead thereof two sermons be preached, most commonly by one Mr Standen and Mr King, men for their opinions not licensed by me to preach at this day. When they are determined to receive the communion they repair to Whiston, where it is their joy to have many out of diverse parishes, principally out of Northampton town and Overstone aforesaid with other towns thereabouts, there to receive the sacraments with preachers and ministers to their own liking . . .[31]

The threat which such activity posed to parochial order and discipline was obvious, and the deprivations of five puritan ministers in 1574 aggravated the situation further. The godly had tried to intervene on behalf of their threatened pastors, for 'the number of those that have been won by preachers are no small number, as it hath appeared when in Billing iij days before the deputation, there did ride to the bishop above xij, coming with them the hands of almost xx more. Likewise did the godly of Collingtree deal with the chancellor,' but they were unsuccessful.[32] From that date small groups of puritans were presented regularly for defecting from the parishes of Collingtree and Hardingstone. At Collingtree the position was later made worse by the institution of William Smith, whose ministry had already aroused the opposition of the puritans in Northampton. During the 1570s groups of godly were also found at Little Houghton, Castle Ashby, and most notably at Abington on the eastern edge of Northampton. The godly in that parish were led by the families of John Ibbs and Richard Leache, and the presentments made against them illustrate the character of their nonconformity. While the menfolk were able to 'gad to sermons' and visit puritan parishes, their wives remained at home and made their stand in their own parish, refusing to kneel at the communion in 1577.

[29]Hist. Mss. Com., *Salisbury Mss.*, xvi. 421; xvii. 26; P.D.R., X613/37, ff. 176v., 199v.; X614/38, f. 208v.; H.I.L., iii. 59; N.R.O., Assembly Minutes, f. 325v.
[30]M. Marprelate, *An Epistle to the Terrible Priests of the Confocation House* (facsimile edn. Leeds 1967), p. 28; P.R.O., SP 14/12/96.
[31]B.L., Lansd. Ms. 17, f. 55; P.D.R., Vis. Bk. 3; X607/7, f. 120v.; 8, f. 2.
[32]Peel, *The Seconde Parte*, i. 122.

Quite often the historian is dependent on the evidence from women to explain the motives behind their husbands' defections from the parish.[33]

Overstone appears to have continued as a local centre until 1580, but thereafter evidence is very sketchy. During the 1580s Whiston and Northampton were the two chief centres of the neighbourhood. The godly at Hardingstone attended All Saints at this time, but the puritans at Abington were able to bring pressure on the patron and secure the services of a puritan minister in their own parish. Half-way between Northampton and Whiston, the parish of Little Houghton continued to be disturbed by a small group of godly. At Castle Ashby a local conflict arose through the attempt of the patron, Lord Compton, to remove the puritan incumbent, Nicholas Williamson. Williamson had been suspended for refusing to subscribe to Whitgift's articles and, in 1586, was presented with 16 of his congregation for not receiving the Easter Communion. Williamson's defence referred to his earlier suspension, which prevented him from entering his church and so administering the sacrament. Later in the year he died and was replaced by a conformist minister, but a substantial minority of the congregation, 18 in all, subsequently took themselves off to other parishes for both sermons and sacraments. In the later 1580s they were joined by a smaller group of adherents from Yardley Hastings, and it is almost certain that they resorted to Whiston.[34]

At Earl's Barton, adjacent to Whiston, a group of six or seven godly were regularly presented for not attending their church, and for deriding the ministers serving the parish. The leader of the group was a local yeoman Robert Welford, a member of a family associated with early protestantism. Although he styled himself a gentleman, it was to the parish gentry rather than the county gentry that he belonged. Nevertheless he would have cut a substantial figure in his own community, and he refused to allow his servants to attend the parish church. Charges levied against him in 1592 reveal his character and also the nature of events at Whiston. He was presented because

> he hath not received the communion in the parish church of many years, the said Robert this xij years seldom or never to common prayer, resorteth to Whiston to hear the minister there, one Francis Foster. Item he, despising the discipline of the church being excommunicate, resorteth to other churches of his own stamp. Item, he so much abused Mr Rainford, late minister of Barton aforesaid, that he exhibited xxvj articles against him, whose answers upon the same remaineth upon record before the High Commissioners, but the matter was ended by gentlemen so that the said Welford remaineth unreformed, a notable Brownist, a Martin, despising government since time he was Hackett's companion . . .[35]

These constitute a comprehensive set of charges which raise a number of questions about the character of puritanism in the area during the troubled years between 1588 and 1591. It is clear that Welford himself was a thoroughgoing radical associated with the separatist group at Oundle, but how far this was characteristic of the Whiston congregation is an open question. The diocesan

[33]P.D.R., X607/9, ff. 40, 41v., Archd. Ct. Bk. 4, f. 28; 5, ff. 16v., 66v., 68, 86, 88, 120v.; Inst. Bk. II. ff. 2, 4v., 34v.

[34]Ibid., X648/1, ff. 73v., 83v., loose leaf between ff. 118–119; Archd. Ct. Bk. 5, f. 12; Archd. Vis. Bk. 7, ff. 43, 95v–96; 9, f. 8; X609/21, f. 203v.; X610/24, ff. 27v–28; Peel, The Seconde Parte, i. 241–242.

[35]Ibid., X648/1, f. 83v.; Archd. Vis. Bk. 7, f. 45; X610/25, f. 19.

authorities, in a time of crisis, were perhaps keen to discredit all puritans in the light of recent events and, if so, they would only be following the example of central government, which sponsored a number of publications linking the *classes* with more radical and eccentric attempts at subversion. In such circumstances it is dangerous to make too much of the references to Brownism and Marprelate in the context of the Whiston congregation though Samuel Clarke later recalled that Brownism was abroad in the county at that time. Welford himself appears to belong to that same social group, the parish gentry, as Hackett's co-conspirators Arthington and Copinger, and he seems to have enjoyed some more powerful protectors. Certainly the charges suggest that proceedings against him in High Commission were stopped by the intervention of some 'gentlemen', and one wonders if Knightley and his friends, at that time themselves busy with Marprelate, were not behind that. It does look as if Welford may have been a link between gentry radicalism, as exhibited by Martin Marprelate, and the more popular radicalism of William Hackett.[36] The majority of the congregation at Whiston may have had more reservations, but it remained a place which received 'diverse persons of other parishes to the communion, such as disobey their own ministers', throughout our period. It was not implicated in the classical movement, but that in itself does not prove that it eschewed radical approaches to reform.

The evidence from Whiston suggests that Welford had powerful supporters, but the tensions between popular radicals and their more substantial puritan friends which we have seen in the county town also affected the rural hinterland. Once again events at Oundle were in the background, for the conflict centred on Francis Wigginton, who had family connections with the town and was schoolmaster at Blisworth. The manor of Blisworth had been purchased in 1593 by Thomas Andrews, himself a puritan. He was clearly behind the attempt to remove Wigginton from his post for maladministration and incompetence, and though the witnesses appear to have been orchestrated, the concern of the godly for education comes out strongly in their testimony. Several of them had kept their children at school for upwards of five years, and at one stage 12 of the children had been sent to school at the nearby parish of Courteenhall because of Wigginton's unsatisfactory behaviour. Courteenhall had a puritan minister and a schoolmaster, Henry Bourne, who was to join the puritans meeting at Northampton in 1603.[37] It was the respectable godly who were choosing to send their children to Courteenhall and, although it seems strange to hear such complaints from the mouths of day-labourers and husbandmen, one of the charges levelled at Wigginton was that he had failed to send any pupil up to the universities during his 12 years tenure of office. Obviously Andrews, with his concern for godly discipline typical of the magistracy, was behind the controversy, and there was no evidence of dissatisfaction before his arrival in the parish, though clearly the godly had voted with their feet, or those of their children, in sending them to school at Courteenhall. The timing of the charges may have been provoked also by fear of the respectable godly, following the activities of Francis' brother Giles in 1590 and 1591. Francis remained in the parish, and his brother's attempt to preach there in 1597 led to further disturbances.

---

[36]See R. Cosin, *A Conspiracie for Pretended Reformation* (1593), *passim*; S. Clarke, *A General Martyrologie*, 389 says that Brownism was rife in Northants. at this time, see below pp. 136–139.
[37]P.R.O., E 134/36 Eliz. H 10; *V.C.H. Northants*, iv. 225; B.L., Sloane Ms. 271, f. 20v.; H.I.L., ii. 177.

The events at Blisworth may well illustrate the reaction of the respectable godly to the scandals following the uncovering of the *classes*, and do at least illustrate that, just as in the county town, tensions existed between the more substantial of the rural godly and their radical sympathizers.[38]

The neighbourhood continued to show a lively attachment to puritanism at successive visitations up to 1610, but the information only shows the tip of the iceberg. It was largely in parishes with unsympathetic clergy and churchwardens that presentments were made. From other places such as Ashton, Horton, and Courteenhall where clergy, churchwardens, and congregation shared an attachment to the puritan cause, no information was forthcoming. The influence of the county town, through the exercise and the *classis*, was paramount in sustaining that tradition. There is little evidence of that antagonism between puritan clergy and their congregations which sometimes came to the surface in the west of the county.

[38]P.R.O., E 134/36 Eliz. H 10; P.D.R., X610/26, ff. 203v., 245.

# 9    THE GODLY PEOPLE: SOME PROBLEMS

*The distribution of the godly*

THE evidence from which rural puritanism can be traced suffers from the limitations of the officials responsible for dealing with it, that is to say the diocesan court officers who heard the cases and the local churchwardens who were responsible for reporting offences. As has already been suggested, such information as exists is most likely to come from parishes with divided religious loyalties like Preston Capes where, ultimately, the incumbent and some of his congregation were forced into separation from the spiritual life of the community.[1] In the neighbouring parish of Woodford Halse the crisis years of 1604 revealed how a rigorous puritan attitude to the eucharist could itself be divisive. A communion was appointed by the minister on 15 July and

> when all things were provided for, fit and convenient for the communion Mr Hawkins received bread and wine standing, and Mr Nicholas Dryden, and Richard Wright, William Moore, John Bisbrooke and his wife, and Edward Marshall. And because the rest of his parishioners would not come to the table (they all kneeling about the table after the customary manner, as they were wont to do) Mr Hawkins would not administer the holy sacrament any more, troubling his parishioners very much.

The lead given by the squire, Nicholas Dryden, and a small godly following was not taken up by the rest of the parish who were consequently deprived of the sacrament. It was probably this that most worried them, for no earlier instances of lay nonconformity are known. In this case the squire may have secured the institution of a puritan minister on an otherwise unwilling congregation which contained a small godly minority.[2]

Elsewhere in the west of the diocese the puritans enjoyed more support in the parishes, and at Weedon Bec they probably invited a neighbouring puritan, William Proudlove, to their parish in 1587. Certainly in 1584 a group of 20 parishioners were already going to services elsewhere and reprimanding their incumbent for adhering too closely to the *Book of Common Prayer*. During Proudlove's trials before the High Commission and Star Chamber the church-wardens refused to cooperate at visitation, failing to appear and, when summoned, objecting to the use of the oath. Their aggressive stance later gained some concessions from authority and in 1590 the godly were granted permission to desert their own parish and attend sermons when none were provided by Proudlove's replacement. The result of this unprecedented concession was that a third of the congregation were absenting themselves from the parish at that

---

[1]Smart proved troublesome to his successor, see R. G. Usher, *The Reconstruction of the English Church*, i. 264; P.D.R., X614/40, ff. 41, 136v.; see above p. 69.
[2]P.D.R., X614/38, f. 111v.

**Map 3** Godly Congregations reported to the Courts.

time. Six years later they had even more success when they secured the reinstatement of their imprisoned pastor and, during the rest of his ministry, the authorities heard no more from the parish. After his death, however, the puritans had
to go 'gadding' again and in 1604 the churchwardens presented certain of their
neighbours for resorting to other churches 'because we have not any minister
among us of good report'. The wardens clearly had some sympathy with the
godly who had by now long experience in the cause, four of those presented in
1604 came from families first reported in 1584.[3]

If the strength of the puritans varied from community to community, so did
their convictions. The puritan rector of Barby, John Ford, had a respectable
history of nonconformity behind him by 1586 when he first ran into difficulties
with a radical sector of his congregation. The source of the disagreement may
have resulted from Ford's social habits, for he was accused of 'siding with the
rich against the poor', but the local prestige of the Daventry *classis*, from which
he remained aloof, compounded his difficulties. During the late 1580s a number
of parishioners were presented for attending services and having their children
christened at Wolston, over the county boundary in Warwickshire. Wolston
was served at that time by Edward Lord, a *classis* member, and was later a base
for the illicit Marprelate Press. Indeed in the very month that the *Protestatyon of
Martin Marprelat* was being printed at Wolston, nine parishioners of Barby were
presented for absenting themselves from church. More importantly the churchwardens were also charged with allowing 'a certain Mr Hodgkins to preach
without authority'. As there are no other obvious candidates it is likely that this
refers to John Hodgkins who had recently printed two of the tracts, probably
at Wolston. If so, and this was allowed by the wardens without the incumbent's
permission, then Ford may have initiated the prosecution. Ford died shortly
afterwards and was replaced by a conformist, who was soon removed after
accusations of simony. When a new incumbent was then required, Simon
Rogers a former *classis* member was appointed. The activities of the puritans
were never brought to the attention of the authorities during his ministry.[4]

Frustration at the hands of a negligent or absentee pastor could also direct the
pious towards puritanism, and the ministry of William Sterne at Green's Norton
was notorious for his neglect of duty. At least one family in the parish, the
Skarold family, sought spiritual refreshment at Bradden where the incumbent
Thomas London, had already been noted as receiving groups of godly from
outside his own parish. The plight of families with no resident pastor could be
serious in times of particular difficulty, and in the late winter of 1590 members
of the Skarold family were reduced to burying their father 'contrary to the
Communion Book without any minister' because they were unable to find a
cleric who could perform the ceremony to their liking in the parish churchyard.
It is probable that Sterne would have withheld permission from a puritan
minister and, rather than accept this, the relatives took it upon themselves to
bury their own dead. The implications of this for the puritans were serious and
resulted in excommunication.[5] These examples, illustrating the different con-
texts in which the rural godly emerged and survived, all came from parishes

---

[3]P.D.R., Inst. Bk. III, ff. 13, 15; Archd. Vis. 7, f. 3v., X609/23, ff. 96v., 177; X610/24, ff.
76, 113v.; X613/37, f. 71; the families of Wawe, Cole, Gare, and Billing.
[4]*Ibid.*, X608/13, f. 1v.; X648/1, f. 148; Arch. Vis. 7, looseleaf between ff. 119 and 120,
f. 130v.; Archd. Ct. Bk. 9, f. 90v., X609/23, ff. 82v.-83v.; X610/24, f. 22; W. Pierce, *An
Historical Introduction to the Marprelate Tracts*, 185-189; *Eliz. Puritan Movt.*, 414.
[5]P.D.R., X609/21, ff. 214v.-215, X610/24, f. 19; Archd. Ct. Bk. 9, f. 95.

K

to the south and west of Watling Street. Elsewhere the picture is more fragmentary.

At Uppingham in Rutland, the ministry of Henry Fletcher had won over a sector of his congregation to puritanism, and when he was succeeded by William Chatburne, an appointee of Bishop Aylmer of London, they withdrew from the parish in 1590. 14 parishioners were named in the presentment and one of them, Aquila Raven, declared that 'it was no matter if twenty such as he were hanged' when asked to express an opinion about Chatburne.[6] During the 1580s the other market town, Oakham, had been a notable preaching centre and some of the inhabitants of the town chose to forsake their parish to seek the ministrations of preachers heard at the market-day lectures; both Robert Johnson and Thomas Gibson attracted small groups of devotees from the town. Gibson also had a following at Aston, the parish adjacent to Ridlington, where four parishioners were presented for refusing the communion from their minister in 1588. Their defence rested on the fact that the incumbent did not preach, and this was also used as an excuse by the godly at Bisbrooke. Clearly the preaching of Gibson and Cawdry at Oakham in 1583 and 1584 had made some impact on the laity, resulting in defections from 'dumb' ministers.[7]

Following his deprivation in 1588 Robert Cawdry was said to be holding private conventicles behind locked doors in his own house, and at Ridlington Thomas Gibson was also accused of preaching at private gatherings. These conventicles certainly worried the diocesan officials who regularly sought information about them at visitation, but no details survive about the conduct of such meetings.[8] We know from the ministry of George Gifford how important they were to Essex puritanism, and the stress which Robert Cawdry placed on household devotion in 1604 suggests that he had valued his experience of them.[9] Glimpses of private gatherings elsewhere in the diocese are all that are offered. Some were clearly sponsored by the gentry, meetings at Fawsley and Whiston have already been noted and, at the end of the century, Sir Edward Montague's house at Boughton was used as a preaching centre. Others, like the meetings held by Roland Nutt at Southwick in 'John Sharman's house' at which strangers to the parish were given the sacrament, probably catered for a different clientele.[10] These isolated references are hardly sufficient to substantiate the rise of a non-separating congregationalist tradition in the diocese, but meeting together privately must have reinforced in the minds of the godly the notion spelled out by Snape to his Northampton charges that they represented 'here one and there one, chosen and picked out from the common multitude'. The godly had not yet chosen to reject contact with the 'common multitude', but they were keenly aware that they comprised a distinctive and necessary élite within the church and were prepared to travel about the countryside to seek each other out.

*Agrarian tensions: Badby*

The puritan clergy of the western parishes were, in the main, introduced to the area by the gentry and sometimes as at Preston Capes and Welton, mentioned earlier, some of the parishioners clearly did not share the enthusiasm of the magnates for their preachers. In those cases the cause of dissension was

[6]P.D.R., Inst. Bk. III, f. 8; X610/23a, ff. 85 and v., 153v.
[7]Ibid., X608/19, f. 72; X609/20, f. 46v.; 21, f. 178; X611/27, ff. 6, 47v.
[8]B.L., Lansd. Ms. 57, f. 172; P.D.R., X609/20, f. 202.
[9]Eliz. Puritan Movt., 372–378; Cawdry, A Short and Fruitfull Treatise, passim.
[10]P.D.R., X611/32, ff. 108, 110; X648/1, f. 24v.

explained, at least by the preachers, in terms of religious disaffection,[11] but in a region recently enclosed on a grand scale there were other possible sources of tension, and the agrarian policy of a godly squire could result in confrontation with his puritan tenants. This happened at Badby, only a mile from Fawsley House. It was probably the meetings at that house which first attracted the puritans from Badby, and in 1574 Matthew Palmer and his wife were enjoined to receive the communion in their own church, and to do so in a kneeling position. Three years later they remained unrepentant and were joined by six other families in the parish, four of whom promised to attend the next parish communion. The Palmer family remained excommunicate and, as such, disturbed the Easter communion of 1578 by demanding to enter the church, although it was illegal for them to do so. A persistent group of godly, including the Goodman, Southam and Rushall families continued to be presented until 1583,[12] and it was they and the Palmers who led the opposition to the lord of the manor, Valentine Knightley, at the end of the 1580s.

Valentine had been granted the manor by his father, Sir Richard, about 1580, and had set about improving its economic potential. This involved transferring a considerable acreage of arable to pasture, and confusion arose as 'to the common rights of pasturage' which copyhold tenants held on that land. In addition Valentine had tried to restrict the tenants' rights to woodland, and had raised the entry fines on copyhold properties. The tenants claimed that they had got a decree in chancery prohibiting infringement of their common rights, and in August 1589 turned their cattle out on the demesne. The beasts were impounded by Knightley's servants who were obstructed by the copyholders, led by Edward Goodman, Anthony and Manasses Palmer, and other members of the Rushall, Goodman, and Smallbone families. Knightley brought a bill in Star Chamber against his tenants, and from then on relations deteriorated. When Knightley's servants set out to plough the demesne, they were disturbed by a group of tenants led by Anthony Palmer, 'a very busy and seditious fellow' and Edward Goodman, 'a man yielding to most of the bad practices of the said Palmer'. The tenants had clearly organized themselves well, and Knightley's lawyer, Christopher Yelverton, added a charge of conspiracy to rebellion to the accusation of forcible entry and obstruction. According to the plaintiff the tenants bore all the marks of a revolutionary agrarian band led by Anthony Palmer, 'being the chief ringleader of them and one as a captain, so named himself or was so named to all the rest, to guide or conduct them in these lewd and riotous enterprises, being mounted upon his horse and armed with a sword and chafing staff, ready to give the onsett'. The tenants claimed that they had a good cause in law and that they had combined to pay the expenses of sending Edward Goodman up to London to get legal advice. They then suggested that Valentine's father, Sir Richard Knightley, should act as arbitrator in the dispute, and accused Valentine of packing the jury at the manorial court with cottagers and youths, thus excluding the principal copyholders.[13] Valentine objected to having his father as arbitrator and it was finally agreed that Sir John Spencer and John Temple should act on behalf of the tenants with Thomas Andrews of Charwelton and Bartholomew Tate representing the lord of the manor. The parties failed to agree and further disturbances took place in the summer of 1590 when the tenants, adopting a common ploy in agrarian disturbances, sent their women-

[11]Peel, *The Seconde Parte*, i. 295–296; see above pp. 37–38, 45.
[12]P.D.R., X607/9, f. 40; X608/13, f. 148; X648/1, ff. IV, 147; Archd. Ct. Bk. 5, f. 91.
[13]P.R.O., STAC 5/K 10/17; 13/10.

folk into the fields to obstruct the servants of Knightley and put them 'in great fear and danger of their lives'. The final outcome, settled by a local commission from Star Chamber, is not known.[14]

The dispute was localized but the tenantry exhibited an aggressive and sophisticated approach to the problem. The effect of the combination of agrarian and religious grievances had been seen more dramatically elsewhere in 1536 and 1549, but the tactics adopted here, sending a representative to London for legal advice and adopting an almost military organization in the fields, were more suggestive of mid-17th-century than of Elizabethan England. How far their puritanism influenced their attitude to their economic problems is difficult to say.[15] They clearly represented the leaders of parochial society. Matthew Palmer was a fairly prosperous tenant of the manor and known to the godly outside his own parish. Other families, in addition to the Palmer's, established a tradition of using biblical Christian names, and the godly showed a generous concern for the poor in their midst. William Smallbone, who desired burial in accordance with the 'ancient and godly custom of christians', left small bequests to the most needy of the parish and John Gibbons also left sums to his poor brethren, the halt and lame, the blind and sick, and 2d. to every household of the poorest in the town. He appointed John Rushall as his overseer and when making his will in 1599 he remembered his church 'which I have often resorted to in the fear of God, in the name of his dear son Christ Jesus, for the forgiveness of my sins and to give him thanks for all his blessings bestowed'. Elizabeth Lyne, one of the women accused in 1590 had mellowed by the time she made her will ten years later. Her attention by then was drawn to the needs of the poor of the parish to whom she left 20s., and also to the school then being built at Daventry, a cause which attracted support from other puritans of the area.[16]

By the end of the century the godly were able to dictate matters to their more cautious pastor, Raphael Heywood, whose ambivalent attitude to the puritans led to unseemly brawls in the churchyard. In 1600 18 of his parishioners were absenting themselves from Heywood's services, but two years later he had compromised and was administering the communion to the puritans while they remained seated or standing. He seemed determined to keep his recalcitrant flock within the fold of the established church and in 1604 pleaded with them to receive the communion in an orthodox fashion and to attend church even when sermons were not preached.[17] From 1574 until 1604 the godly were prepared to stand up to squire or minister and to insist, even when both were sympathetic to puritan aims, that they too had a rightful place in the formation of the godly commonwealth. Theirs was a radicalism which remained outspoken but, for the most part, within the broad spectrum of puritan activity. This was not true of all radicals.

### Separatists and extremists: Oundle

Events at Oundle between 1585 and 1600 and their repercussions in London in 1591 discredited the whole puritan movement. The conspiracy revolved around the unstable personality of William Hackett, whose decision to move from the local to the national arena ended in his execution and proved disastrous

---

[14]Ibid., K 1/16.
[15]A. G. Dickens, The English Reformation (1964), 124–128, 220–222.
[16]See P.D.R., will volume V 570; W 413, 422, 521, 762; P.R.O., P.C.C. wills, Rutland 53.
[17]Ibid., X612/34, ff. 20, 59, 114v.; 35, f. 70v.; X614/38, f. 114.

to the puritan movement as a whole. The affair, which culminated in Hackett being declared King of Europe by his accomplices, was seized on by the authorities who used Hackett's links with the more respectable wing of puritanism, mainly through the person of Giles Wigginton, to discredit the whole movement.[18] Following the propaganda of Bancroft and Cosin, who stressed the lunatic and unstable nature of the affair in order to pour scorn on the 'presbyterian faction', the attention of subsequent historians has remained on those aspects of the case. The conspiracy has rightly been called 'preposterous' and receives brief treatment from recent historians of puritanism, who have generally viewed it as an abberation beyond the pale of puritan history.[19] Just as Bancroft was wrong in making too close an identification between the *classes* and Hackett, the view of recent historians requires some reconsideration. Whether the conspiracy was an aberration is questionable, for it had its roots firmly in local puritan developments.

Prior to the mid 1580s the chief nonconformists at Oundle were catholic recusants in the household of a tenant of Sir Thomas Tresham, Gilbert Hussey. Hackett had himself been a member of Hussey's retinue and, as Cosin suggested, had served there for 10 years. During that time he was said to have been a catholic himself, and was probably the man of that name listed with other catholics of the parish in 1577.[20] Events changed radically when Giles Wigginton, after a stormy career in the north of England where he had seen catholicism at close quarters, returned to his native parish as a deprived minister. This was sometime late in 1585 or in 1586 and within two years the activities of radical dissenters in the town were attracting the attention of the local courts.[21] The earliest appearance by a member of this group was that of William Bradshaw, on 16 September 1587, who claimed that nobody in the nearby village of Lilford 'hath either care of God or his service'. One month later Bradshaw's wife and three other women were presented for refusing to be churched after childbirth, and they were followed soon after by William Hackett who characteristically was said to have taken 'the surplice from the desk in the church of Oundle where it did stay, and contemptuously in the time of service laid it under his tail'.[22] Thus launched on his public career Hackett soon attracted the attention of a wider audience. He was evidently known to the godly of Whiston and was taken up by the squire of Stoke Doyle Anthony Palmer, a signatory of the 1605 petition, with whom he visited the Hampshire home of Paul Wentworth, brother of the puritan champion Peter. Palmer, who was himself a kinsman of Sir Richard Knightley, returned to Oundle with Hackett who, bound and tormented for 20 days, claimed to have assumed the spirit of John the Baptist. If it was his intention to proclaim the second coming, and there was a strong millenarian strand in the whole affair, he was to be disappointed. The immediate result was a more prosaic bondage in Northampton gaol, imposed upon him by that vastly different puritan zealot, Sir Walter Mildmay. Even in

[18]See the accounts by Bancroft, *Daungerous Positions*, 141–176; Cosin, *A Conspiracie for Pretended Reformation*, *passim*; and the 'confession' of one of the conspirators H. Arthington, *The Seduction of Arthington by Hacket* (1592). Arthington also had recusant connections, see H. Aveling, 'The Catholic Recusants of the West Riding of Yorkshire', in *Proceedings of the Leeds Philosophical and Literary Society*, x pt. 6, 287.

[19]Knappen, *Tudor Puritanism*, 297; *Eliz. Puritan Movt.*, 424.

[20]See P.D.R., X607/9, f. 40v., X608/21, f. 141v., X610/23a, f. 110v.; Archd. Ct. Bk. V. f. 39; R. Cosin, *A Conspiracie*, 2.

[21]Venn, *Alumni Cantab.*, iv. 402.

[22]P.D.R., X609/21, ff. 104v., 116v.; 23, f. 143v.

these circumstances Hackett arranged a spectacle for his followers and, on the night before his incarceration, he claimed to have been visited by an angel so that 'by this tale, the erronious opinions afore conceived of him, were greatly increased'.[23]

On his release Hackett proceeded to London, fell in with two other zealots, Edmund Copinger and Henry Arthington, and tried to assist the imprisoned *classis* leaders. He remained in close touch with them through Giles Wigginton and John Bentley, a servant of Sir Richard Knightley. As the activities of the so-called conspirators became more unstable, the *classis* leaders became concerned about the consequences of their actions for the puritan cause. Nevertheless condemnation was not forthcoming from that quarter, and it was a policy of caution that was advised. This ambivalence on the part of the leadership played into the hands of the government, and once Hackett was arrested and executed it was too late for the puritans to disassociate themselves.[24] Of course the conspiracy took place when the puritan leadership was demoralized and the clerical leaders in prison. They were thus less able to control affairs, but this cannot excuse them entirely. During the 1570s and 1580s one of the features of puritan preaching was a confident assertion in the rightness of their cause, which bred an equally confident expectation of speedy reformation. However much the clerical leadership recognized the problems involved in this, it was a constant feature of the sermons delivered to sustain their congregations. Often they expressed their dislike of the established church and their hopes for reformation in inflammatory terms; Edmund Snape had asked his congregation in 1589, 'How say you if we devise a way whereby to shake off all the antichristian government and authority of bishops? ... peradventure it will not be this year and a half?' He went on to say that the discipline 'should be directed all in one day'. These hopes of reform, expressed in quasi-revolutionary terms, were an intrinsic feature of puritan preaching and thought, and it is not surprising that, in the aftermath of the Star Chamber trial, some of the more hot-headed godly attempted to bring that reformation about by revolutionary means in order to fulfil that prophecy.[25]

Hackett was not central to the history of puritanism, but neither can he be disowned by it. Cosin suggested that he had supporters in his home town at Oundle and this is supported both by the court records and also from puritan sources. In fact Samuel Clarke, in his biography of his father Hugh, confirms the impression of a community largely sympathetic to traditional morality subsequently and suddenly infected with radical extremists. It was among these people 'that for the generality of them, were very ignorant and ungodly' that Hugh Clarke found himself trying to introduce the discipline and a sabbatarian ethic. Clarke took to preaching against Whitsun ales and morris dancing soon after his arrival in the town, but it was an uphill struggle and the inhabitants were not to be deprived of their amusements. It was only through a miraculous warning

upon a Sabbath day which they had highly profaned by drinking, dancing etc. In the night when they were returned to their several homes there was heard a great noise and rattling of chains up and down the town, which was

---

[23]Cosin, *A Conspiracie*, 8–9, 43–44.
[24]Bancroft, *Daungerous Positions*, 144, 148, 151, 154.
[25]Cosin, *A Conspiracie*, 23, 32; P.R.O., STAC 5/A 27/33; Bancroft, *Daungerous Positions*, 143.

accompanied with such a smell and stink of fire and brimstone, that many of their guilty consciences suggested to them that the devil was come to fetch them away quickly to hell. This so terrified and wrought upon them, that thay began to give better heed to the ministry of God's Word, and to break off their profane courses for the greatest part, so that there was an eminent reformation wrought amongst them; at least sixteen of those poor souls being effectively wrought upon, and brought home to Christ ...

Oundle was certainly an exciting and confusing place in which to live in the late 1580s. Such a visitation upon the wordly and its stress on divine retribution may have created an atmosphere in which the godly, like Hackett, also had their visions. The struggle against antichrist needed theological and ecclesiological debate, but out in the field the weaponry was often more direct and less subtle. In the face of ignorance and indifference the traditional fear of divine retribution through direct intervention was likely to be more effective in bringing about reform.[26]

Just when it seemed that Clarke was winning over the prophane he was out-flanked on the left by radicals, said by his son to be Brownists, with whom he 'had many bickerings and disputations with some of the chief of them, whom he mightily confuted, and through God's grace, reclaimed some of them'. From the local court records, this group appears to have comprised Hackett's former associates. Their leader was Robert Pamphlin, a schoolmaster in the town, who was presented with eight of his friends for not attending the exercise in September 1589. Others also charged included William Bradshaw. Pamphlin had already been before the court for associating with Giles Wigginton, and it was later claimed that he acted as a scribe for Hackett in his correspondence with Copinger and Arthington.[27] On 20 January 1590 four parishioners were charged with harbouring Wigginton, and later in the year, eight women were charged with refusing to be churched. Four months before Hackett's execution, his wife and four others were presented for not attending church, and some of the group were involved in the clandestine burial of the schoolmaster's infant child.[28]

They soon withdrew from Oundle to Stoke Doyle, where Anthony Palmer was squire, because according to Cosin 'the minister fitted his [Hackett's] humour better', but if this was the case it was not the incumbent Thomas Deacon. Deacon was a puritan and later recommended Robert Catelin to the townsmen of Northampton, but he reported the events in his parish to the bishop. The minister involved must have been a friend of or perhaps in the household of Palmer, but we have no information about him. The form of service used by the group included psalm-singing and preaching, and the defectors from Oundle were welcomed by a group of sympathizers in the parish, led by Palmer. How far they were separatist is difficult to say without evidence of their opinions, but according to Clarke Brownism was 'abroad in Northamptonshire' at that time.[29] Robert Browne himself was living at his father's home at Tolethorpe near Stamford, but was about to be reconciled to the established church and to take the living at Thorpe Achurch, four miles south of Oundle. Whether he had already established contacts in the area is not known, but despite

[26]S. Clark, A General Martyrologie, 387–388.
[27]Ibid., 389; P.D.R., X609/23, ff. 144v–46; 23a. f. 51; Cosin, A Conspiracie, 23.
[28]P.D.R., X610/23a, ff. 57, 100v. Archd. Ct. Bk. 9, f. 129. One of those involved was Richard Dickens, identified by Cosin as a travelling companion of Hackett, A Conspiracie, 44.
[29]P.D.R., X610/23a, f. 66, 111; Cosin, A Conspiracie, 44; see above p. 100.

his return to the fold his lengthy ministry at Achurch was to lead some parishioners to schism in the early 17th century. It may be that his presence was already an unsettling influence.[30]

By 1591 Clarke was moving on from Oundle to Wolston in Warwickshire to fill the gap left by a deprived *classis* minister, but before his departure he claimed to have won over some of the radicals. His successor, however, was not a puritan and so the group were once more in conflict with their pastor. Most of these presented between 1587 and 1591 appeared in a list of excommunicated persons drawn up in 1595 and they remained aggressively stubborn in their refusal to attend church. Indeed when called before the diocesan courts in 1596 Richard Wigginton's wife challenged them to 'proceed against me and spare me not, I pray God you may be ashamed of your doings and repent you, you call [*sic* summon] all honest women. Good is evil with you, and evil good'. Continued excommunication led to clandestine burial services for members of the group, and their separation from their own parish must have been complete.[31] By the end of the century the trouble at Oundle appeared to have subsided and the radicals, even if not reconciled to their own parish, were drawn back into communion with the godly of neighbouring villages. On 12 November 1599 George Jernon, one of the group, was presented for absenting himself from his parish church and going to Stoke Doyle and Barnwell for services; when he appeared he also admitted attending the house of Sir Edward Montague in order to hear sermons.[32] The gap between the godly magistrate and the radical people appears to have narrowed and they seem to have found common ground again. Separatism was no more an issue in the diocese.

## The contribution of the people

The events at Oundle and at Badby are instructive for the light they throw on the tensions that existed between the aims of the lay and clerical leadership, and how those aims were interpreted by the godly. In times of stress the information from Northampton, Blisworth, and these two communities suggest that puritanism contained within it a radical appeal to the godly which the leadership could not always control. It may be that, as has been suggested in Kent, puritanism turned 'committed Protestantism into a principal pillar of provincial order and stability', but in Northamptonshire the pillar rested on insecure foundations and showed a potential to threaten that stability. The puritan leadership was well aware of this.

Apart from illustrating their radical capacity, the evidence from the godly in the diocese shows that, although they could not do without their ministers and the support of the gentry, the people too had a dynamic role to play in puritan history, if not on the national at least in the local arena. This the puritan clergy recognized in 1605 when the advice of the godly was sought by the ministers, and it has recently been pointed out that 'the puritans also use that deceptive expression "the people" which is scarcely valid in the discussion of Tudor political history, but which already has some meaning in the discussion of protestant affairs'.[33] The expression is, of course, deceptive for who were the people?

[30]F. I. Cater, 'Robert Browne and his Treatise of Reformation', *Trans. Congreg. Hist. Soc.*, i. 117, 120; 'The Later Years of Robert Browne' *Trans. Congreg. Hist. Soc.*, iii. 307–316.
[31]Clark, *A General Martyrologie*, 389–390; P.D.R., X611/28, ff. 1, 29v., 48, 78.
[32]P.D.R., X611/32, ff. 108, 110.
[33]Clark, *English Provincial Society*, 184; *Eliz. Puritan Movt.*, 94.

Where did they fit into their local community? George Carleton, in the 1570s, described the godly in the following terms, 'This people consist of all degrees from the nobility to the lowest. And so hot is the desire of God's truth in them, that they will not train themselves to favour any of the laws or ordinances set forth by the Queen in God's matters, but such as are void of all offence and reformed according to sincerity. This people, as they do not like the course of our church, so they do and will practise assemblies of brethren in all parts of this realm and have their own churches in companies.'[34] Subsequent events in the diocese of Peterborough show Carleton to have been prophetic, not just in his assessment of the strength of puritanism, but in his stress on the congregational tendencies of that brotherhood. The godly may have accepted the presbyterian platform of the puritan clergy as a desirable end for the nation, and they certainly subscribed to the necessity of removing the abuses of the established church, but it was within their local community that most of them sought to bear witness to and further the reformation.

The puritans at Badby claimed to be the leading copyholders, and the wills of members of the Palmer and Smallbone families suggest that this was indeed the case. At Oundle the Wigginton family were among the more prosperous of the townsmen and the steady progression of the Welford family through the strata of agrarian society from husbandmen to gentlemen suggests that the puritans were, in fact, often to be found among the leaders of parish society. This was certainly so in Northampton also.[35] The information is, of course, impressionistic and imprecise but the evidence of wills suggest that the godly brethren were often, in addition to being a spiritual élite, set apart socially from others in their congregations. Much more work needs to be done on this, but a few comments are worthwhile. In several parishes the godly all adopted the convention, often at the instigation of their pastors, of giving their children biblical Christian names, which in itself marked them out from their fellow parishioners. Thomas Fryer of Northampton, mayor of the town in 1590, christened his children Samuel, James, Prudence, Hannah, and Bethiah, and the Fosbrookes of Cranford included an Eleazar, Nathaniel, and Samuel.[36] The godly often enjoyed a close relationship with a particular pastor, often remembered when making their wills. Snape and Catelin did particularly well from small tokens of affection from their charges, though no one profited as much as Thomas Gibson of Ridlington who received £10 from a parishioner, John Dive, in 1601. A further £3 went to the schoolmaster Abel Mellors. These tokens of affection were occasionally accompanied by responsibilities, like that laid on Jonas Chalenor by John Merrill a husbandman of Byfield in 1599. Merrill asked Chalenor to ensure that his daughter married an honest man and also asked him to dispose of 2s. to a poor but worthy scholar at Oxford. William Wakelin, a husbandman of Cranford, simply asked the ministers of the town to be responsible for sorting out his legacies in 1591, and several others appointed clergy as their overseers, particularly when they had young families.[37]

By the end of the century bequests to the poor are commonplace in several

[34]P.R.O., SP 12/21/121, f. 268, quoted in *Eliz. Puritan Movt.*, 144.

[35]E.g. P.D.R., Will Volume V 1, 19, 570, 698; W 105, 296, 422, 494, 572, 660; Y, ff. 178–179, see Chapter 8 above.

[36]*Ibid.*, Will Volume Y 1; P.R.O., P.C.C. wills, Neville 20. There are several other examples from wills and parish registers, particularly in the west of the county. This is a subject worth exploring in some depth.

[37]See for example P.R.O., P.C.C. wills Drake 44, Bolein 9, Woodhall 53, Wallop 61; P.D.R., Will Volume Y ff. 13v.–16; W 334 and refs. for n. 35 above.

communities with puritan traditions such as Northampton, Badby, Lamport, Byfield, Earls Barton, Castle Ashby, Preston Capes, Cogenhoe, and Daventry, and provide one testimony to the social concern of the godly. The poor were to be remembered, but in such a way as suggested that within their local community there was a distance between the godly (or at least those whose names we know of) and their poorer neighbours. By their example of a worthy life, and through the practice of loving-kindness, the more prosperous godly provided support for their ministers and for each other, and an example to their less fortunate neighbours. Several illustrations of this could be taken from the probate records of the diocese, but it is perhaps best here to return to Oundle for an example. Robert Easton, a tanner from Oundle, made his will on 15 February 1585 and began with a fervent statement of Calvinist belief in salvation through Christ's passion. He went on

> I give and bequeath to the minister of the town of Oundle for the time being, so that he be a preacher of the pure word of the eternal God and do labour faithfully in the word and in doctrine, forty shillings of good English money yearly until such time as my son William Easton shall come to the age of one and twenty years if he live so long, or otherwise to the end of fourteen years after my decease . . .

Two separate bequests followed to the poor.

> I will and bequeath unto the poor people of the parish of Oundle forty shillings of good English money to be given and distributed amongst them indifferently according to their several necessities at the discretion of the minister of the town for the time being, John Rysley, William Dennis, John Chapman the younger, and John Belderby, or three of them . . . And further for the better relieving of the poor needy members of Christ inhabiting within the same town, I will and bequeath more unto them and their relief, forty shillings of good English money yearly until the term abovesaid (as for preacher) be expired. To be also distributed to them according to the discretion of the parties above named or, for default of them, by as many others the most godly and approved christians inhabiting the same town.

Easton went on to leave his Bible to the minister on condition that it be restored to his son when the latter reached twelve years of age. Clearly the town was not yet to be disturbed by the radical extremists, but already in Easton's eyes, there was a distinction to be drawn between the godly poor and the common multitude. The will conveys a strong impression of a godly concern for that caring discipline and mutual support which was to characterize provincial dissent for the next two hundred years, but radicalism was not far off. Among the witnesses to Easton's will were Robert Catelin, still to play his part at Northampton and William Pamphlin, a brother and associate of the radical schoolmaster, Robert.[38]

[38]P.R.O., P.C.C. wills, Windsor 3.

# ASSESSMENT

NATIONALLY, the state of the church in 1610 was a disappointment to the puritans. The hopes of the returning exiles in 1559 and the proposals put forward by Thomas Cartwright and the presbyterians a decade later had not been realized and the church was still governed by bishops at the head of an essentially pre-reformation judicial system. Furthermore the liturgy, enshrined in the *Book of Common Prayer*, still contained many traces of popish superstition. Nevertheless, despite these institutional set-backs, the puritans were well-entrenched in the diocese by that date. There had been much solid achievement in the locality, most notably in the reform of the ministry and in the close cooperation that existed between the puritan clergy of the diocese and the godly magistracy, whether urban or rural. The exercises, and later experiments to maintain a preaching ministry, had not only been attractive to young radical clergy but, beginning as they did in the 1570s, they had also restored some self-respect to the older members of a depressed and neglected profession battered by two decades of religious upheaval.[1] The concern of the puritans for standards of learning among the clergy gained acceptance among a wide sector of the laity and, as an ideal, was not disputed by the established church. Thus by the end of the 16th century the puritan concept of a preaching ministry regularly expounding the word of God was generally accepted as a desirable end, even if it could not yet be achieved. The pulpit had replaced the altar at the centre of religious life and, moreover, the preaching tradition established in provincial England during this half century was a mainspring of the nation's religious life for the following 100 years at least.

In this the ministers of the diocese had played a prominent part and they were ably supported by their patrons, who formed a godly magistracy over the area. The puritan gentry of the diocese had replaced their catholic peers as commissioners and justices far more quickly than was the case in either Cheshire or Sussex, where recusants held on to office rather longer. In this the gentry of south-west Northamptonshire were most forward, and only in Rutland, where landed gentry were rather thin on the ground, did catholics hold on to office much after 1580. So successfully did the puritans exclude the catholics from local office-holding that otherwise loyal recusant households produced in a second generation some political hot-heads who became involved in the Gunpowder Plot. Catholicism was defeated locally, but its potential for subversion made the puritans ever watchful, and radicalized some of the godly people in ways not always acceptable to magistrate or minister.

The years between 1558 and 1610 also saw considerable changes of emphasis within puritanism which did not always get immediate acceptance among its adherents. The optimistic hopes of reform in the early years of Elizabeth's reign were largely placed on the success of preaching by ministers to their fellow clergy and the landowning classes of society. It was hoped that this would bring about, by political and constitutional means, the institutions necessary to the establishment of the godly commonwealth, namely, presbyterianism or something approximating to it. It was, in effect, a policy of revolution by constitutional means in which the word of God as interpreted by the puritan clergy would gain acceptance among the leaders of society and subsequently by their inferiors. The cause was right and, as such, would inevitably triumph. The success of this policy, which might be described as disciplined millenarianism, was frustrated by two obstacles; firstly, the intransigent opposition of the Queen and, secondly, the degree of apathy and ignorance among the mass of the people who clung tenaciously to traditional values and superstitions.[2] Both necessitated a change of direction in puritan strategy. The total opposition of the Queen became clear during the 1580s and drove some puritans to abandon constitutional attempts at reform and replace them by a policy of stealth. If reformation could not be brought about at the centre, then it was to be introduced into the provinces by the clergy and leaders of local society. This form of 'presbytery in episcopacy' was the aim of the *classes* and in some parishes the presbyterian discipline was established in spirit if not formally. In a few places, the tradition of locally controlled discipline survived for some time; for example, at Maxey in 1612 the incumbent, squire, and four laymen were presented for attempting to impose a self-devised form of penance on a woman convicted of fornication.[3] The discovery of the *classes* in the late 1580s, however, put a stop to most of these intiatives and led to a reconsideration of strategy. For some puritans the eventful years between 1588 and 1592 led to separation from a church which appeared irredeemably corrupt. For others, the earlier puritan rhetoric seeking speedy reform encouraged ill-advised attempts by the laity to bring that reformation about. Both of these responses attracted widespread contemporary comment and had significant short-term consequences for puritanism, but it was a quieter change of direction that was to be of fundamental importance. The failure of the attempts at constitutional reform and at institutional reform by stealth led the puritans to reconsider their concept of their mission. Once attention was turned to reformation in the parishes it became clear to some of the puritan clergy that their preaching had not always met with the expected success. The experiences of the 1590s, when harvest failures had caused tithes to become an issue between pastor and congregation even in Northampton, further underlined how tenuous was the hold of the ministers over the mass of the people.[4] Attention to the pastoral side of the ministry was required, and the revolutionary hopes of the earlier years gave way to a policy of gradualism. Just as in the puritan literature of the early 17th century, the disciplined godly life came to be seen as the hallmark of a true Christian, so, in the nation, a gradual grass-roots reformation was to bring about more fundamental changes than constitutional solutions imposed from above. Even former radicals like Robert Cawdry and Francis Merbury were converts to this view. It was a view which had always had a place in puritan thought, particularly among Cambridge

[2]For the Queen see Neale, *Elizabeth I and Her Parliaments, passim*; for the people see K. Thomas, *Religion and the Decline of Magic* (Penguin edn., 1973), 179–206.

[3]E. J. I. Allen, 'The State of the Church in the Diocese of Peterborough 1601–42' (Unpub. Oxford B.Litt. thesis, 1972), p. 116.

[4]N.R.O., Assembly Minutes, f. 266 and v.; *The Borough Records* ii. 398. The effects of the economic difficulties of the 1590s on the relationship between Minister and people in terms other than simple economic ones needs more attention.

men like Edward Dering, but was one which had spent two decades in the background.[5]

This change of emphasis did not gain acceptance overnight, nor did it mean that attempts to influence government and parliament were abandoned. The struggle now took place on two fronts, the political and the pastoral, but the experiences of half a century led many puritans to doubt the effectiveness of reformation by government edict. The consequences of a policy of gradualism were awesome for those who were to undertake it. The established church, despite its official policy, had fortunately allowed the puritans and their followers a reasonable degree of latitude in the practice of their religion. This state of affairs suited the puritans, most of whom wished to stay within the church and reform it from there. In fact, in the face of ignorance and apathy, it was a sacred duty of the godly to convert the whole population by example. The godly commonwealth remained as the desired end, but the means of bringing it about had changed. It was not only possible for the puritans to remain within the established church, but also proper for them to do so if they wanted to convert the people.

It is the impact of puritanism among the people that is most difficult to assess. In terms of numbers the godly remained as a tiny fraction of the population as a whole, but their importance cannot be measured in quantitative terms alone. In many cases they were drawn from the parochial élites. In 1605, the ministers themselves recognized that 'the people' had a positive contribution to make to puritan growth and were not simply the passive recipients of preaching and exhortation. At the same time the contribution which the people made to puritanism in times of stress was not always welcome to ministers or magistrates. Puritan rhetoric did not always respond quickly to shifts in policy, and the people could more easily respond to the appeals for sudden reformation and to the violent denunciation of the abuses of the church than to the more sophisticated demands for gradual reform. In several parishes the godly folk worked in close harmony with their clergy and gentry leaders, sharing their concerns for education and for discipline, but in some places they proved difficult to control. The radicalism of the people might appear in advance of the ministers when viewed in the light of the upheavals of the mid 17th century, but in the context of puritan history since 1558 it is more clearly seen as a frustrated expression of a policy which had been abandoned by much of the leadership after 1588. Whether the radicalism of the people at Oundle and Northampton laid foundations which provided continuity with the Civil War period has yet to be established, but at Badby the mixture of religious dissent and social concern does seem to point forward in time.

By 1610 the puritans were well represented among all sectors of society in the diocese, but the tradition had become a more diffuse and less dogmatic one than had appeared likely in the 1580s. In such a tradition tensions existed between the different groups that constituted the whole. There was a close harmony between puritan clergy and godly magistrates in both town and country, but the people still remained something of an unknown quantity. Their numbers were small, and the evidence so far unearthed suggests that only one-third of the parishes in the diocese had direct experience of puritan evangelism.[6] Doubtless people

[5]P. Collinson, 'A Magazine of Religious Patterns: an Erasmian Topic transposed in English Protestantism', D. Baker (ed.), *Renaissance and Renewal in Christian History* (Oxford 1977), 226, 228, 233–234, 237–240.
[6]See Map 1; C. Haigh, *Reformation and Resistance*, 305–315 points out the geographical limitations of puritan evangelism in Lancashire also.

from other places attended major centres like Northampton and Whiston but, even so, it is as well to remember that the success of puritanism was limited in this way. The limitation did, in fact, influence the character of puritan activity. The growing awareness that reformation of the whole nation was unlikely, if not impossible, encouraged the godly to place more emphasis on contacts between themselves. They did not separate from 'the world' and reject contact with it but, as with Robert Easton of Oundle, they were increasingly aware of a distance between themselves and the rest of the community. It was from this experience that the tradition of non-separating congregationalism emerged alongside and out of presbyterianism. They were not as yet distinct traditions in the local context but remained intermingled for some time to come.[7]

With substantial support from the gentry, who saw themselves as the guardians of local rights and traditions, and a reasonable following among the people, the puritan clergy had made considerable impact on the diocese by 1610. The durability of the tradition thus established needs to be considered, for the puritans were soon under attack by a diocesan administration dominated by anti-Calvinistic Arminians. The Arminians attempted the early policy of the presbyterians in seeking to impose their form of churchmanship from above, but they chose the hierarchy and the court rather than parliament as the vehicles to effect this change. The diocesan officials were thus out of touch with the views of the majority of the parochial clergy and almost all the laity of the diocese. The Arminians had some able support among the clergy of Northampton in Samuel Clarke, and also at Uppingham where Jeremy Taylor was incumbent, but these were the exceptions.[8] In the county town the puritan pattern of worship was, however, maintained throughout the 1620s and 1630s by Jeremiah Lewys of All Saints. After fifty years of Calvinism, the Arminian policies were unpopular with the clergy and the gentry, and the expenses involved in beautifying churches in accordance with their beliefs brought them few friends among the people at large.[9] Moreover, the puritan preaching tradition established at All Saints was also continued elsewhere. We know already that Oakham continued as a preaching centre, and in the two former *classis* centres, Daventry and Kettering, lectureships were established between 1610 and 1630. At Kettering Robert Bolton preached a series of sermons which were published, as were those of other members of the combination lecturing there in the 1620s.[10] Other towns with lectureships included Rothwell between 1607 and 1613 and Brackley in 1639, and in the parishes of Titchmarsh, Pytchley and Brigstock there were preachers whose reputations extended beyond the parochial boundaries.[11] These lectures by combination brought together the clergy of several neighbourhoods in common opposition to the authorities, and the survival of Calvinism itself became identified with these puritan initiatives. If it was the puritans that appeared dogmatic and intransigent in the 1580s, it was the establishment that was to appear so in the 1620s and 1630s, when the puritans were defending a more broadly-based churchmanship. With the support of the gentry, the puritan ministers easily withstood the offensive of the Arminian faction that ruled the diocese.

[7]P. Collinson, 'Early Dissenting Tradition', 15–26.

[8]N. R. N. Tyacke, 'Puritanism, Arminianism, and Counter-Revolution', 137–139; Allen, *op. cit.* 140–146.

[9]Allen, *op. cit.* p. 146 ff.; *The Borough Records*, 391–398; Serjeantson, *A History of All Saints*, p. 205.

[10]P. Collinson, 'Lectures by Combination', 198–199; see above pp. 44–46.

[11]Allen, *op. cit.* pp. 124–125, 129, 131–136 gives details and references.

Moreover, the preaching tradition remained strong throughout the Civil War. The *Ministers' Testimony* of 1648 had 69 signatories from Northampton-shire, almost 35 per cent of the clergy in the county at that time and a greater proportion than either Warwickshire or Norfolk, two other noted puritan centres, could muster. When, in 1660, the monarchy was restored and the Church of England re-established an awkward choice had to be made. Some puritans remained within the established church as did most of the gentry, but the clergy of 65 parishes in the diocese were silenced or removed, among them the aged Jeremiah Lewys of Northampton. The withdrawal of most gentry support for dissent was important, but the most striking thing about the lists from 1648 and 1660–1662 is the continuity of tradition which appears when they are examined against the evidence of the late 16th and early 17th century. Many of the same communities were represented at each stage.[12] Once a puritan tradition took root in a locality it often proved to be durable, and the years between 1610 and 1660 provide plenty of examples of continuity between Elizabethan puritanism and later dissent. In the years between 1558 and 1610 the puritans not only laid foundations strong enough to withstand the threat from Arminianism in the 1620s and 1630s, but also established the main outlines of the ecclesiastical topo-graphy of the diocese for the next 150 years. At Daventry in the 1660s, for example, 'secret meetings for worship were frequently held late at night, and conducted occasionally by ministers, at a house in the hamlet of Drayton, where considerable numbers from the town and neighbourhood often assembled', and at Kettering the ejected minister 'frequently preached in his own house, and in other houses in the town'. Other former puritan centres in town and country later had dissenting groups, though their dispersal mostly in the east and the forest areas, suggest that continuity with dissent was strongest where gentry domination of puritanism had been weakest.

At Northampton in 1695 the following convenant was made; 'We, this church of Christ, whose names are underwritten, having given up ourselves to the Lord and to one another according to the will of God, do promise and covenant, in the presence of God, to walk together in all the laws and ordinances of Christ, according to the rules of his Gospel . . .' It was to this congregation that Philip Doddridge was called in 1729.[13] Encouraged in his youth by a grand-son of Hugh Clarke, the puritan minister of Oundle during the 1580s,[14] Dod-dridge represented a less dogmatic nonconformity than any of the puritans had done. His ministry reached a far wider audience than the town itself, and during his 21 years there, Northampton again provided an example of an alternative churchmanship to that represented in the cathedral city of Peterborough. In this respect at least Doddridge's ministry continued a tradition established by his predecessors, Percival Wiburn, Edmund Snape and Robert Catelin. In his more ecumenical approach to church affairs Doddrige may also have represented an important stage in the puritan withdrawal from dogmatism, but that is a hypothesis which remains to be tested by a local study of religious affairs between 1610 and 1730.[15]

[12]A. G. Matthews (ed.), *Calamy Revised* (Oxford, 1934), 556 and index; F. Bate, *The Declaration of Indulgence, 1672* (1908), pp. vi, xlii–xliii, xlv.

[13]T. Coleman, *Memorials of the Independent Churches in Northamptonshire* (1853), 9, 81, 186, also at Oakham, Oundle and Rothwell.

[14]D.N.B., Doddridge, Philip; Clarke, Samuel (1684–1750).

[15]G. Nuttall, *Richard Baxter and Philip Doddridge: a study in a tradition* (1951).

# SOURCES USED AND BIBLIOGRAPHY OF WORKS CITED

## MANUSCRIPT SOURCES

*Public Record Office*

| | |
|---|---|
| C.3 | Chancery Proceedings, Elizabeth. |
| E 134 | Exchequer Depositions. |
| E 178 | Exchequer Commissions. |
| P.C.C., wills | Prerogative Court of Canterbury, registered wills. |
| SP. 12 | State Papers Domestic, Elizabeth. |
| SP. 14 | State Papers Domestic, James I. |
| SP. 15 | State Papers Domestic, Elizabeth, Additional. |
| STAC 5. | Star Chamber Proceedings, Elizabeth. |
| STAC 7. | Star Chamber Proceedings, Elizabeth. |
| STAC 8. | Star Chamber Proceedings, James I. |

*British Museum*

| | |
|---|---|
| Lansdowne Mss. | 6; 17; 38; 50; 55; 68; 76; 102; 103; 443; 444; 445; 737. |
| Harleian Mss. | 69; 120; 280; 398; 594; 871; 6849; 7042. |
| Additional Ms. | 22473. |
| Sloane Ms. | 271. |
| Stowe Ms. | 570. |

*Lambeth Palace Library, London*

| | |
|---|---|
| Carte Miscellanee | xiii. 56, 65. |
| MS. | 178. |

*Corpus Christi College, Cambridge*

MS. 122.
MS. 294

*Magdalene College, Cambridge*

Pepys Ms., Papers of State, ii.

*Northamptonshire Record Office*

Peterborough Diocesan Records

Correction Books:

| | | |
|---|---|---|
| ML 558 | Jan. 1566–Jan. | 1570. |
| ML 559 | Jan. 1570–Jul. | 1572. |
| ML 560a | Jun. 1571–Feb. | 1574. |
| ML 560b | May 1570–May | 1571. |

ML 561 Oct. 1571–Feb. 1572.
X 607/6 Apr. 1572–Dec. 1572.
X 607/7 Jan. 1573–Nov. 1573.
X 607/8 Dec. 1573–Aug. 1574.
X 607/10 Apr. 1575–Apr. 1576.
X 607/11 Aug. 1575–Oct. 1576.
X 607/12 Mar. 1575–Oct. 1576.
X 608/13 Apr. 1576–Jul. 1577.
X 608/14 Nov. 1576–Mar. 1582.
X 608/15 Aug. 1577–Mar. 1583.
X 608/16 Jun. 1582–Jul. 1582.
X 608/17 Mar. 1582–Mar. 1583.
X 608/18 Jun. 1583–Oct. 1584.
X 608/19 Jun. 1585–Nov. 1586.
X 609/20 Feb. 1586–Nov. 1586.
X 609/21 Jan. 1587–Jan. 1589.
X 609/22 Oct. 1588–Feb. 1589.
X 609/23 Jul. 1588–Nov. 1580.
X 610/23a Oct. 1589–Nov. 1592.
X 610/24 May 1590–Jan. 1595.
X 610/25 Nov. 1588–Jun. 1595.
X 610/26 Sep. 1594–Oct. 1597.
X 610/27 May 1595–Dec. 1595.
X 610/28 Oct. 1595–Jun. 1597.
X 610/29 Jun. 1597–Mar. 1598.
X 611/31 Dec. 1598–Jun. 1599.
X 612/32 May 1598–May 1601.
X 612/34 Jul. 1600–Jun. 1601.
X 612/35 Jul. 1601–Oct. 1603.
X 613/36 Jun. 1601–Feb. 1606.
X 614/38 Dec. 1603–Sep. 1603.
X 614/39 Oct. 1605–Jul. 1608.
X 612/33 Mar. 1606–May 1611.
X 614/40 Mar. 1607–Dec. 1608.
X 613/37 May 1607–Jul. 1609.

Visitation Books:
1 Aug. and Sep. 1561.
2 Apr. 1570.
3 1573.
4 1585–1589.
4a 1588 (a working copy of part 4).
5 1591–1597.
6 1607.
7 1600–1608.

Institution Books:
1 1541–1574.
2 1574–1584.
3 1584–1602.
4 1599–1610.

Miscellaneous Books:
4   Consistory Court Book 1550–1566.
5   Consistory Court Book 1571–1572.
6   Court of Arches Proceedings (copies 1585–1602).
8   Registers of licences, caveats, etc.
9   Bishop Howland's clergy book 1586.
12   Church Survey of Rutland 1605.

Miscellaneous items:
Mainly loose leaf and strays from court books, some fragments of cause papers, three letters to the bishops 1578–1591, and a list of excommunicants 1600 (169 items under call mark X 950/1–169).

Probate Registers 1549–1611. (17 volumes)

Ecclesiastical Commissioners:
X 607/9   Mar. 1573–Jan. 1578.

Archdeaconry of Northampton:
X 648/1   Comperta and Detecta 1581–1584.
Visitation Book 2   1538, 1543.
Visitation Book 3   1546–1550.
Visitation Book 4   1576–1580.
Visitation Book 5   1574–1580.
Visitation Book 7   1584–1588.
Visitation Book 9   1586–1500.
Court Books          1589–1613.   (5 volumes)

Isham Correspondence.

Minutes of the Northampton Town Assembly 1549–1627.

*National Register of Archives, Quality Court, London*
Baskerville Transcripts, De L'isle and Dudley Papers.

*History of Parliament Trust, Tavistock Square, London*
Elizabethan members' files.


## PRINTED SOURCES

*Acts of the Privy Council of England*, v–xxxii, ed. J. R. Dasent (1892–1907).
*An Abridgement of that Booke which the Ministers of Lincoln Diocese delivered to his Maiestie upon the first of December last, 1605* (1605).
*An answer at large to a most hereticall, trayterous, and Papisticall Byll, in English Verse, which was cast abroad in the streetes of Northampton, and brought before the judges at the last Assises there, 1570* (Northampton, 1881).
*A Paper on Puritans in Northamptonshire, dated 16 July 1590, With Particulars of the Classics holden at the Bull in Northampton; and of one Edmond Snape beeinge or pretendinge to be Curate of S. Peters in Northampton* (Northampton, 1878).
Ed. E. Arber, *An Introductory Sketch to the Martin Marprelate Controversy* (1879).
Ed. G. J. Armytage, *The Visitation in the County of Rutland. 1618–19* (Harleian Soc. 3, 1870).
H. Arthington, *The Seduction of Arthington by Hacket* (1592).

*Articles to Bee enquired of by the Churchwardens and Swornmen within the diocese of Peterborough ... 1594* (1594).

R. Bancroft, *Daungerous Positions and Proceedings* (1593).

Ed. M. Bateson, 'A Collection of original letters from the bishops to the Privy Council 1564, with returns of the justices of the peace and others within their respective dioceses, classified according to their religious convictions', *Camden Miscellany*, ix. (Camd. Soc. New Series, liii. 1895).

J. Beatniffe, *A Sermon Preached at Towcester 1588* (1590).

*Cabala sive scrinia sacra* (1691).

E. Cardwell, *Synodalia* (Oxford, 1842, repr. 1966) 2 vols.

Ed. L. H. Carlson, *The Writings of John Penry* (1967).

R. Cawdry, *A Short and Fruitfull Treatise, of the profit and necessitie of Catechising* (1604).

R. Cawdry, *A Treasorie or Store-House of Similies* (1600).

Ed. P. Collinson, *The Letters of Thomas Wood, Puritan* (B.I.H.R., Supplement no. 5, 1962).

*Commons Journals*, i. (1803).

*The Correspondence of Archbishop Parker*, eds. J. Bruce and T. T. Perowne (Parker Society, 1853).

R. Cosin, *A Conspiracie for Pretended Reformation* (1593).

Ed. M. C. Cross, *The Letters of Sir Francis Hastings* (Somerset Record Society, 1969).

D. Defoe, *A Tour through the Whole Island of Great Britain* (Penguin edn, 1971).

'Diocesan returns of recusants for England and Wales, 1577', *Miscellanea* xii (Cath. Rec. Soc., vol. 22, 1921).

J. Field, *A Caveat for Parsons Howlet and the rest of his darke broode* (1581).

T. Gibson, *A Fruitfull sermon preached at Occam in the countie of Rutland, the 2 November 1583* (1584).

Eds. J. Goring and J. Wake, *Northamptonshire Lieutenancy Papers 1580–1614* (N.R.S. xvii, 1976).

*Gray's Inn Admissions Registers*, ed. J. Foster (priv. print, 1889).

Hist. MSS. Com., *Buccleuch MSS.* iii. (1926).

Hist. MSS. Com., *Montague MSS.* (1900).

Hist. MSS. Com., *Salisbury MSS*, (1883–1970), 21 vols.

Hist. MSS. Com., *Various Collections* iii (1904) Tresham Papers.

R. Hooker, *The Laws of Ecclesiastical Polity* (Everyman edn) 2 vols.

J. Howlet (pseud.), *A brief discours contayning certayne reasons why catholiques refuse to goe to churche* (Douai, 1580).

E. A. Irons, 'A Calendar of a Court Book' *Northants N. & Q.* (New Series) ii.

E. A. Irons, 'An Episcopal Visitation in 1570' *Northants N. & Q.* (New Series) ii.

Ed. W. P. M. Kennedy, *Elizabethan Episcopal Administration* (Alcuin Club xv-xvii, 1924), 3 vols.

Ed. S. E. Lehmberg, 'Archbishop Grindal and the Prophesyings', *Historical Jnl. of the Protestant Episcopalian Church* (1963).

Eds. C. A. Markham and J. C. Cox, *The Records of the Borough of Northampton* (Northampton, 1898), 2 vols.

M. Marprelate, *The Marprelate Tracts* (facsimile edn, 1967).

Ed. F. C. Metcalfe, *The Visitations of Northamptonshire made in 1564 and 1618–19, with Northamptonshire Pedigrees from various Harleian MSS.* (1887).

J. Norden, *Speculi Britannia Pars Altera, or a Delineation of Northamptonshire* (1720).

*Ed.* A Peel, *The Seconde Parte of a Register* (Cambridge, 1915), 2 vols.

*Eds.* W. P. W. Phillimore and H. I. Longden, *Northamptonshire Marriage Registers* (1909), 2 vols.

*Recusant Roll, no. 2, ed.* H. Bowler (Catholic Record Society, lvii, 1965).

R. G. Usher, *The Presbyterian Movement 1582–9* (Camden Society, 3rd series, vii).

Visitation Articles 1600, 1602, 1605, 1607, 1613 1617, 1623, 1626. Printed copies bound together at Lambeth Palace Library, call mark 1599. 18 (7a).

*Ed.* J. Wake, *A Copy of Papers relating to Masters, Beacons, and Subsidies in the County of Northampton. A.D. 1586–1623,* with an introduction by J. E. Morris (N.R.S. iii, 1926).

*Ed.* J. Wake, *The Montagu Masters Book, A.D. 1602–1623* (N.R.S. vii, 1935).

P. Wiburn, *A checke Reproofe of Mr. Howlet's Untimely Schreeching in her Majestie's Eares* (1581).

R. Winwood, *Memorials of affairs of state in the reigns of Queen Elizabeth and King James I* (1729) 2 vols.

*Zurich Letters, ed.* R. Robinson (Parker Society, 1842–1845) 2 vols.

## SECONDARY WORKS

*The Agrarian History of England and Wales iv, 1500–1640, ed.* J. Thirsk (Cambridge, 1967).

K. J. Allison, M. W. Beresford, and J. G. Hurst, *The Deserted Villages of Northamptonshire* (Leicester, 1966).

G. Anstruther, *Vaux of Harrowden* (Newport, Mon., 1953).

H. Aveling, 'The Catholic Recusants of the West Riding of Yorkshire', *Proceedings of the Leeds Philosophical and Literary Society* (vol. x, part vi, 1963).

S. B. Babbage, *Puritanism and Richard Bancroft* (1962).

G. Baker, *The History and Antiquities of the County of Northampton* (1822–30), 2 vols.

O. Barron, *V.C.H., Northamptonshire Families* (1906).

F. Bate, *The Declaration of Indulgence, 1672* (1908).

T. Blore, *The History and Antiquities of the County of Rutland* (1811).

J. Bridges, *The History and Antiquities of Northamptonshire, ed.* Whalley (Oxford, 1791).

V. J. K. Brook, *Whitgift and The English Church* (1964 edn).

L. H. Carlson and R. Paulson, *English Satire* (Los Angeles, 1972).

F. I. Cater, 'Robert Browne and his Treatise for Reformation', *Trans. of the Congregational History Society,* i.

F. I. Cater, 'Robert Browne's Ancestors and Descendants', *Trans. of the Congregational History Society,* ii.

F. I. Cater, 'The Later Years of Robert Browne', *Trans. of the Congregational Historical Society,* iii.

P. Clark, *English Provincial Society from the Reformation to the Revolution* (1977).

S. Clarke, *A General Martyrologie . . . Lives of Sundry Modern English Divines* (1651).

T. Coleman, *Memorials of the Independent Churches in Northamptonshire* (1853).

P. Collinson, 'A Magazine of Religious Patterns: an Erasmian topic transposed in English Protestantism', in D. Baker (*ed.*), *Renaissance and Renewal in Christian History* (Oxford, 1977).

P. Collinson, *A Mirror of Elizabethan Puritanism: the Life and Letters of 'Godly Master Dering'* (1964).

P. Collinson, *The Elizabethan Puritan Movement* (1967).

P. Collinson, 'John Field and Elizabethan Puritanism', in S. T. Bindoff, J. Hurstfield, and C. H. Williams (*eds.*), *Tudor Government and Society* (1961).

P. Collinson, 'Lectures by Combination: Structures and Characteristics of Church Life in 17th-century England', *Bulletin of the Institute of Historical Research*, xlviii.

P. Collinson, 'Towards a Broader Understanding of the Early Dissenting Tradition', Cole & Moody (*eds.*), *The Dissenting Tradition: Essays for Leland Carlson* (Ohio, 1975).

J. S. Coolidge, *The Pauline Renaissance in England* (Oxford, 1970).

M. C. Cross, *The Puritan Earl: Henry Hastings, 3rd Earl of Huntingdon* (1966).

M. H. Curtis, *Oxford and Cambridge in Transition* (Oxford, 1939).

A. G. Dickens, *The English Reformation* (1964).

*Dictionary of National Biography*, eds. Leslie Stephen and Sidney Lee (1908–1909).

A. Everitt, *Change in the Provinces; The seventeenth century* (Leicester, 1969).

A. Everitt, *The Pattern of rural dissent. The nineteenth century* (Leicester, 1972).

A. Everitt, 'Nonconformity in Country Parishes', in J. Thirsk (*ed.*), *Land, Church and People* (Reading, 1970).

A. Everitt, *The Local Community and the Great Rebellion* (1969).

M. E. Finch, *The Wealth of Five Northamptonshire Families 1540–1640* (N.R.S. xix, 1956).

A. J. Fletcher, *A County Community in Peace and War, Sussex 1600–1660* (1975).

J. Foster, *Alumni Oxonienses, 1500–1714* (Reprinted 1968) 4 vols. in 2.

T. Fuller, *The Church History of Britain* (Oxford, 1845), J. S. Brewer (*ed.*) 6 vols.

C. Garrett, *The Marian Exiles* (Cambridge, 1938).

E. F. Gay, 'The Midland Revolt and the Inquisitions of Depopulation of 1607', *Trans. Roy. Hist. Soc.* (New Series, xviii).

H. Gee, *The Elizabethan Clergy and the Settlement of Religion 1558–1564* (Oxford, 1898).

G.E.C., *Complete Peerage* (1910–1959) 14 vols.

J. H. Gleason, *The Justices of the Peace in England, 1558–1640* (Oxford, 1969).

C. Haigh, 'Puritan Evangelism in the reign of Elizabeth I', *English Historical Review*, xcii.

C. Haigh, *Reformation and Resistance in Tudor Lancashire* (Cambridge, 1975).

W. Haller, *The Rise of Puritanism* (New York, 1957).

C. Hill, *The Economic Problems of the Church* (Oxford, 1956).

C. Hill, *Society and Puritanism in Pre-Revolutionary England* (1964).

W. G. Hoskins, *Provincial England* (1963).

R. A. Houlbrooke, 'The decline of ecclesiastical jurisdiction under the Tudors', in R. O'Day and F. M. Heal (*eds.*), *Continuity and Change, Personnel and Administration of the Church in England* (Leicester, 1976).

R. A. Houlbrooke, 'The Protestant Episcopate 1547–1603', in R. O'Day and F. Heal (*eds.*), *Church and Society in England; Henry VIII to James I* (1977).

E. A. Irons, 'A Paper on Sir Robert Cawdrie; rector of South Luffenham 1571–87', *Rutland Archaeological and Natural History Society, 14th Report* (1917).

E. A. Irons, 'Mr. Abraham Johnson' *Rutland Archaeological and Natural History Society, 10th Report* (1913).

Sir Gyles Isham, *All Saints Church, Lamport* (Rugby, 1959).

Sir Gyles Isham, *Easton Mauduit and the Yelvertons* (1962).

M. Knappen, *Tudor Puritanism* (Phoenix edn, 1965).

S. J. Knox, *Walter Travers* (1962).

*Ed.* H. I. Longden, *The Visitation of the County of Northampton in the year 1681* (Harleian Soc. 87, 1935).

H. I. Longden, *Northamptonshire and Rutland Clergy, 1500–1900* (Northampton, 1939–1943) 15 vols, with volume of addenda by G. Anstruther (Northampton, 1952).

R. B. Manning, 'The Making of a Protestant aristocracy; the ecclesiastical commissioners of the diocese of Chester, 1550–98', *Bulletin of the Institute of Historical Research*, xlix.

R. B. Manning, *Religion and Society in Elizabethan Sussex* (Leicester, 1969).

R. A. Marchant, *The Church under the Law* (Cambridge, 1969).

*Ed.* A. G. Matthews, *Calamy Revised* (Oxford, 1934).

J. E. Neale, *Elizabeth I and her Parliaments, 1559–1601* (1953–1957) 2 vols.

J. E. Neale, *The Elizabethan House of Commons* (1963 edn).

G. Nuttall, *Richard Baxter and Philip Doddridge: a study in a tradition* (1951).

R. O'Day, 'The Reformation of the Ministry', in R. O'Day and F. M. Heal (eds.), *Continuity and Change* (Leicester, 1976).

A. F. Scott-Pearson, *Thomas Cartwright and Elizabethan Puritanism* (1925).

P. A. J. Pettit, *The Royal Forests of Northants* (N.R.S. xxiii, 1968).

*Ed.* W. P. W. Phillimore, *A Calendar of Wills Relating to the Counties of Northampton and Rutland, proved in the Court of the Archdeacon of Northampton, 1510–1652* (1898).

W. Pierce, *An Historical Introduction to the Marprelate Tracts* (1908).

H. C. Porter, *Reformation and Reaction in Tudor Cambridge* (Cambridge, 1958).

W. Prest, *The Inns of Court under Elizabeth I and the early Stuarts, 1590–1640* (1972).

F. D. Price, 'Bishop Bullingham and Chancellor Blackleech', *Transactions of the Bristol and Gloucestershire Archaeological Society*, xci.

P.R.O., *List and Index IX, List of sheriffs to 1831* (1898).

C. Read, *Mr Secretary Cecil and Queen Elizabeth* (1965 edn).

C. Read, *Lord Burghley and Queen Elizabeth* (1965 edn).

R. C. Richardson, *Puritanism in North West England* (Manchester, 1972).

*Ed.* A. Rogers, *The Making of Stamford* (Leicester, 1965).

A. L. Rowse, *Tudor Cornwall* (1941).

J. C. Sainty, *Lieutenants of Counties, 1585–1642* (B.I.H.R., Supplement 8, 1970).

R. M. Serjeantson, *A History of the Church of All Saints, Northampton* (Northampton, 1901).

R. M. Serjeantson, *A History of the Church of St. Peter, Northampton* (Northampton, 1904).

W. J. Sheils, 'Some Problems of government in a new diocese: the bishop and the Puritans in the diocese of Peterborough, 1560–1630' in R. O'Day and F. M. Heal (eds.), *Continuity and Change* (Leicester, 1976).

A. Hassell Smith, *County and Court, Government and Politics in Norfolk 1558–1603* (Oxford, 1974).

M. Spufford, *Contrasting Communities* (Cambridge, 1974).

M. Spufford, 'The scribes of villagers' wills in the 16th and 17th centuries and their influence', *Local Population Studies*, vii.

J. M. Steane, *The Northamptonshire Landscape* (1974).

L. Stone, 'The Educational Revolution in England, 1560–1640', *Past and Present*, xxviii (1964), 41–80.

J. Strype, *Annals of the Reformation . . . during Queen Elizabeth's Reign* (Oxford, 1824).

K. Thomas, *Religion and the Decline of Magic* (Penguin edn, 1973).

J. A. F. Thomson, *The Later Lollards, 1414-1520* (Oxford, 1965).

N. R. N. Tyacke 'Puritanism, Arminianism, and Counter Revolution' in C. S. R. Russell (*ed.*) *The Origins of the English Civil War* (1973).

R. G. Usher, *The Reconstruction of the English Church* (London and New York, 1910) 2 vols.

*V.C.H. Northamptonshire, ii–iv* (1906-1937).

*V.C.H. Rutland ed.* W. Page (1908-1935), 2 vols.

J. and J. A. Venn, *Alumni Cantabridgienses*, part one (Cambridge 1922-1927) 4 vols.

*Visitation Articles and Injunctions*, eds. W. H. Frere and W. M. Kennedy (Alcuin Club, 1910) 3 vols.

J. Wake, *The Brudenells of Deene* (1953).

C. Wise, *The Montagues of Boughton* (Kettering, 1868).


UNPUBLISHED THESES

E. J. I. Allen, 'The State of the Church in the Diocese of Peterborough 1601-42' (Unpublished Oxford B.Litt. thesis, 1972).

D. C. Chalmers, 'Puritanism in Leicestershire 1558-1633' (Unpublished Leeds M.A. thesis, 1962).

C. Kightly, 'The Early Lollards 1382-1428' (Unpublished York D.Phil. thesis, 1975).

W. J. Sheils, 'The Puritans in Church and Politics in the Diocese of Peterborough 1570-1610' (Unpublished London Ph.D. thesis, 1974).

E. E. Trafford, 'Personnel of Parliament, 1593' (Unpublished London M.A. thesis, 1948).

# GENERAL INDEX

Abbreviations; c., curate; r., rector; v., vicar